# RDA
AND

# SERIALS
# CATALOGUING

# RDA
## AND
## SERIALS
## CATALOGUING

Ed Jones

**f** facet publishing

Published by Facet Publishing,
7 Ridgmount Street, London WC1E 7AE
www.facetpublishing.co.uk

Facet Publishing is wholly owned by CILIP: the Chartered Institute of Library and Information Professionals.

First published in the USA by the American Library Association, 2013.
This UK edition 2013.

*British Library Cataloguing in Publication Data*
A catalogue record for this book is available from the British Library.

ISBN 978-1-85604-950-4

Printed and bound in the United Kingdom by Lightning Source.

# CONTENTS

*Introduction* vii

## PART I: PREPARATION   1

*Chapter 1*   An Introduction to Serials and Serials Cataloging   3

*Chapter 2*   Getting to Know RDA: A New Structure and Other Changes
from AACR2   27

## PART II: SERIALS CATALOGING USING RDA   43

*Chapter 3*   Searching and the Universe of Serials   45

*Chapter 4*   Cataloging Serials and Ongoing Integrating Resources Using RDA   51

     1. *General Instructions Relating to Serials Cataloging Using RDA
and MARC 21*   53

     2. *Attributes of Resources: Manifestations and Items and the Works
and Expressions They Embody (by ISBD Area)*   67

     3. *Relationships between Resources*   126

     4. *Identifying Works and Expressions [RDA 6]*   135

     5. *Identifying Related Entities: Authorized Access Points for Persons,
Corporate Bodies, and Other Resources Related to the Resource
Being Described*   152

     6. *Online Serials and CONSER Provider-Neutral Records*   168

     7. *Ongoing Integrating Resources*   177

*Epilogue*   RDA and Linked Data   193

*Index* 207

# INTRODUCTION

HIS MANUAL PROVIDES AN INTRODUCTION TO Resource Description and Access (RDA) as it applies to the cataloging of serials and ongoing integrating resources. It is designed to be used by serials catalogers who are new to RDA and by monograph catalogers who are new to both serials cataloging and RDA. It assumes a working knowledge of the *Anglo-American Cataloguing Rules* (AACR2) and of the MARC 21 formats, but not necessarily as they apply to the cataloging of serials and ongoing integrating resources.

In addition to providing an introduction to RDA, this manual provides a context for the work of serials cataloging. Those new to serials cataloging will be introduced to both the infinite variety of the objects of serials cataloging—*serials*—and the sometimes arcane mysteries of the craft itself. This context is given in chapter 1, which delineates the salient characteristics of serials, and also describes the variety of cataloging practices that have held sway at one time or another during the last hundred years or so, along with the arguments offered in support of these practices and those raised in opposition. These arguments tend to get replayed from time to time—occasionally when the original context is long forgotten—and it is useful to understand that a solution designed for one environment may not be suitable once that environment no longer exists, or has changed beyond recognition. It is also useful to understand that nearly every solution imaginable has been deemed appropriate at one time or another, but none has proved permanent, nor is any likely to.

Chapter 2 also elaborates the context of RDA in terms of the Functional Requirements for Bibliographic Records (FRBR) conceptual model and the changes that have occurred from AACR2 cataloging.

Chapter 3 provides some rudimentary hints on searching for serial records in large bibliographic databases, recognizing problematic situations, and avoiding pitfalls.

In terms of RDA itself, this manual assumes the reader has a basic familiarity with FRBR, the conceptual model that underlies RDA, and with CONSER (Cooperative ONline SERials), the cooperative cataloging program that, since 1975, has heavily influenced the cataloging of serials and ongoing integrating resources in North America. A familiarity with FRBR will help immensely in understanding the discussion of RDA, while a familiarity with CONSER will help understand some elaborations of practice at certain points in the manual. However, both FRBR and CONSER will be discussed only as necessary to provide context for a particular point.

## RDA IMPLEMENTATION SCENARIOS

RDA is designed to work competently in three environments or "implementation scenarios." These are numbered 3 to 1 in order of increasing sophistication:

Scenario 3: "Flat file" database structure (no links between bibliographic and authority records)
Scenario 2: Linked bibliographic and authority records
Scenario 1: Relational/object-oriented database structure

MARC record exchange in North America currently takes place in the flat file environment described by scenario 3, and consequently this manual is written for implementation scenario 3. Although the MARC 21 formats are capable of supporting linked bibliographic and authority records as described in implementation scenario 2, the mechanism for doing so—subfield $0—is not yet in widespread use.

When it occurs, the transition to a scenario 2 environment will occur first as a *potential* transition, made possible by the machine generation and population of subfield $0 in MARC 21 records.

Subfield $0 is already employed in MARC 21 records used by the German-language cataloging community for records created following their cataloging rules, the Regeln für die alphabetische Katalogisierung für wissenschaftlichen Bibliotheken (RAK-WB).

### Example of Linked RAK-WB Record (Scenario 2) from Deutsche Nationalbibliothek

[100] 1# $a Dickens, Charles $d 1812-1870 *$0 (DE-101)118525239* ← LINK TO RELATED AUTHORITY RECORD FOR DICKENS
[245] 10 $a Great expectations $c Charles Dickens. [Vol. ed.: Rod Mengham]

Note that while record *exchange* still takes place in a scenario 3 environment, record *storage* in individual libraries and bibliographic utilities may occur in a hybrid scenario 2/3 environment, where pattern matching has been used to generate links between bibliographic records and authority records within the local system, or such linking has been facilitated by the cataloger. OCLC Connexion's "control heading" function is an example of this.

Scenario 1—the optimal environment for RDA data—still lies some distance down the road. An introduction to linked data and the Semantic Web—prerequisites of a scenario 1 environment—is provided as the epilogue to this manual.

## THE MEAT OF THE MANUAL: CHAPTER 4

### (Cataloging serials and ongoing integrating resources using RDA)

Cataloging manuals are typically organized either according to the sequence of rules presented in the cataloging code or the sequence of fields presented in the MARC 21 bibliographic format. An example of the former is Maxwell's *Handbook for AACR2;* an example of the latter is the *CONSER Editing Guide.* The *CONSER Cataloging Manual* is in a class by itself, generally following the sequence of AACR2 but with special chapters devoted to features specific to serials and to special classes of serials.

Given that RDA is designed as an online tool rather than as a publication to be read sequentially, and given that the *structure* of catalog records—what RDA calls record syntaxes—are not integrated into the text of RDA, the designer of a manual for RDA is presented with challenges in terms of organization, but is also presented with a certain freedom. The challenge is to recast this online tool in a form that be consumed as sequential text; the freedom is that one can do so in whatever way seems most useful, since the source material is independent of a sequential context.

That said, this manual adopts a conservative approach (at least for this first edition). It assumes that current catalogers, having cut their teeth on AACR2, are most comfortable with the structure of that code. Because the content of RDA is for the most part continuous with that of AACR2, and because the International Standard Bibliographic Description (ISBD), which underlies part 1 of AACR2, is recognized as the standard for descriptive data in the Statement of International Cataloguing Principles (ICP) that informs RDA, it seems reasonable in the current manual to try to hew fairly closely to the structure of AACR2 and ISBD, at least in its general outlines. At the same time, where the FRBR conceptual model provides a more useful point of departure, this structure is superimposed.

Because of its central role and necessarily elaborate structure, chapter 4, "Cataloging Serials and Ongoing Integrating Resources Using RDA," requires a more detailed exposition for the reader. Given that RDA is initially being implemented in a scenario 3 environment, RDA elements relating to the four FRBR Group 1 entities (work, expression, manifestation, item) are presented here in the rough sequence that catalogers encounter them via bibliographic records rather than segregated according to the relevant FRBR entity.

Chapter 4 takes as its point of departure the cataloging of print serials, including reproductions of print serials in other media. Exceptional practices for cataloging online serials and ongoing integrating resources are given at the end of the chapter (sections 6 and 7 respectively). These are addressed only to the extent that their cataloging varies from the cataloging of print serials.

Chapter 4 generally adheres to the following structure:

1. General instructions relating to RDA and MARC 21
2. Attributes of resources (manifestations and items and the works and expressions they embody):

   - Generally organized by ISBD area
   - ISBD-prescribed punctuation is integrated into the examples
   - MARC 21 coding is integrated into the examples
   - Notes that relate to a particular element are given with the instructions for that element, not with instructions relating to the Notes area
   - Where RDA provides more instructions covering a class of element (e.g., titles) these are addressed at the point where that element is first encountered
   - Where RDA indicates access may be appropriate for a particular element to support a particular user task, this is noted

3. Relationships between resources
4. Identifying works and expressions (authorized access point for the resource)
5. Identifying related entities (authorized access points for persons, corporate bodies, and other resources related to the resource being described)
6. Special instructions relating to online serials
7. Special instructions relating to ongoing integrating resources

The epilogue provides a short excursion into the future of RDA scenario 1. It is necessarily speculative, but it provides an introduction to the world of linked data and a very different way of viewing the products of cataloging.

## REPRESENTATION OF MARC 21 CONTENT DESIGNATION IN EXAMPLES

Because the display conventions for MARC 21 content designation vary, depending on the system doing the displaying, this manual adopts a system-neutral approach, hewing as closely as possible to the actual structure of MARC records. Three-digit field tags are presented in square brackets, and all subfield codes (including subfield $a) are identified by a preceding dollar sign ($). Blank values in field indicator positions and fixed-length field positions (in fields 006–008) are represented by hash marks (#). Elements in these positions are not explicitly identified, though they are outlined in examples whenever mentioned in related text.

## A NOTE ON SOURCES

AACR2 used the phrase "sources of information," further differentiated into a "chief source of information" (the source from which the title proper was taken), and "prescribed sources of information" (a hierarchy of prescribed sources from which to record elements in a given area of the bibliographic description). If a given element was taken from a source other than a prescribed source, it was recorded within square brackets in the bibliographic description. In common parlance, catalogers spoke of the chief source and prescribed sources when discussing these matters.

RDA uses the term "preferred source of information" instead of "prescribed sources of information," and elements taken from a source other than a preferred source may be identified by a variety of means (note, special coding, or brackets). The chief source is no longer distinguished from other preferred sources. Instead, instructions refer, when necessary, to "the same source as the title proper."

In this manual, we will simply refer to the *source* (meaning the source from which the information is taken) unless it is necessary to differentiate one source from another.

## ACKNOWLEDGMENTS

This manual is best seen as a work in progress. Its long-term success or failure will depend heavily on the extent and quality of reader feedback. Readers are encouraged to contact the author with any and all questions, corrections, and suggestions for improvement.

On this point, I have already benefited greatly from the advice and suggestions of colleagues, among them Everett Allgood, Carroll Davis, and Robert Maxwell, all of whom generously agreed to review drafts of the text at various stages in its evolution, a time-consuming process that tests one's professional mettle, and Diane Hillmann, who helped me negotiate the potential minefield (for me) of linked data. The final product has benefited greatly from their suggestions. I would also like to acknowledge those who provided answers to questions as I puzzled my way along, especially Judith Kuhagen at the Library of Congress, who helped ensure that the text would not deviate from the intent of RDA.

Finally, I would like to acknowledge one of the greatest and most successful creations of modern librarianship: the CONSER Program. I have had the honor of being involved with CONSER on and off over the decades and have seen it evolve from an intimate and somewhat tentative group of a dozen or so institutions to full and confident maturity as the premier international cooperative cataloging program. I have made extensive use of the documentation that CONSER has produced over the years, not least the *CONSER Editing Guide* and the *CONSER Cataloging Manual* (both massive and ongoing integrating resources). There are few questions in serials cataloging that these products, or the related SCCTP training materials, have not addressed in much more detail than I can here.[1] I would also like to acknowledge the four successive CONSER coordinators at the Library of Congress. Since Dorothy Glasby got CONSER up and running (1977–1981), CONSER has been served by a succession of coordinators—Linda Bartley (1981–1993), Jean Hirons (1993–2003), and Les Hawkins (2003– )—whose longevity testifies to the pleasure they took (and take) in the work. They have guided the program along a path of innovation that its originators could hardly have imagined. CONSER continues to serve as a model for all cooperative cataloging programs.

---

**NOTE**

1. *CONSER Editing Guide,* 1994 ed. (Washington, DC: Library of Congress, Acquisitions and Bibliographic Access Directorate, 1994– ); *CONSER Cataloging Manual,* 2002 ed. (Washington, DC: Library of Congress, Serial Record Division, 2002– ). Training materials from the Serials Cataloging Cooperative Training Program (SCCTP) can be found on the website of the CONSER program: www.loc.gov/aba/pcc/conser/scctp /scctp-materials.html.

# PREPARATION

# CHAPTER 1

# AN INTRODUCTION TO SERIALS AND SERIALS CATALOGING

## WHAT IS A SERIAL?

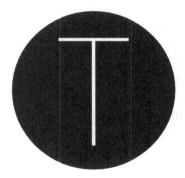

his is in fact an interesting question, because serials are not born,[1] they are made. To be exact, they are the invention of serials catalogers (and who better?). The definition of a serial in the sense we will be using here—the *cataloging* sense—will be found not in the *Oxford English Dictionary* but in RDA:

> **Serial.** A resource issued in successive parts, usually bearing numbering, that has no predetermined conclusion (e.g., a periodical, a monographic series, a newspaper). Includes resources that exhibit characteristics of serials, such as successive issues, numbering, and frequency, but whose duration is limited (e.g., newsletters of events) and reproductions of serials. (RDA Glossary)

This definition is interesting in that it includes several examples, suggesting you might not get the idea from the definition by itself. In fact, the former definition, in the *Anglo-American Cataloguing Rules* (AACR2), gave even more examples (journals, magazines, electronic journals, continuing directories, annual reports, newspapers, and monographic series). The RDA definition of *monograph*, on the other hand, is given without examples (though, tellingly, examples are included with the definition of serial's sibling, *integrating resource*). So one could say that a serial is like a good work of art: you may not know what a serial is, but you know one when you see one.

Be that as it may, using the RDA definition, we can view *serials* as encompassing most of the physical universe—including all living things—and the truly committed serials cataloger may argue for such a broad definition, if only for reasons of professional territoriality. But in the day-to-day world of serials cataloging, the division is made along more pragmatic lines, *viz.,* to minimize the amount of time and effort expended by the library cataloging its resources, without unnecessarily compromising the user's access to those resources.

In the end, this is the whole point of the definition. It recognizes that certain objects, to which we give the label "serials," have properties that lend themselves to one or more time-saving library practices, specifically:

1. A single description representing all the individual parts (saving cataloging time, at least as long as the title remains comparatively stable)
2. The availability of an ongoing subscription or standing order (saving acquisitions staff time)
3. An efficient mechanism for recording and summarizing the individual parts held (enabling (a) the efficient claiming of any part that fails to turn up and (b) the efficient reporting of holdings to the user)

Over time, pragmatic considerations have expanded and contracted the range of materials that are subject to serials cataloging. When AACR2 was implemented in 1981, the definition of *serial* was much stricter than it is today. Numbering was absolutely required—dates of publication were no substitute. Objects that failed this test—even those published year after year with an unchanging title—were necessarily cataloged individually as monographs. As time has gone by, however, the need to control costs has encouraged a more pragmatic approach. The numbering requirement has long since been abandoned. Likewise, there has been a gradual progression toward ever more accommodating definitions of what constitutes a minor title change (in the sense of a title change that does not trigger the creation of a new catalog record).

So serials cataloging is by its nature a pragmatic activity. But what then causes certain catalogers to be drawn to this field, first tempted in from the periphery, then finally and irrevocably captured by its alluring siren song?

## IT'S ALIVE!

The major attraction of serials cataloging is that serials are alive. Not only are they alive, but they share our life events, and then some. They are born; they marry; they divorce (sometimes messily); they remarry; they may have—how to put this?—"informal" relationships; they have offspring; and they die, sometimes quickly, sometimes in a slow, painful, lingering, degenerative fashion. Some are even born again, with theological implications that have yet to be adequately explored. One consequence of all this is that a serials catalog record is never finished, not even when you're absolutely sure it's dead, not even when you've ritualistically driven a stake through its heart, pounding with all your might.

There are many examples that can demonstrate the organic nature of serials. One of my favorites is *Saturday Review,* in its heyday an influential journal of serious thought and opinion, and an anchor for serious people, comparable to journals such as *The New Yorker, The Atlantic,* or *Vanity Fair* today. For much of its existence *Saturday Review* was under the close and remarkable editorship of a man named Norman Cousins.[2]

## AND THEREIN LIES A TALE

*Saturday Review* first emerged in 1924 as *The Saturday Review of Literature,* having technically begun life four years earlier as the Saturday book review supplement to *The New York Evening Post. The Saturday Review of Literature* was the brainchild of a group including the supplement's founder and editor, Henry Seidel Canby, who also served as its first editor (1924–1936). In 1942 Norman Cousins, already involved with the *Post* and the *Review,* became editor, and the review changed from a strictly literary journal to one that delivered informed commentary on all aspects of contemporary life. (The title was shortened to *The Saturday Review* in 1952.) In 1958, Cousins became owner as well as editor, subsequently distributing 49 percent of the shares among the staff. Circulation had grown more than tenfold since he had taken the reins, and would reach more than 260,000 in 1960.

After that, things got interesting. In 1961, the stockholders sold their share in the company to McCall's Publishing Company, which in 1972 was itself sold to an investment group headed by the owners of *Psychology Today.* By this time *Saturday Review* had achieved a circulation of 650,000, its all-time high. But Cousins could not abide the new owners, who had decided the weekly magazine would be better off as four monthlies, each devoted to a particular aspect of contemporary life: the arts, education, science, and society. Cousins left to form his own biweekly magazine, which he named *World*—Cousins was a long-time world federalist—and had soon regathered his old stable of *Saturday Review* hands under the new roof. From his perch at *World,* which had 100,000 charter subscriptions, Cousins quietly watched as the four *Saturday Review* monthlies first floundered, then sank. The owners declared bankruptcy, and Cousins came in to pick up the pieces, purchasing rights to the now-defunct title and relaunching it as *Saturday Review/World,* which he subsequently shortened to *Saturday Review.* But after all the turmoil, even Cousins was unable to restore *Saturday Review* to its former prestige, though it would hobble along in fits and starts for another decade or so under various ownerships. In 1977, illness forced Cousins to retire from active involvement in *Saturday Review,* though he remained as chairman of the editorial board for three more years. The last issue of the journal appeared in late 1986, by which time *Saturday Review,* once—as its name implies—published weekly, was struggling to come out every other month.

So what, you may ask, does this tale of obscure origins, a slow but steady rise to fame and influence, dastardly betrayal, improbable resurrection, and finally decrepitude and decline have to do with serials cataloging? It is this: The history just related vividly describes the organic nature of a serial. To put it in terms of the relation-ships that form the superstructure of serials cataloging, we have reproduced the story below, in the form of brief bibliographic records and, using OCLC's xISSN History Visualization Tool, in the form of a somewhat simplified family tree (see figure 1.1):

> *New York evening post (New York, N.Y. : 1920)* [published 1920-1934]
> Its Saturday book review supplement spun off as: Saturday review of literature
>
> *Saturday review of literature* [published 1924-1951]
> Spun off from: New York evening post (New York, N.Y. : 1920)
> Continued by: Saturday review (New York, N.Y. : 1952)
>
> *Saturday review (New York, N.Y. : 1952)* [published 1952-1973]
> Continues: Saturday review of literature
> Split into: Saturday review of the arts; Saturday review of education; Saturday review of the sciences; and: Saturday review of the society
>
> *Saturday review of the arts* [published 1973]
> Continues in part: Saturday review (New York, N.Y. : 1952)
> Merged with: Saturday review of education; Saturday review of the sciences; Saturday review of the society; and: World (New York, N.Y. : 1972); to become: Saturday review/world
>
> *Saturday review of education* [published 1973]
> Continues in part: Saturday review (New York, N.Y. : 1952)
> Merged with: Saturday review of the arts; Saturday review of the sciences; Saturday review of the society; and: World (New York, N.Y. : 1972); to become: Saturday review/world
>
> *Saturday review of the sciences* [published 1973]
> Continues in part: Saturday review (New York, N.Y. : 1952)
> Merged with: Saturday review of the arts; Saturday review of education; Saturday review of the society; and: World (New York, N.Y. : 1972); to become: Saturday review/world
>
> *Saturday review of the society* [published 1973]
> Continues in part: Saturday review (New York, N.Y. : 1952)
> Merged with: Saturday review of the arts; Saturday review of education; Saturday review of the sciences; and: World (New York, N.Y. : 1972); to become: Saturday review/world
>
> *World (New York, N.Y. : 1972)* [published 1972-1973]
> Continues in spirit: Saturday review (New York, N.Y. : 1952)
> Merged with: Saturday review of the arts; Saturday review of education; Saturday review of the sciences; and: Saturday review of the society; to become: Saturday review/world
>
> *Saturday review/world* [published 1973-1974]
> Formed by the merger of: Saturday review of the arts; Saturday review of education; Saturday review of the sciences; Saturday review of the society; and: World (New York, N.Y. : 1972)
> Continued by: Saturday review (New York, N.Y. : 1975)

*Saturday review (New York, N.Y. : 1975)* [published 1975-1986]
    Continues: Saturday review/world

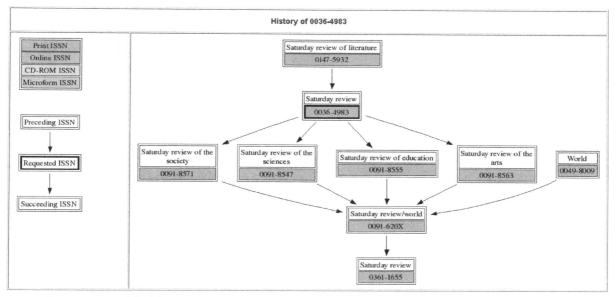

*figure 1.1: Simplified family tree generated by OCLC's xISSN History Visualization Tool*
*http://worldcat.org/xissn/titlehistory*

## SERIALS CHANGE TITLES

"I see you've gone and changed your name again . . ."
—*Leonard Cohen, "So Long, Marianne"*

On the outside, the most obvious thing that happened to *Saturday Review* was that its name changed. This happens to serials with alarming regularity—or, more accurately, irregularity. Publishers tend to do what they want, despite catalogers forever urging them to do what *we* want. This urge to be able to control our fate reached its zenith in a National Information Standards Organization (NISO) standard for the format and arrangement of periodicals (NISO/ANSI Z39.1). Quite reasonably—from our point of view—we wanted serials to appear with a predictable layout, one that would facilitate serials cataloging. Alas, publishers didn't pay attention. To put it bluntly, publishers want to sell the product. More specifically, they want to sell the current issue of the product. And they'll do whatever it takes to increase the chance of a sale. Such frenetic activity on the part of publishers seldom bodes well for serials catalogers.

Which brings us to title changes, publisher changes, etc.

The first question every cataloger must answer before cataloging a new item is "Is this or something like it already in our collection?" Or, in our world of cooperative cataloging, "Is this or something like it already in existence?" This latter question is much more difficult to answer. In terms of the FRBR conceptual model, the question breaks down into a hierarchy: Is this a new work, a new expression, a new manifestation, or a new item? The cataloger's task becomes more difficult the farther up the hierarchy one is driven to answer it.

For serials catalogers, the question is also complicated by what might be called the question of the *boundaries* of the serial—the things that define a serial's beginning and end, and distinguish it from other serials—which in RDA, as in AACR2 and its predecessors, are necessarily fuzzy. In such an environment the answer to the question is often not yes or no but maybe. Serials catalogers must cultivate a tolerance for ambiguity.

One reason for this is that serial titles tend to be rather common (though we're not making any judgment here). The creators of serials repeatedly come up with titles that have already been used many times before on other serials. In addition, serial titles can be subject to seemingly capricious changes, which RDA considers either "major" or "minor" depending on the nature of the change and the type of words involved.

If the cataloger is lucky, the serial to be cataloged will have a unique title, such as the *Canadian Journal of Jabberwocky Studies/Revue canadienne d'études jabberwock-iennes*. In such a case the title will either be in the catalog or not, and if it is, a quick examination of its description will establish whether or not it's the same serial.

However, titles are often not distinctive. If the title in hand is the *Journal of Science,* for example, the cataloger may be tempted to slip it into another cataloger's work-flow rather than confront the arduous task of distinguishing it from its numerous namesakes. Hopefully, it carries an International Standard Serial Number (ISSN). Hopefully, when the cataloger searches the ISSN in the catalog, a matching record is retrieved, and it becomes simply a case of verifying that no important bibliographic details need updating on that record. If no record is found, it is back to the arduous task. One can search for the serial using other attributes or entities associated with it, but if nothing turns up, then there is little left to do but go through the other candidates—the other *Journals of Science* in this case—and eliminate them from consideration one by one.

Or there may be one of these capricious title changes, which can occur at any time without warning, and often without acknowledgement. Since serial issues typically arrive in isolation, a title change may be suspected only because the library has no record of a subscription to the title in hand, and it is not listed among the many titles tossed in the recycling bin because they arrive uninvited. Fortunately, what drives the normal cataloger mad becomes a challenge to the serials cataloger, and there is an inexpressible satisfaction that comes from being the first to discover that Journal *Y* is actually Journal *X* in clever disguise. The more obscure the evidence that clinches this conclusion, the better.

Before we leave this section, however, it may be helpful to visit briefly with some of the more peculiar animals that inhabit the serials menagerie. For while the term *serial* itself is an invention of librarianship, defining publications that exhibit a certain set of characteristics, the concept encompasses many recognizable publication types that have an independent existence outside the world of librarianship.

# THE UNIVERSE OF SERIALS

As mentioned above, cataloging definitions of serials invariably include a bunch of "for examples," because the definition seems somehow incomplete without something concrete to hang it on. RDA retains three of these: newspapers, periodicals, and monographic series. These are treated below, as well as some examples from earlier definitions, since each in its way represents a unique type of publication, posing its own dangers for the unwary cataloger.

## Newspapers

Newspapers emerged in the early days of printing when printers realized that, rather than printing a special broadsheet every time something interesting happened, they could make more money by printing one on a regular basis, regardless of whether or not something interesting had happened. The first such, published December 2, 1620, had the fetching title *New Tydings Out of Italie Are Not Yet Com.* (For the etymologically inclined, tidings is cognate with the German Zeitung [newspaper]).

The first real newspaper in English—like many firsts, it had a disputed title—is said to have been the *London Gazette*.[3] It began publication in 1665 in Oxford, whither the court had retired to escape the Plague, but returned to London in time to cover the Great Fire three years later. It is still being published today but is much less interesting, being mainly a vehicle for official government announcements.

Newspapers have a distinctive format in that the text begins on the first page, beginning just under the title. Older newspapers often filled this valuable real estate with classified advertising, reflecting an editorial judgment on what was most likely to entice the customer, especially on slow news days (which were most days). For catalogers, one consequence of the typical newspaper layout is that titles of newspapers are invariably caption titles—titles appearing at the top of the text—with other details of publication appearing either in the masthead (a special box on an inside page reserved for such stuff) or the colophon (the bottom of one of the last pages).

## Periodicals 1: Magazines

Magazines are periodicals aimed at a popular audience (as opposed to a scholarly audience), sold mainly on newsstands, in supermarkets, drug stores, book stores, etc. Originally they had a physical appearance similar to newspapers but were published less frequently and contained longer articles. Famous examples from the nineteenth century include the *Illustrated London News* and *Harper's Weekly*.

Like newspapers, magazines were originally characterized by caption titles—still the norm for newsletters and similar publications aimed at a narrow and well-defined audience—but over the years, especially as illustrations became more sophisticated (and so more seductive for enticing customers), text was pushed off the first page by ever-larger illustrations until finally there was no text left. The title began to merge into the illustrated first page, often now published on sturdier paper, and the cover title was born.

## Periodicals 2: Scholarly Journals

Scholarly journals had their origins in the circular letters used by scholars to keep one another abreast of developments in the scientific world (much as preprint servers do today). The first purely scientific journals were the *Philosophical Transactions of the Royal Society* (or, to give its full title, *Philosophical Transactions: Giving Some Accompt of the Present Undertakings, Studies, and Labours of the Ingenious in Many Considerable Parts of the World*) and the French *Journal des sçavans*, both initially published in 1665.

Scholarly journals are distinguishable from magazines in that they aspire to be books. Indeed, one of the banes of an acquisitions librarian's existence is discovering that the book just purchased for an astronomical sum is in fact already in the library's collection, because it was simultaneously published as volume 31, issues 1–2 of the *Journal of Devious Book Publishing*.

Scholarly journals also sometimes try to facilitate their physical transformation into books by banishing advertising to the front and back of each issue and by issuing a volume title page and index once each volume is complete. The covers and advertising are removed prior to binding, the volume title page is slapped on the front, the index is slapped on the back, the pages are already numbered continuously from issue to issue, and voila! A book.

Removing advertising has become easier over the years as the amount of advertising in scholarly journals has diminished, even as librarians have become less interested in removing said advertising in the first place (both for cost reasons and because the ever-looming future historians might curse them for removing artifacts of popular culture). So the scholarly journal as book survives chiefly as a means to get libraries to purchase the same content twice and in the now quaint custom of continuously paginating multiple issues within a single volume.

## Monographic Series

Cataloging a group of monographs as a series is sometimes a tricky business, since it's often not clear whether they constitute a series or not. But to paraphrase comedian Tom Lehrer, "when correctly viewed, everything's a series," and historically serials catalogers have done their best to shoe-horn as many publications as possible into this category, especially research reports and such. It's a lot cheaper to check in RR1975-035 as one of 2,500 research reports represented in the series *RR (Freedonia*

*Ministry of War*) than to catalog it as a monograph (along with each of its 2,499 fellows). Twinges of conscience occur only when someone impertinently asks whether anyone would ever actually be looking for one of these reports under such a contrived title. Fortunately, in an online world where individual research reports are often freely available under their individual titles—bypassing the library catalog altogether—catalogers are confronted with this unhappy choice less and less often.

## Annual Reports

Annual reports are examples of serials that don't really have titles but we pretend that they do. This is because the intended audience of annual reports—shareholders, for example—receive them whether they want them or not. Others may request the annual report and, no matter what it's called, the organization will know just what to send the requester. From the point of view of the issuing body, the purpose of the cover is to visually impress the audience, and an actual title is superfluous. In fact, it's not uncommon for annual reports to lack a title altogether (in which case the name of the organization, however it appears on the report, becomes the default title—a sort of cataloger's revenge).

Similar publications (in terms of unstable or absent titles) include newsletters sent to contributors to charities, members of clubs, etc.

## Statistical Serials

Statistical publications have been around as long as writing systems, for which one of the first purposes was to make a record of what the ruler owned and what the ruled owed. When this began to be recorded on a periodical basis, the first statistical serial was born.

Statistical serials are an example of a class of publication that moves in and out of the serial model. Because they consist of data, statistical serials have been particularly susceptible to disruption by online migration. A publication that appears in print as page after page of massive tables in stately progression, brought together in successive monthly issues (perhaps with an annual cumulation) is represented online instead by a workbook made up of multiple worksheets, the whole being replaced each month in its entirety. Or perhaps by a gradually accruing database containing all the data back to the beginning, the tables to be derived according to the whim of the user. Or perhaps by some combination of these, along with PDFs of issues in the still extant print publication. Online the once proud statistical serial may have been absorbed into a single overarching data website, no longer retaining its distinctive title, its unique data now part of a great data pool. The data may now be available for use by other applications entirely outside the originating organization—something especially likely with government data. In these cases, the serial experiences something of an existential crisis: What have I become? Do I still exist? Statistical serials are more likely than others to exist today in the murky middle ground between serials and ongoing integrating resources, exhibiting characteristics of both and of neither, leaving it to the serials cataloger to determine which predominates.

So welcome to the world of serials cataloging! And specifically, welcome to the world of serials cataloging using RDA. The remainder of this chapter will try to reassure you that however you're feeling, you are not the first to be faced with a new cataloging code,. This has happened before. The path is well trodden, and the questions we confront today are similar to the questions serials catalogers have confronted in the past, only—these being serials—different.

## A BRIEF HISTORY OF SERIALS CATALOGING

Much like serials, serials cataloging has changed over the years, often in quite remarkable ways. Given this, it is useful to know where we've come from, if only to get a better idea of how we got where we are. In the following brief survey, we will discover that our current practice does not reflect eternal verities but rather the practical adaptations we have made over time to changes in our catalogs and changes in the materials we catalog: serials.

Until 1967 (1971 in the United States), a serial was defined by the continuity of its numbering. No matter how often the title changed, a serial was treated as a unit if the numbering was continuous from one title to the next. Likewise, if a serial was entered under the name of a corporate body, no matter how often the name of the body changed—so long as it was essentially the same body—a serial was treated as a unit if the numbering was continuous from name to name (or if issues were distinguished by dates rather than by numbers).

After 1967 (1971 in the United States), a new serial was deemed to exist whenever the title changed or the name of the body under which it was entered changed. Although this change in cataloging practice occurred more than forty years ago, in some ways we are still living with its consequences.

How did it happen? Why was one way of cataloging serials dominant from the beginning of cataloging to the late twentieth century and another way dominant since? Were they crazy? Are we crazy? If we look back, we can see that the answer to both questions is no, but we can also gain an understanding of how and why cataloging practice changes over time.

Although modern Anglo-American cataloging practice can be said to begin with the *91 Rules for the Compilation of the Catalogue* developed for the British Museum's Department of Printed Books (1841), those rules were but the first of a cacophony of competing cataloging codes to emerge over the course of the nineteenth century. Everyone who was anyone produced a cataloging code. To spare the reader, I will here ignore all nineteenth-century codes but one, the most influential in the United States: Cutter's *Rules,* first published in 1876.

## Cutter

1876 was the year of the founding of the American Library Association and the centennial of American independence, and in that year Charles Ammi Cutter published his *Rules for a Printed Dictionary Catalogue* (part II of his magisterial *Public Libraries in the United States of America: Their History, Condition, and Management*). Built on a diversity of earlier cataloging codes, Cutter's code would provide the foundation for all that followed.

Hard as it is to imagine, serials in those days came in just one format: print. No online versions, no microforms, no CD-ROMS, no downloadable audio, etc. Just print. There was little to complicate serials cataloging other than constraints imposed by the form of the catalog.

In 1876, the predominant form of library catalog was the *book catalog*. This was not a catalog of books but rather a catalog that was itself a book (often running to several volumes), and one that needed to be continually kept up to date. A book catalog was typically maintained in manuscript—at least the working copy—though printed catalogs of the more important libraries were common. This was both for convenience, because copies could be available at several points in the library, and as a source of revenue, because other libraries would pay good money to know what you owned. When entries were made or amended, there was a strong incentive to minimize the impact on the physical catalog. Real estate in book catalogs was expensive. If a serial mischievously changed its title, it was easiest in such a catalog to continue using the existing entry under the old title and indicate the change of title in a note, with a reference or added entry made under the new title at the appropriate place in the catalog. (This reference or added entry might be made directly on the page if there was space, or via a slip of paper "tipped in" if there was not.) Cutter set out this practice of *earliest-entry cataloging* for periodicals in his rule 54, along with an alternative practice of entering "each part" under its own (successive) title.[4]

Although rule 54 continued right through the last edition of Cutter's cataloging code in 1904, the introduction of printed cards from the Library of Congress and other sources—available on subscription—signaled the twilight of the book catalog in the United States, and its rapid displacement by the card catalog. This change in the form of the catalog removed the physical constraint that had favored earliest entry for serials.

Reflecting on the expected impact of ready-made card sets from the Library of Congress, the H. W. Wilson Company, and others, Cutter famously observed, "I cannot help thinking that the golden age of cataloging is over."[5] It was at least the end of a world where a single individual could have complete control over the shape of a cataloging code. The success of the LC printed cards also meant that libraries receiving them would have a strong interest in applying rules that were compatible with those used by LC catalogers. Subsequent codes, therefore, have necessarily been the product of collective activity, with the Library of Congress playing a major role in their shaping.

But while the change from book catalog to card catalog removed the principal rationale for earliest-entry cataloging, it did not remove the incentive to describe serials in the most economical way possible. If the real estate in a book catalog was limited, the real estate on a catalog card was even more so.

Cutter was a great advocate of shortening titles, a practice that made sense in those days before keyword searching, when titles were used more to identify than to find a serial. He provides a number of rules for shortening titles, including the wonderful rule 113: "Omit all other unnecessary words." It is clear from his examples that he would be merciless, but this is also spelled out in his general introduction to abridgment, where he makes an argument that resonates today: "Many a title a yard long does not convey as much meaning as two well chosen words."[6] In fact, Cutter's guiding principle, given the limited space available in a book catalog, was to pack as much information as possible into that space. Anyone who has perused his five-volume catalog of the Boston Athenæm Library will marvel at his skill in doing just this.[7]

Abridging titles was aided in particular by the concept of corporate authorship, which encouraged the entry of the publications of government agencies, societies, and institutions under the heading for the issuing body. Cutter's broad definition of corporate authorship seemed to be aimed in particular at serials: "Bodies of men (societies, cities, legislative bodies, countries) are to be considered the authors of their memoirs, transactions, journals, debates, reports, &c."[8] As a consequence of entering a serial under its issuing body, any occurrence of that body's name in the title proper became, by the terms of rule 113, "unnecessary words."

## The 1908 Anglo-American Code (American Text) and Its Elaborations

The introduction of LC printed cards and the increasing acknowledgment of the value of applying a common set of cataloging rules led in 1901 to the formation of a committee to revise the condensed rules of the American Library Association and align them as much as possible with those of the Library of Congress (based principally on Cutter's rules) and with Melvil Dewey's *Library School Rules*. This committee, under the direction of J. C. M. Hanson, Chief of the Catalog Division at the Library of Congress, received in 1904 a proposal from the (British) Library Association for the development of a joint code. The result was the first Anglo-American cataloging code, reflecting agreement on most issues (but not so much agreement as to obviate the need for separate British and American texts).

With the spread of card catalogs in the United States, American cataloging practice had come to favor not earliest-entry cataloging but its inverse, that is, entry under the latest title or issuing body, the presumption being that most catalog users would be looking for the latest issue or edition of a given serial. This preserved what was seen as a strong advantage of earliest-entry cataloging: its ability to provide in one place of a complete (or nearly complete) bibliographic history of a serial. This was especially true for the cards now being produced by the country's foremost research library, the Library of Congress. The bibliographic history was especially appreciated by other libraries with less complete holdings. References or added entries were made under earlier titles and issuing bodies.

Latest-entry cataloging was incorporated into the American text of the 1908 Anglo-American code: "If a periodical has changed its name, enter it under the latest form" (rule 121), and was continued in substance in its more elaborate American successors (1941, rule 214; 1949, rule 5C), as well as in a couple of specialized Library of Congress publications devoted to the cataloging of periodicals and the serial publications of societies and institutions.[9-13] (The British text of the 1908 code continued to favor earliest-entry cataloging.)

The change from earliest-entry cataloging was not without controversy. As late as 1919 the Library of Congress tried to address these concerns, offering the following rationale in response to an argument by T. Franklin Currier (Harvard College Library) for retaining earliest-entry cataloging:

> Societies and their publications are known to the public under their current names and titles. Earlier names are, even after a short interval, not distinctly remembered, or are entirely forgotten. It is therefore the current name under which the reader will usually look for the publications in the catalogue, and if he finds only a reference there to an earlier name or title he is annoyed, even though the inconvenience and loss of time be slight. To spare many readers on many occasions this annoyance and delay, a little time and labor spent once on the part of the cataloguer to transfer the entry to the new name or title when a change has occurred seems to us profitably spent.[14]

Of course, latest-entry cataloging applied not just to changes in title, but also to changes in the name of a body under which the serial was entered—a large number of serials, thanks to the definition of corporate authorship. When a corporate body changed its name, serials entered under the earlier name were re-cataloged under the latest name. Even serials issued entirely under the earlier name would be recataloged, since the earlier heading was retired from use. A reference in the catalog led the user from the earlier name to the latest.

Cutter's rules for abridging titles disappeared in the 1908 code, though abridged titles were permitted in a "written" card catalog (rule 136). Here the desire for a complete bibliographic history of a serial triumphed. Of course, given the predilection of serial titles to change, this could be an expensive rule to follow in practice. In an attempt to address the seemingly contradictory objectives of economy and bibliographic fidelity, the Library of Congress directed its catalogers to present a "short title" on the first card, with the full titles borne by the serial over time given as a note on a second card.[15]

By the time the American text of the 1908 code was revised in 1949, the "abridgement" pendulum had swung back in Cutter's direction. The so-called Green Book (*Rules for Descriptive Cataloging in the Library of Congress*) instructed that long titles be abridged if this could be done "without loss of essential information" (rule 3:5 A). An accompanying example showed how *The Works of William Shakespeare* could be reduced to *Works* (sensible, since the main entry would be Shakespeare, providing the necessary context). With serial publications, the Green Book went further:

> A short title is generally used in cataloging serial publications if this makes it possible to disregard minor variations in the wording on various issues, especially if these occur in subtitles. . . . Adjectives denoting the frequency of the publication are also omitted (without mark of omission) from the titles of reports; e.g., *Report* instead of *Annual report* and *Biennial report, Financial statement* instead of *Monthly financial statement, etc.* (rule 7:4)

The net effect of abridgement was to eliminate a lot of noise from the catalog. If a title appeared first as the *Journal of the East Finchley Historical Society* and later as the *East Finchley Historical Society Journal,* rule 7:4 would reduce it in both instances simply to *Journal* (in which form it might well appear on some future issue). With the society as the main entry, there was no confusion:

> East Finchley Historical Society.
> Journal. v. 1- Jan. 1970- [East Finchley, Eng., H. Grytpype-Thynne]

The user of a card catalog in those days would have naturally looked under the name of the society for its journal and so would have found it. Giving the full name of the journal would have added no information and would have cluttered the limited real estate of the card.

Despite the evident shift toward principles of economy in this case, it was a solitary instance. American libraries were by this time dealing with a huge postwar surge in publishing—especially of serials—and research libraries, including the Library of Congress, were accumulating larger and larger processing backlogs. At the same time, the application of a cataloging code that had grown increasingly complex over time—the 89 pages of Cutter's 1876 code had by 1949 ballooned into the combined 433 pages of the Red Book (choice and form of entry) and Green Book (bibliographic description)—was creating a crisis in cataloging.[16]

To address this crisis and propose a path forward, the American Library Association (ALA) Board on Cataloging Policy called on the talents of Seymour Lubetzky.

## Lubetzky, the Paris Principles, and AACR1

Lubetzky had earlier produced a thorough-going analysis of bibliographic description for the Library of Congress, and the ALA board now asked him to do the same for choice and form of entry. The result was *Cataloging Rules and Principles,* Lubetzky's classic 1953 analysis of the Red Book. Among the many recommendations he made, Lubetzky set out a succinct argument for the successive entry of serials, taking the point of view of a researcher approaching the catalog with a bibliographic citation:

> [I]n the case of a periodical or serial which appears over a long period of time and is subject to various changes of title, it is not to be expected that a writer

citing a given volume will inquire what the original title was, or what the relation of the given title is to any other title, and the purposes of the catalog will therefore better be served if each title is entered separately and provided with notes indicating its relation to any other titles.[17]

There was also a practical aspect to successive-entry cataloging, in that for any title change, only the cards for the immediately preceding title needed to be pulled and revised.

Lubetzky also pondered the concept of corporate authorship, one of the bedrock principles of Anglo-American cataloging, but easier to invoke in theory than to apply in practice, tending to a code based on cases rather than on underlying principles. Reviewing the history of corporate authorship up to that time, Lubetzky asked, "In the face of this long and weary experience, can we continue on the same course?"[18]

The answer was no. Revision of the catalog code began in 1956, with Lubetzky appointed editor of the revised code. Work progressed through the ensuing years, but Lubetzky left in 1960 to take up a teaching position with the UCLA library school. At the International Conference on Cataloguing Principles (ICCP) held the next year in Paris his work gained international recognition. There Lubetzky's arguments in the area of serials cataloging, as in much else, were well received, and they greatly influenced the *Statement of Principles* that form the conference's lasting monument.

Two principles deserve special mention[19]:

1. Principle 11.5 endorsed successive-entry cataloging in most cases:
   When a *serial publication* is issued successively under different titles, a *main entry* should be made under each title for the series of issues bearing that title, with indication of at least the immediately preceding and succeeding titles. For each such series of issues, an added entry may be made under one selected title. If, however, the variations in title are only slight, the most frequently used form may be adopted as a uniform heading for all issues.
2. Principle 9.1 restricted the application of corporate authorship to cases where "the work is by its nature necessarily the expression of the collective thought or activity of the corporate body" or "the wording of the title or title-page, taken in conjunction with the nature of the work, clearly implies that the corporate body is collectively responsible for the content of the work." A footnote used as an example of this latter condition "serials whose titles consist of a generic term (Bulletin, Transactions, etc.) preceded or followed by the name of a corporate body, and which include some account of the activities of the body."

The Paris Principles in turn reinforced Lubetzky's approach in the revision of the cataloging rules, now called the *Anglo-American Cataloging Rules,* which endorsed both principles. However, a footnote to rule 167G stated that the Library of Congress would continue to catalog serials under the latest entry. This was at the request of the

ALA Catalog Code Revision Committee, "which cited the need for the bibliographic information provided by the LC cards when a serial is cataloged as one entry under its latest title or corporate author."[20]

Thus Lubetzky's argument for successive-entry cataloging, based on a hypothetical researcher, bibliographic citation in hand, came into conflict with the argument for latest-entry cataloging, based on a need to know and understand the bibliographic history of a given serial.

In the area of corporate authorship, the impact in the United States was even more muted. In 1967, when AACR1 came into force, the dominant catalog form in American libraries was still the card catalog, and it was expected that the changes in cataloging practice embodied in AACR1 would have crippling economic consequences in terms of maintaining the integrity of those catalogs, especially for research libraries. Wholesale recataloging under AACR1 headings was out of the question, as was a split catalog with only new materials following AACR1. For this reason, what Carolyn Frost termed "the infamous rules 98 and 99" (which continued the earlier practice of entering churches and many institutions under local place) were incorporated into the North American text of AACR1, with the result that "this long and wearying experience" would continue a while longer.[21] To further limit the effect of implementing AACR1 in the area of headings, the new rules were applied only to headings *entirely new* to the catalog. Headings already present in the catalog continued to be used, even though they did not conform to AACR1. Headings for entities that were new to the catalog, but whose headings included *components* that were already present—for example, a parent body—were added to the store. In this way, AACR1 practice was *superimposed* on the existing catalog. New editions of works already in the catalog, new works by authors already in the catalog, etc., were cataloged using the old (Red Book) headings rather than new AACR1 headings.

Gradually, the more egregious departures from the Paris Principles were eliminated. In 1971, latest-entry cataloging of serials was abandoned on practical rather than theoretical grounds: "to expedite the handling and cataloging of serials."[22] And rules 98 and 99 were deleted from the North American text of AACR1 in 1972.[23] But the policy of *superimposition* continued right up to the implementation of AACR2 in 1981.

## Winds of Change: MARC, ISDS, ISBD(S), and the CONSER Project

The early 1970s introduced a sea-change for serials cataloging, a consequence of mechanization, international developments, and the interaction of the two.

With the growth in the use of computers to assist library operations, especially to assist in the compilation of abstracting and indexing services, the search was on for a standard identifier for serials to facilitate accurate citations. One such was the standard serial number (SSN), developed in 1970 and defined by the American National Standards Institute (ANSI) as a US national standard a year later (ANSI Z39.9-1971).

Much as the International Standard Book Number (ISBN) grew out of the Standard Book Number (SBN) developed in the UK in the late 1960s, so the ISSN (ISO 3297) grew out of the SSN.[24] A plan was developed within Unesco's UNISIST program for scientific and technical information for a system—the International Serials Data System (ISDS)—that would have an international center in Paris and various national and regional centers responsible for assigning ISSNs within their territory. In the United States, responsibility for assigning ISSNs was given to the National Serials Data Program (NSDP) at the Library of Congress.

ISDS, the network for assigning ISSNs, was created to achieve the following purposes:

- To create and maintain an international registry of serials (today's ISSN Portal)
- To define and promote the ISSN, to facilitate the retrieval of scientific and technical information in serials and make it available internationally
- To encourage communication along the serials information chain
- To promote international standards for serials in the areas of bibliographic description and data exchange[25, 26]

The ISSN is a serial identifier, where each ISSN corresponds to a "key title" based on the title proper and augmented as necessary with other data to render it unique. There is no abridgement of titles as under AACR1.

This was the situation when in February 1973 the Library of Congress began to produce printed cards for its roman alphabet serials using a new MARC format for serials (preliminary edition, 1970).[27, 28] Hardly had serials catalogers at the Library of Congress begun typing their cataloging data onto the new MARC worksheets—other staff actually entered the data into the system—when the International Federation of Library Associations issued recommendations for an ISBD for serial publications, the International Standard Bibliographic Description for Serials (ISBD(S)).[29] Mimicking the key title of ISDS, the ISBD(S) called for augmenting generic titles by adding a space-hyphen-space followed by the transcribed name of the issuing body. It also gave preference to the key title and ISSN when referring to another serial in a note. In anticipation of adopting the ISBD(S), the Library of Congress began applying this new treatment of generic titles in May 1974 (deleting at the same time the AACR1 rules that called for omitting the name of a body when it formed an integral part of the title).[30] Two years later it adopted the practice of referring to related serials by key title.[31, 32] Because under AACR1 many serials continued to be entered under corporate body, the latter practice often entailed following the key title of the related serial with the catalog entry for its issuing body, in order to make it findable in the catalog, e.g.,

Continued by: Hawaii's in-migrants, ISSN 0361-2252, issued by: Hawaii. Dept. of Planning and Economic Development. Research and Economics Analysis Division.

This remained the extent of the impact of ISBD on serials cataloging until ISBD usage was made general for all types of material with the implementation of AACR2 in 1981.

The high-water mark for the key title as the defining characteristic of a serial catalog record was also achieved at this point, at least in practice. There would be a brief theoretical triumph at the 1975 conference of the American Library Association in San Francisco, where ALA's Catalog Code Revision Committee voted—much to Lubetzky's horror—to recommend that all serials be entered under title in the new code, but the committee later rescinded its recommendation.[33,34]

This is the world into which the CONSER Project—today's CONSER Program—was born. Like the ISSN, CONSER arose in response to the potential application of the computer to mechanizing labor-intensive manual activities, especially in the compilation of union lists of serials. Many such projects were under way in the late 1970s.

Arising from a desire to create quality serial catalog records and avoid unnecessary duplication of effort, the CONSER Project was the first cooperative cataloging program of the MARC era. To create its database, the project chose to use the new online cataloging system of the Ohio College Library Center (OCLC), using as its seed files the small but growing file of LC MARC serial records and larger files of brief records from a number of machine-readable union lists of serials. Initially, project participants comprised the national libraries of the United States and Canada, along with their respective national ISSN centers, and a number of other key American libraries. The project adopted AACR1 as the basis for entries rather than the corresponding entries superimposed from the earlier rules, an arrangement that required CONSER records to contain duplicate heading fields that could be "flipped" as necessary when generating output, depending on whether the product would be pure AACR1 or not. It also, out of necessity, accepted latest-entry cataloging in the interest of building a viable database as rapidly as possible. Successive-entry cataloging had only been in force for a couple of years, and the initial purpose of the project was to convert existing card files. The Library of Congress and National Library of Canada (NLC) "authenticated" records as they were completed by the various CONSER participants. Once authenticated, a record could only be changed by requesting modification from the Library of Congress or NLC.

Although latest-entry cataloging was allowed within CONSER, successive-entry cataloging was preferred, and a desire to prepare for future online check-in of issues encouraged the transcription of titles proper as they appeared on the piece, unabridged.

So the triumph of Cutter's abridged titles proper in AACR1 was brief indeed. AACR2 would consign such titles to history and encourage the opposite of abridgement—augmentation—by severely restricting the circumstances under which a serial could be entered under a corporate name. Common titles, formerly safely tucked away under a variety of corporate headings, would now be exposed for what they were. This presented a huge potential for bibliographic chaos, especially for monographic series, one that the rules themselves did not entirely anticipate.[35]

## AACR2

The introduction of AACR2, like that of AACR1, was accompanied by a certain unease. In fact, implementation, originally planned for 1980, was postponed a year to 1981 to allow libraries to better prepare. Several large research libraries, including the Library of Congress, decided to close their existing card catalogs and either open a new temporary card catalog for their AACR2 records or begin producing their AACR2 catalog on a different medium such as microfilm or microfiche.

In some ways, the publication of AACR2 can be seen as "having a second go" at AACR1. For the first time, there were no separate British and North American texts, though national differences persisted in options and alternative rules. The most noticeable difference from AACR1 came from the fact that the new code evolved symbiotically with a General ISBD, something that strongly influenced the rules for bibliographic description (chapters 1–13). Additionally, in rule 21.1B2, AACR2 severely restricted the circumstances under which a serial—or any publication, for that matter—might be entered under the heading for a corporate body, abandoning the very notion of corporate authorship, a change that met some resistance at the time, including from Lubetzky.[36]

This resulted in many more serials being entered under title proper, presenting a problem not anticipated in the code: multiple serials—sometimes hundreds—with the same catalog entry. Because AACR2 contained no special rule for distinguishing among entries in such cases, the Library of Congress and NLC proposed the temporary remedy of "unique serial identifiers," analogous to key titles but coded as uniform titles, with qualifying data based on name headings rather than transcribed data.[37] In 1982 this interim policy was incorporated into AACR2 by adding to the two existing glossary definitions of "uniform title" a third: "The particular title used to distinguish the heading for a work from the heading for a different work."[38]

While all these changes had a significant impact on serials cataloging, the main difficulty accompanying the introduction of AACR2 related to the state of library systems software. While the practice of superimposition would be ended when the new code was implemented, the large number of headings involved—and the fact that instances of these headings would have to be updated one-by-one in the LC MARC database—produced a compromise in the form of so-called *AACR2-compatible* headings: existing headings that, while not in strict compliance with the rules of AACR2, were nonetheless deemed "close enough."

It is sometimes forgotten that, while AACR2 was developed with an eye to the online catalog, it was introduced in a working environment that was still overwhelmingly oriented toward the card catalog. In fact, Margaret Maxwell's classic *Handbook for AACR2* (1980) operates entirely in a card catalog environment.[39] The user will look in vain in its index for a reference to the MARC format, which was introduced some thirteen years earlier but was still used, like the even younger OCLC cataloging system, mainly for producing catalog cards. Nonetheless, librarians were anticipating a migration to online catalogs, and limitations in the MARC format and in the systems then in existence to process and manipulate its products—the primitive online catalogs of the day—led necessarily to a "dumbing down" of the filing rules. In 1980, a year before the delayed introduction of AACR2, both the American Library Association and the Library of Congress published new filing rules, revised to take into account the comparative lack of sophistication of machine catalogs. No longer would there be a human being explicitly interfiling "3rd" and "third." Henceforth, character strings would file "as is" rather than "as should be." Abbreviations and numerals that had once interfiled with their spelled out forms would now form separate sequences. To compensate, whenever a form occurred—a number or abbreviation, for example—that would formerly have been filed in its spelled out form, an added entry would be made explicitly using that spelled out form. For serials, however, there was no corresponding mechanism for the problem of those "unique serial identifiers" interfiling among longer titles:

> History (Albany, N.Y.)
> History and memory
> History and science
> History as a discipline
> History (Aspen, Colo.)
> . . .
> History (Washington, D.C.)

Eventually, filing sequence became less problematic as more and more online catalogs—and more and more of their users—began favoring keyword searching over index browsing.

With the 2002 revision of AACR2, the scope of chapter 12 was expanded to include:

1. Integrating resources (updating loose-leaf publications and online resources that undergo internal change rather than change by the addition of discrete units)
2. Reprints of serials
3. Serial-like publications of limited duration, such as those connected with a conference or expedition

This revision of chapter 12 grew out of changes in the serials world since the original publication of AACR2 in 1978, especially the rapid evolution and expansion of the World Wide Web during the 1990s.[40]

As happened with AACR1 and latest-entry cataloging, the coping mechanisms that accompanied the introduction of AACR2, such as AACR2-compatible headings, were eventually abandoned. The differing national options and alternative rules were gradually removed from the text, clearing the way for the adoption of a common "Anglo-American" name authority file in 1994. Finally, in 2007 the Library of Congress announced the goal of eventually eliminating AACR2-compatible headings entirely from its files.[41]

The 1990s also saw the development of the FRBR conceptual model, from its inception in a resolution of the 1990 Stockholm Seminar on Bibliographic Records to the publication of the final report that embodies the model—Functional Requirements for Bibliographic Records—in 1998.[42] The development of the FRBR model, which underlies RDA, and its application to the cataloging of serials, is covered in the next chapter.

**NOTES**

1. In a later paragraph I will assert that serials are in fact born.

2. In addition to editing *Saturday Review,* Cousins was a crusader for nuclear disarmament and world government, and helped bring about the 1963 Nuclear Test Ban Treaty which prohibited the atmospheric testing of nuclear weapons.

3. *The Oxford Companion to English Literature,* 7th ed., ed. Dinah Birch (Oxford: Oxford University Press, 2009), s.v., "newspapers, origins of," www.oxfordreference.com/views/ENTRY.html?subview=Main&entry=t113.e5414.

4. Charles A. Cutter, *Rules for a Printed Dictionary Catalogue* (Washington, DC: Government Printing Office, 1876), http://hdl.handle.net/2027/wu.89101448959.

5. Charles A. Cutter, *Rules for a Dictionary Catalog,* 4th ed., rev. (Washington, DC: Government Printing Office, 1904), http://hdl.handle.net/2027/mdp.39015030341468.

6. Cutter, *Rules for a Printed Dictionary Catalogue,* 1st ed., 55.

7. *Catalogue of the Library of the Boston Athenæum,* 1807–1871 (Boston: Boston Athenæum, 1874–1882), http://nrs.harvard.edu/urn-3:HUL.FIG:004106506.

8. Cutter, *Rules for a Printed Dictionary Catalogue,* 1st ed., 10.

9. *Catalog Rules, Author and Title Entries,* US edition, comp. by committees of the American Library Association and the (British) Library Association (Chicago: American Library Association Publishing Board, 1908), http://hdl.handle.net/2027/mdp.39015033881775.

10. *A.L.A. Catalog Rules, Author and Title Entries,* prepared by the Catalog Code Revision Committee of the American Library Association with the collaboration of a committee of the (British) Library Association. Preliminary American, 2nd ed. (Chicago: American Library Association, 1941), http://hdl.handle.net/2027/mdp.39015033890123. "The preliminary American second edition of A.L.A. catalog rules, on Part I of which the present volume is based, was prepared by: American Library Association, Catalog Code Revision Committee." The 1st ed., published in 1908, has title: *Catalog rules, author and title entries.*

11. *A.L.A. Cataloging Rules for Author and Title Entries,* prepared by the Division of Cataloging and Classification of the American Library Association, 2nd ed. Clara Beetle (Chicago: American Library Association, 1949), http://hdl.handle.net/2027/mdp.39015074108591.

12. Mary Wilson MacNair, *Guide to the Cataloguing of Periodicals* (Washington, DC: Government Printing Office, Library Branch, 1918), http://hdl.handle.net/2027 /mdp.39015027883514.

13. Harriet Wheeler Pierson, *Guide to the Cataloguing of the Serial Publications of Societies and Institutions* (Washington, DC: Government Printing Office, Library Branch, 1919), http://hdl.handle.net/2027/mdp.39015033895858; 2nd ed., 1931.

14. Ibid., 9.

15. *Catalog Rules, Author and Title Entries,* 37.

16. Andrew D. Osborn, "The Crisis in Cataloging," *Library Quarterly* 11 (October 1941): 393–411, www.jstor.org/stable/4302882.

17. Seymour Lubetzky, *Cataloging Rules and Principles: A Critique of the A.L.A. Rules for Entry and a Proposed Design for Their Revision* (Washington, DC: Processing Department, Library of Congress, 1953), 47, http://hdl.handle.net/2027/ucl. b3400542.

18. Ibid., 36.

19. "Statement of Principles Adopted by the International Conference on Cataloguing Principles, Paris, October 1961," http://www.nl.go.kr/icc/paper/20.pdf.

20. Judith Proctor Cannan, "Serials Cataloging: Successive Entry," *Library Resources & Technical Services* 17 (Winter 1973): 74, http://downloads.alcts.ala.org/lrts/lrtsv17no1.

21. Carolyn O. Frost, "A Comparison of Cataloging Codes for Serials: AACR2 and Its Predecessors," in *AACR2 and Serials: The American View,* ed. Neal Edgar (New York: Haworth Press, 1983), 27–40. Also published as *Cataloging & Classification Quarterly* 3, 2/3 (Winter 1982/Spring 2983), doi:10.1300/J104v03n02_04.

22. "Cataloging of Serials," *Cataloging Service* 99 (April 1971): 1, http://hdl.handle. net/2027/mdp.39015036863457.

23. "Deletion of AA98 and 99," *Cataloging Service* 104 (May 1972), 4, http://hdl.handle .net/2027/mdp.39015036863457.

24. *National Serials Data Program; Phase I Final Report* (Washington: Information Systems Office, Library of Congress, 1969), www.eric.ed.gov/ERICWebPortal /detail?accno=ED076220.

25. *Report on the Feasibility of an International Serials Data System, and Preliminary Systems Design,* prepared by M. D. Martin and C. I. Barnes for UNISIST/ICSU-AB Working Group on Bibliographic Descriptions, DM/CB/284, London: INSPEC, April 1970, http://unesdoc.unesco.org/images/0009/000985/098515eb.pdf.

26. United Nations Educational, Scientific, and Cultural Organization, UNISIST Steering Committee (First Session), International Serials Data System (ISDS) (Item 6 of the Provisional Agenda), SC-73, CONF.201/8, Paris, 6 September 1973, http://unesdoc .unesco.org/images/0000/000057/005789EB.pdf.

27. *Serials: A MARC Format,* preliminary ed. (Washington, DC: Library of Congress, 1970).

28. "Serial Entries in Machine-Readable Form," *Cataloging Service* 106 (May 1973): 5, http://hdl.handle.net/2027/mdp.39015036863457.

29. *ISBD(S)—International Standard Bibliographic Description for Serials,* Joint Working Group on the International Standard Bibliographic Description for Serials (London: IFLA Committee on Cataloguing, 1974).

30. "Cataloging Rules—Additions and Changes," *Cataloging Service* 108 (April 1974): 2, http://hdl.handle.net/2027/mdp.39015036863457.

31. "Serials with Generic Titles," *Cataloging Service* 109 (May 1974): 9, http://hdl.handle .net/2027/mdp.39015036863457.

32. "Notes on Serial Entries which Refer to Other Publications," *Cataloging Service* 117 (Spring 1976): 9, http://hdl.handle.net/2027/mdp.39015036863440.

33. Josephine S. Pulsifer, "The Special Problems of Serials," *Library Trends* (January 1977): 691, http://hdl.handle.net/2142/8766.

34. Seymour Lubetzky, "Ideology of Bibliographic Cataloging: Progress and Retrogression," in *The Nature and Future of the Catalog: Proceedings of the ALA's Information Science and Automation Division's 1975 and 1977 Institutes on Cataloging,* eds. Maurice J. Freedman and S. Michael Malinconico (Phoenix: Oryx Press, 1979), 5–19.

35. John K. Duke, "AACR2 Serial Records and the User," in *AACR2 and Serials: The American View,* Neal Edgar, ed. (New York: Haworth Press, 1983), 115.

36. Seymour Lubetzky, "The Fundamentals of Bibliographic Cataloging and AACR2," In *The Making of a Code: The Issues Underlying AACR2,* ed. Doris Hargrett Clack (Chicago: American Library Association, 1980), 16–25.

37. "Unique Serial Identifiers," *Cataloging Service Bulletin* 5 (Summer 1979): 4, http://hdl .handle.net/2027/mdp.39015005102895.

38. Jean Weihs and Lynne C. Howarth, "Uniform Titles from AACR to RDA," *Cataloging & Classification Quarterly* 46, no. 4 (2008): 366, doi:10.1080/01639370802322853.

39. Margaret F. Maxwell, *Handbook for AACR2* (Chicago: American Library Association, 1980).

40. Jean Hirons and Crystal Graham, "Issues Relating to Seriality," *International Conference on the Principles and Future Development of AACR, Toronto, October 23– 25, 1997,* http://epe.lac-bac.gc.ca/100/200/300/jsc_aacr/issues/r-serial.pdf.

41. "'AACR2 Compatible' Headings," www.loc.gov/catdir/cpso/AACR2-d.pdf.

42. IFLA Study Group on Functional Requirements for Bibliographic Records, *Functional Requirements for Bibliographic Records: Final Report* (München: Saur, 1998).

# CHAPTER 2

# GETTING TO KNOW RDA

A new structure and other changes from AACR2

## RDA: CONCEPTUAL MODELS AND A NEW APPROACH

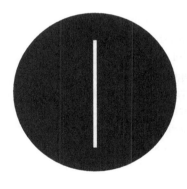

f you squint hard enough, the overall structure of RDA mirrors that of AACR2, though much of the vocabulary is unfamiliar. What had been called bibliographic description is now called recording the attributes of the resource. What was called choice of entry is now called using some of these attributes to identify the work, expression, manifestation, and item. What was called form of entry is now called using some of the attributes of these and other entities to identify those entities. But the sequence is roughly the same (if you squint), and sometimes the text is verbatim the corresponding text from AACR2, so there is occasionally that warmth that arises with recognition.

In AACR2 bibliographic description was addressed in part I and choice and form of entry in part II. In RDA bibliographic description is addressed in sections 1 and 2 and choice and form of entry is addressed all over the place but mainly in sections 3, 4, 6, and 8. Beyond this very general correspondence, the underlying structure of RDA is radically different from that of AACR2. AACR2 was largely the linear descendent of the 1908 Anglo-American code, inheriting along the way Lubetzky's reforms and generalizing the international work on standard descriptions (ISBD) first introduced into AACR1 with the 1974 revision of chapter 6 (separately published monographs). While textually RDA can be traced to AACR2 and its predecessors—should one wish to perform such exegesis—its structure is radically different, bearing a much greater resemblance to the data dictionary associated with a database.

There is a reason for this.

RDA is based on a pair of conceptual models that were hammered out in the decades after the introduction of AACR2. These are FRBR and Functional Requirements for Authority Data (FRAD).[1,2] FRBR was the product of a study on the functional requirements of bibliographic records commissioned following the 1990 Stockholm Seminar on Bibliographic Records, while FRAD arose in response to a recommendation in the FRBR final report to extend the model to authority records. FRBR and FRAD are entity-relationship models, so called because they describe a domain (for example, cataloging) where the key concepts—called entities—are described in terms of their attributes or properties (for example, the title of a resource) and their relationships to other entities (other resources, persons, families, corporate bodies, and subjects). In our current world, bibliographic and authority data are typically aggregated into discrete records, with bibliographic data corresponding to a mix of FRBR entities, but this will not always be the case. Conceptually, *records* were being superseded by *data* even as these two conceptual models were wending their way through the international review process. Indeed, while the Stockholm Seminar envisaged requirements for *records,* as did the charge of the working group that produced FRAD (called the IFLA Working Group on Functional Requirements and Numbering of Authority *Records*), its final product discusses authority *data* rather than authority *records.*

Approaching cataloging rules in this new way produces interesting results. One of the ways in which RDA differs from AACR2 is in separating instructions for recording the attributes of the carrier (the manifestation and item) from those for recording the attributes of the content (the work and expression). Under AACR2, attributes of resources—though not called attributes—were dealt with together, first in general terms (chapter 1), then specifically in terms of particular carriers (e.g., chapter 11, microforms) or particular forms of content (e.g., chapter 3, cartographic materials), and, for serials—and later integrating resources—in general terms again, based on mode of issuance (chapter 12, continuing resources). The internal structure of these chapters—the rule numbering—mirrored one another in order to facilitate their concurrent use when cataloging a resource that had characteristics dealt with in more than one chapter, and followed the order of the ISBD. In RDA, instructions relating to the attributes of carriers are given in section 1 while those relating to the attributes of content are given in section 2.

RDA also differs from AACR2 in intermingling instructions for attributes and relationships normally recorded in authority records with those normally recorded in bibliographic records. Given that most of us still operate in a world where these records are distinct from one another, this can be a bit confusing. The mappings to the MARC formats in appendixes D.2 (MARC 21 Bibliographic) and E.1 (MARC 21 Authorities) can help mitigate the confusion. It is also helpful to be mindful of situations where this problem may arise.

Instructions relating to the attributes of persons, families, and corporate bodies are given in RDA section 3, while those relating to the attributes of concepts, objects, events, and places are given in section 4. Instructions in these sections (as well as section 2, which deals with works and expressions) will sometimes apply to bibliographic records, sometimes to authority records, and sometimes to both (for example, attributes that form part of an authorized access point). Keep calm and carry on. Bear in mind that RDA is not meant to be read in a linear fashion.

Having said that, the sections and chapters of RDA do constitute conceptual wholes that can usefully be summarized in order to provide an overall understanding of the code.

# ORGANIZATION OF RDA

The following outline describes RDA as initially published. For ease of readability, it omits sections and chapters that have yet to be developed, do not apply to the current implementation scenario, or relate purely to authority data. It also shortens the names of sections and chapters whenever this can be done without confusing the reader. The FRBR Group 2 entities (person, family, corporate body) and Group 3 entities (concept, object, event, and place) are referred to as such, both to encourage the reader to think in terms of FRBR entity groups and simply to save the time of the reader.

## Introduction

The introduction (chapter 0) places RDA in its broader context, relating it to the FRBR and FRAD conceptual models and to the objectives and principles in the ICP. Additionally, it explains key concepts that will be encountered again and again, such as CORE elements, alternatives and options, exceptions, and the use of examples.

## Sections 1 and 2

Taken together, sections 1 and 2 (chapters 1–7) contain the instructions relating to description. Unlike in AACR2, they do not include the prescribed punctuation of ISBD, nor do they prescribe an order for recording the attributes of the resource. The attributes of the manifestation and item, and the physical or digital carrier of the resource, are dealt with in section 1, while the attributes of the work and expression embodied in the manifestation, and the intellectual or artistic content of the resource, are dealt with in section 2.

### SECTION 1: RECORDING ATTRIBUTES OF MANIFESTATION AND ITEM
1. General guidelines
2. Identifying manifestations and items

3. Describing carriers
4. Providing acquisition and access information

**SECTION 2: RECORDING ATTRIBUTES OF WORK AND EXPRESSION**

5. General guidelines
6. Identifying works and expressions
7. Describing content

## Section 3

Section 3 (chapters 8–11) deals with the attributes of access points for persons, families, and corporate bodies. When constructing those access points, use the record syntax in appendix E. Examples in section 3 incorporate this syntax.

**SECTION 3: RECORDING ATTRIBUTES OF GROUP 2 ENTITIES (PERSON, FAMILY, AND CORPORATE BODY)**

8. General guidelines
9. Identifying persons
10. Identifying families
11. Identifying corporate bodies

## Section 4

In its present state, section 4 might usefully be seen as an extension of section 3. It deals initially only with the attributes of access points for places (chapter 16, which includes the AACR2 presentation syntax for places). Places can be used both on their own, when they represent territorial authorities (places as corporate bodies), and as attributes of FRBR Group 1 or Group 2 entities.

**SECTION 4: RECORDING ATTRIBUTES OF GROUP 3 ENTITIES (CONCEPT, OBJECT, EVENT, AND PLACE)**

16. Identifying places

## Section 6

Section 6 deals with the relationships between Group 2 entities (persons, families, and corporate bodies) and the resource. Appendix I gives terms for expressing the relationships.

**SECTION 6: RELATIONSHIPS TO GROUP 2 ENTITIES
(PERSONS, FAMILIES, AND CORPORATE BODIES)**
    18. General guidelines
    19. Group 2 entities associated with a work
    20. Group 2 entities associated with an expression
    21. Group 2 entities associated with a manifestation
    22. Group 2 entities associated with an item

## Section 8

Section 8 deals with relationships between resources. Appendix J gives terms for expressing the relationships.

**SECTION 8: RELATIONSHIPS BETWEEN GROUP 1 ENTITIES (WORKS,
EXPRESSIONS, MANIFESTATIONS, AND ITEMS)**
    24. General guidelines
    25. Related works
    26. Related expressions
    27. Related manifestations
    28. Related items

## Appendixes

Appendixes
    A. Capitalization
    B. Abbreviations
    C. Initial articles
    D. Record syntaxes for descriptive data
    E. Record syntaxes for access point control
    F. Additional instructions on names of persons
    G. Titles of nobility, terms of rank, etc.
    H. Dates in the Christian calendar
    I. Relationship designators: Relationships between a resource and persons, families, and corporate bodies associated with the resource
    J. Relationship designators: Relationships between works, expressions, manifestations, and items
    K. Relationship designators: Relationships between persons, families, and corporate bodies
    L. Relationship designators: Relationships between concepts, objects, events, and places
    Glossary

## WHERE'S THAT RULE?

Among the handy resources in RDA Toolkit is a copy of the final version of AACR2 with each rule linked to its corresponding RDA instruction(s). Despite this, a number of AACR2 rules are so important for serials cataloging that their corresponding RDA instructions are identified here for easy reference.

> 21.1B (Entry under corporate body) → RDA 19.2.1.1.1 (Corporate bodies considered to be creators)
>
> 21.2B (Changes in titles proper: Integrating resources) → RDA 2.3.2.12.3
>
> 21.2C (Changes in titles proper: Serials: Major and minor changes) → RDA 2.3.2.12.2 / RDA 2.3.2.13
>
> 21.3B (Changes of persons or bodies responsible for a work) → RDA 6.1.3.2.1
>
> 24.13 (Corporate bodies (except government agencies): Subordinate entry) → RDA 11.2.2.14
>
> 24.14 (Corporate bodies (except government agencies): Direct or indirect subheading) → RDA 11.2.2.15
>
> 24.18 (Government agencies: Subordinate entry) → RDA 11.2.2.19
>
> 24.19 (Government agencies: Direct or indirect subheading) → RDA 11.2.2.20

## THE APPROACH OF THIS MANUAL

Although RDA Toolkit is designed to be used as an online tool, this manual is designed to be used as a book. Consequently, any aspects of RDA Toolkit that have been optimized for an online environment will not be carried over to this manual. In particular, the record syntaxes relegated to RDA appendix E—ISBD and MARC 21 Bibliographic—will be integrated with the instructions taken from RDA proper in the following chapters. Likewise, while the approach in this manual will adhere fairly closely to the section arrangement of RDA, it will depart from it when this seems in the best interest of the reader. For example, instructions relating to the attributes of works, expressions, manifestations, and items will be intermingled, because these attributes are intermingled in the resource itself. The organization of attributes will follow the International Standard Bibliographic Description as recorded in the MARC 21 Bibliographic format. Instructions to record a relationship with a FRBR Group 1 or Group 2 entity will occur when a given attribute of the resource suggests such a relationship.

Relationships with resources present a particular problem in the current record-based implementation scenario. Whereas the FRBR model envisages most relationships between Group 1 entities occurring between works and expressions, in the current record-based environment these relationships typically occur between manifestations. This manual will likewise describe most relationships in these terms, though relationships that require an authorized access point for the related resource will be expressed in terms of works and expressions in accord with the letter of RDA.

While this manual aims to be a stand alone product to the extent possible, it assumes a certain familiarity on the part of the reader with the cataloging products from which it draws much of its content: RDA itself, the FRBR conceptual model, the MARC 21 formats, and the ISBD. For the uninitiated, good introductions to all but the ISBD are available:

> Chris Oliver. *Introducing RDA: A Guide to the Basics* (Chicago: ALA Editions, 2010), ISBN 978-0-8389-3594-1.
>
> Robert L. Maxwell. *FRBR: A Guide for the Perplexed* (Chicago: ALA Editions, 2007), ISBN 978-0-8389-0950-8.
>
> *Understanding MARC Bibliographic: Machine-Readable Cataloging*, 8th ed. (Library of Congress, 2009), www.loc.gov/marc/umb.
>
> *Understanding MARC Authority Records: Machine-Readable Cataloging* (Library of Congress, 2004), www.loc.gov/marc/uma.

Also it cannot be emphasized enough that this manual, like all static products, was already out of date when it was published. Readers are urged to consult RDA Toolkit and related local policies for the most current information.

## CHANGES FROM AACR2 TO RDA

There have been several noteworthy changes from AACR2 to RDA. These changes adhere to the general principles outlined in the ICP, and in fact the motivation for many of these changes lies in the desire to conform to these principles:

1. *Convenience of the user.* Decisions taken in the making of descriptions and controlled forms of names for access should be made with the user in mind.
2. *Common usage.* Vocabulary used in descriptions and access should be in accord with that of the majority of users.
3. *Representation.* Descriptions and controlled forms of names should be based on the way an entity describes itself.
4. *Accuracy.* The entity described should be faithfully portrayed.
5. *Sufficiency and necessity.* Only those data elements in descriptions and controlled forms of names for access that are required to fulfill user tasks and are essential to uniquely identify an entity should be included.
6. *Significance.* Data elements should be bibliographically significant.
7. *Economy.* When alternative ways exist to achieve a goal, preference should be given to the way that best furthers overall economy (i.e., the least cost or the simplest approach).
8. *Consistency and standardization.* Descriptions and construction of access points should be standardized as far as possible. This enables greater consistency, which in turn increases the ability to share bibliographic and authority data.

9. *Integration.* The descriptions for all types of materials and controlled forms of names of all types of entities should be based on a common set of rules, insofar as it is relevant.

The principle of *common usage,* for example, accounts for the replacement of certain cataloger-supplied Latin abbreviations in the bibliographic description with statements in the vernacular (e.g., replacing "[s.n.]" with "[publisher not identified]"). These vernacular words and phrases are much more likely to be understood by most catalog users, and ideally they will be able to be machine-generated from coded values, which are especially useful in the context of a multilingual catalog.

Similarly, the principle of *representation* accounts for changes to several transcription practices in part I of AACR2. These practices typically involved abbreviating or omitting text appearing in the source being transcribed that was deemed too lengthy to be accommodated on catalog cards (still the predominant form of catalog when AACR2 was implemented in 1981). While RDA descriptions will consequently be lengthier than AACR2 descriptions, the process of transcription will be greatly simplified. For example, catalogers will no longer need to know when, where, and how to abbreviate a given word or phrase (such as "Government Printing Office"). Making this a more mechanical process also facilitates the so-called *ingestion* of text from other sources, including the scanning of an area of the source using optical character recognition (OCR) products.

Beyond these, the general material designator (GMD), whose introduction was the most visible change in bibliographic description from AACR1 to AACR2, is being retired in favor of a matrix of three elements for resource categorization created in collaboration with the publisher community and intended to facilitate the interoperability of metadata created by the library and publisher communities. (Analogous changes are taking place in the revised ISBD.) These new elements specify the general media type and the more specific carrier type—both applying to the manifestation—and the content type, which applies to the work.

## SPECIFIC CHANGES BY AACR2 CHAPTER AND VERSE

The specific changes from AACR2 to RDA are elaborated in the following paragraphs, arranged by the affected AACR2 rule. In general, only changes that are expected to affect serials cataloging have been included.

## Part I: Description

## CHAPTER 1: GENERAL RULES FOR DESCRIPTION

### 1.0C PUNCTUATION

ISBD prescribed punctuation:

- Square brackets: When square brackets are required, enclose each element in its own brackets. (Adjacent elements are no longer bracketed together.)
- Full stops: When a full stop is required, it is recorded in addition to any full stop that is already present (e.g., at the end of an abbreviation).

### 1.0D LEVELS OF DETAIL IN THE DESCRIPTION

The three levels of detail are replaced by the distinction in RDA between elements that are CORE and those that are not.

### 1.0E LANGUAGE AND SCRIPT OF THE DESCRIPTION

RDA 1.4 permits the recording of elements in a transliterated script as well as in the script in which they appear on the resource. (This is a cosmetic change, retroactively sanctioning current practice.)

### 1.0F INACCURACIES

In RDA inaccuracies are transcribed as found, though the inaccuracy may be noted and the corrected form may be recorded if considered important for access. *An exception is made for an inaccuracy limited to the title proper of the first issue of a serial.*

### 1.1B TITLE PROPER

The title proper is now transcribed as is with regard to punctuation. Formerly, certain marks of punctuation that might have been confused with ISBD prescribed punctuation were replaced. No special instructions are now given for punctuating alternative titles, though marks of punctuation may be added if needed for clarity.

### 1.1C GENERAL MATERIAL DESIGNATION

The general material designation is replaced by a combination of three new elements: media type, carrier type, and content type.

### 1.1D PARALLEL TITLES

Parallel titles may now be taken from anywhere in the resource, not just the chief source. There are no limitations on how many parallel titles may be recorded.

### 1.1E OTHER TITLE INFORMATION

Other title information is no longer supplied by the cataloger if the title proper is felt to need explanation (e.g., when the name of a corporate body has been used as the title proper of its annual report).

### 1.1F STATEMENT OF RESPONSIBILITY

- The statement of responsibility is recorded in square brackets *only* if it is taken from outside the resource.
- There is no longer a limit on the number of persons, etc., that may be recorded in a statement of responsibility, though there is an option to record only the first, followed by a bracketed summarization (e.g., [and 4 other agencies]).
- Statements of responsibility are now transcribed *as is,* though an option permits the omission of certain information.
- The instruction to treat a noun phrase as other title information if it is "indicative of the nature of the work" (e.g., dramatized adaptations / by Barry Campbell) has been removed. Such phrases are now treated as part of the statement of responsibility.

### 1.2B EDITION STATEMENT

Edition statements are now transcribed *as is,* without abbreviation or the substitution of arabic numerals for roman numerals or numbers expressed as words.

### 1.4C PLACE OF PUBLICATION, DISTRIBUTION, ETC.

- Places of publication, distribution, etc., are transcribed *as is,* without abbreviation or clarification (other than adding the name of a larger jurisdiction [as an option]).
- For multiple places of publication, distribution, etc., the hierarchy of preferences given in 1.4C5 has been replaced by an instruction to simply follow "the sequence, layout, or typography of the names" in the source. The limit on the number of places that may be recorded has also been removed, but only the first recorded place is considered a core element.
- [S.1.] has been replaced by a bracketed statement in the vernacular (e.g., [Place of publication not identified]).

### 1.4D NAME OF PUBLISHER, DISTRIBUTOR, ETC.

- Names of publishers, distributors, etc., are transcribed *as is,* without abbreviation or shortening.
- For multiple publishers, distributors, etc., the hierarchy of preferences given in 1.4D4 has been replaced by an instruction to simply follow the "sequence, layout, or typography of the names" in the source. The limit on the number of publishers, distributors, etc., that may be recorded has also been removed.
- [s.n.] has been replaced by a bracketed statement in the vernacular (e.g., [publisher not identified]).
- When the name of a distributor is available rather than the name of a publisher, the one is no longer substituted for the other. Rather, [publisher not identified] is explicitly recorded and the name of the distributor is recorded as its own separate element.

### 1.4F DATE OF PUBLICATION, DISTRIBUTION, ETC.

- When the date of publication, distribution, etc., is unavailable and cannot be supplied, this is now recorded (e.g., [date of publication not identified]) in addition to any copyright date or date of manufacture that may be available. Formerly only the copyright date (or, failing this, the date of manufacture) was recorded in these circumstances.
- New instructions for the format of supplied dates are given. Earliest/latest possible dates are indicated by "not before/after" (e.g., [not before 2007]). Approximate dates will be indicated by a question mark (e.g., 2007?) rather than "ca." (e.g., ca. 2007).
- The form in which dates are recorded is now left up to the cataloging agency. Formerly, arabic numerals were substituted for roman numerals.

### 1.5B EXTENT OF ITEM (INCLUDING SPECIFIC MATERIAL DESIGNATION)
Terms that were abbreviated (e.g., "v." for "volumes") are no longer abbreviated in RDA.

### 1.5C OTHER PHYSICAL DETAILS
Terms that were abbreviated (e.g., "ill." for "illustrations") are no longer abbreviated in RDA.

### 1.5D DIMENSIONS
RDA prefers metric units. Alternatively, the cataloging agency may choose the system of measurement. Metric symbols (e.g., cm) are no longer followed by full stops.

### 1.6G NUMBERING WITHIN SERIES
Numbering is transcribed *as is,* without abbreviation, though numerals may be recorded in the form in which they appear on the resource, in the form preferred by the cataloging agency, or in both forms.

### 1.6H SUBSERIES
Omitting the ISSN of a series when the ISSN of its subseries was present is now optional.


## CHAPTER 2: BOOKS, PAMPHLETS, AND PRINTED SHEETS
No changes relevant to the cataloging of serials or ongoing integrating resources.


## CHAPTER 3: CARTOGRAPHIC MATERIALS

### 3.3B STATEMENT OF SCALE
The scale can now be taken from any source.

### CHAPTER 4: MANUSCRIPTS (INCLUDING MANUSCRIPT COLLECTIONS)

No changes relevant to the cataloging of serials or ongoing integrating resources.

### CHAPTER 5: MUSIC

No changes relevant to the cataloging of serials or ongoing integrating resources.

### CHAPTER 6: SOUND RECORDINGS

#### 6.5B EXTENT OF ITEM (INCLUDING SPECIFIC MATERIAL DESIGNATION)

Terms beginning with "sound" have generally been replaced by terms beginning with "audio."

#### 6.5D DIMENSIONS

Dimensions are always given, even when they conform to a commonly accepted standard.

### CHAPTER 7: MOTION PICTURES AND VIDEORECORDINGS

#### 7.5B EXTENT OF ITEM (INCLUDING SPECIFIC MATERIAL DESIGNATION)

Added: "film roll" and "videodisc"; changed: "video cartridge" and "videotape reel."

#### 7.5D DIMENSIONS

Dimensions of films and videotapes now include width.

### CHAPTER 8: GRAPHIC MATERIALS

No changes relevant to the cataloging of serials or ongoing integrating resources.

### CHAPTER 9: ELECTRONIC RESOURCES

#### 9.5B EXTENT OF ITEM (INCLUDING SPECIFIC MATERIAL DESIGNATION)

Added: "online resource"; changed: "computer disc" replaces both "computer disk" and "computer optical disc."

### CHAPTER 10: THREE-DIMENSIONAL ARTEFACTS AND REALIA

No changes relevant to the cataloging of serials or ongoing integrating resources.

## CHAPTER 11: MICROFORMS

### GENERAL

The American practice of describing the original publication when cataloging a microform reproduction of a previously published work will not continue under RDA. (Technically this is not a change from AACR2 to RDA, since it is permitted under neither code.)

### 11.5D DIMENSIONS

Dimensions are always given, even when they conform to a commonly accepted standard. Dimensions of microfilms now include width.

## CHAPTER 12: CONTINUING RESOURCES

### 12.1B TITLE PROPER

The mark of omission is now used regardless of where the omitted data is taken from. AACR2 had an exception for the beginning of the title proper. (A cosmetic change was also made to remove an obsolete instruction relating to the presence of a corporate body name in the title proper.)

### 12.1E OTHER TITLE INFORMATION

The instruction that other title information be recorded only if considered important has been removed, since this element is not CORE under RDA.

### 12.3B NUMERIC AND/OR ALPHABETIC DESIGNATION

Designations are transcribed *as is,* without abbreviation, though numerals may be recorded in the form in which they appear on the resource, in the form preferred by the cataloging agency, or in both forms.

### 12.3C CHRONOLOGICAL DESIGNATION

Designations are transcribed *as is,* without abbreviation, though numerals may be recorded in the form in which they appear on the resource, in the form preferred by the cataloging agency, or in both forms.

### 12.3D NO DESIGNATION ON FIRST ISSUE OR PART

There is no longer a prescribed form for the supplied designation when the form on future issues is not available as a model.

## CHAPTER 13: ANALYSIS

No changes relevant to the cataloging of serials or ongoing integrating resources.

**Part II: Headings, Uniform Titles, and References**

## CHAPTER 21: CHOICE OF ACCESS POINTS

### 21.0D OPTIONAL ADDITION: DESIGNATIONS OF FUNCTION
RDA appendix I greatly expands the designators that can be used to relate a person, family, or corporate body to a resource.

### 21.2B CHANGES IN TITLE PROPER: INTEGRATING RESOURCES
A change in mode of issuance and/or media type requires a new description. Likewise a new set of base volumes for an updating loose-leaf publication.

### 21.2C CHANGES IN TITLE PROPER: SERIALS
A change in mode of issuance and/or media type requires a new description.

### 21.6B WORKS OF SHARED RESPONSIBILITY: PRINCIPAL RESPONSIBILITY INDICATED
RDA removes the limit (the so-called Rule of Three) on the number of access points for persons, etc., involved in a work of shared responsibility.

### 21.6C WORKS OF SHARED RESPONSIBILITY: PRINCIPAL RESPONSIBILITY NOT INDICATED
RDA removes the limit (the so-called Rule of Three) on the number of access points for persons, etc., involved in a work of shared responsibility.

## CHAPTER 22: HEADINGS FOR PERSONS

### 22._ INITIALS IN PERSONAL NAME HEADINGS
RDA contains instructions for adding a full stop after an initial. The practice was undocumented in AACR2 (as indicated by the underline mark).

### 22.3D DIFFERENT SPELLINGS OF THE SAME NAME
Prefer the form found on the first resource received.

### 22.5C ENTRY UNDER SURNAMES: COMPOUND SURNAMES
The detailed instructions on recording compound surnames, based on the IFLA publication *Names of Persons: National Usages for Entry in Catalogues,* have been replaced by a reference to the publication itself.[3]

### 22.15C ADDITIONS TO NAMES ENTERED UNDER SURNAME: OTHER ADDITIONS
Terms indicating relationship (e.g., Jr.), formerly excluded unless absolutely needed to distinguish identical names, are now treated as part of the name.

### 22.17 ADDITIONS TO NAMES: DATES

- Names of months are no longer abbreviated.
- "century" is no longer abbreviated.
- "ca." is replaced by "approximately".
- "fl" is replaced by "active" (Library of Congress policy). There is no longer a restriction on using dates of activity in the twentieth century.

### 22.18 ADDITIONS TO NAMES: FULLER FORMS

There is no longer a restriction on when fuller forms can be added to names.

### 22.19 ADDITIONS TO NAMES: DISTINGUISHING TERMS

Terms of address and initials indicating academic degrees and society memberships are no longer added to names, except in very limited circumstances. Terms indicating profession or occupation or field of activity are added only to names not conveying the idea of a person (e.g., Sting).

## CHAPTER 23: GEOGRAPHIC NAMES

No changes relevant to the cataloging of serials or ongoing integrating resources.

## CHAPTER 24: HEADINGS FOR CORPORATE BODIES

### 24.2C DIFFERENT SPELLINGS OF THE SAME NAME
Prefer the form found on the first resource received.

### 24.7A CONFERENCES, CONGRESSES, MEETINGS, ETC.: OMISSIONS
Terms of frequency will no longer be omitted from headings for conferences, etc. (RDA treats conferences, etc., and exhibitions, etc., alike.)

### 24.7B CONFERENCES, CONGRESSES, MEETINGS, ETC.: OMISSIONS
If a conference, etc., is held in three or more places, each place is recorded, separated by a semicolon.

### 24.8A EXHIBITIONS, FAIRS, FESTIVALS, ETC.: OMISSIONS
The year of convocation will now be included. (RDA treats conferences, etc., and exhibitions, etc., alike.)

## CHAPTER 25: UNIFORM TITLES

### 25.3B WORKS CREATED AFTER 1500
Introductory phrases (e.g., Here beginneth the tale of) are no longer routinely omitted from preferred titles.

**25.3C WORKS CREATED AFTER 1500: SIMULTANEOUS PUBLICATION UNDER DIFFERENT TITLES**
Prefer the form found on the first resource received.

**25.5C ADDITIONS: LANGUAGE**

- Languages of subtitles of motion pictures, etc., are added.
- When a single expression involves multiple languages, the name of each language is added, rather than "Polyglot."

## CHAPTER 26: REFERENCES

**26.1E EXPLANATORY REFERENCES**
General explanatory references (as opposed to those that clarify a specific relationship) are no longer made.

**26.1H WHEN NOT TO MAKE REFERENCES**
The instruction not to make references when the reference is so similar to a heading or other reference as to be unnecessary has been removed.

---

**NOTES**

1. IFLA Study Group on Functional Requirements for Bibliographic Data, *Functional Requirements for Bibliographic Records: Final Report,* as amended and corrected through February 2009. www.ifla.org/files/cataloguing/frbr/frbr_2008.pdf.

2. *Functional Requirements for Authority Data: A Conceptual Model,* ed. Glenn E. Patton. (München: K. G. Saur, 2009).

3. *Names of Persons: National Usages for Entry in Catalogues,* 4th ed. (München: K. G. Saur, 1996), www.ifla.org/files/cataloguing/pubs/names-of-persons_1996.pdf.

# SERIALS CATALOGING USING RDA

# CHAPTER 3

# SEARCHING AND THE UNIVERSE OF SERIALS

**T**HE FIRST STEP IN CATALOGING A SERIAL IS PRAY-ing that someone else has already cataloged it. The prayer is short, and each religion has its own variation. There are believed to be versions for agnostics and atheists, though this may be more legend than fact. Most cataloging departments are tolerant of their serials catalogers mumbling the Prayer of the Serials Cataloger from time to time throughout the day. Some provide a special room.

The second step is determining whether your prayer has been answered. This is done by searching in your particular database, which hopefully includes the CONSER database of more than a million serials catalog records. Having such a large database is both a blessing and a curse. On the one hand, there is a greater probability that someone else will have already cataloged your serial—waiting for someone else to do so is a venerable tradition in all types of cataloging—but on the other hand, having such a large number of records makes it much more difficult to determine that someone has actually accomplished the task, especially if the serial does not have a very distinctive title.

## BEFORE SEARCHING

Before searching, familiarize yourself with the class of minor title changes set out in RDA 2.3.2.13.2. This is necessary because you may not otherwise recognize the catalog record when you find it. RDA 2.3.2.13.2 lists various types of title change that do *not* result in the creation of a new description. Knowing the nature of these *minor* changes allows you to recognize the various guises under which your serial might possibly appear in the catalog. For example, the *JSC Journal of RDA Studies* may appear in the catalog as *RDA Studies*. Rather than creating a new record in such a case, you should simply modify the existing record by adding an access point and/or note for your variant title.

Armed with the Knowledge of Minor Changes, you are ready to search for your serial.

Serials catalogers have developed a hierarchy of searching techniques, which can be summarized as follows:

1. If the serial has an ISSN, use it.
2. If the serial has a distinctive title, use it.
3. If the serial does not have a distinctive title, try to narrow your results set by:
   - Identifying a related corporate body;
   - Identifying its earliest possible date of publication; or
   - Identifying a related serial with a distinctive title.

Each of these will be covered in turn.

## SEARCHING BY ISSN

An ISSN is to serials what an ISBN is to books. Well, not really, but I'm trying to let you down easy. Whereas the ISBN is assigned by the publisher and printed on every book, the ISSN is assigned by an ISSN center, typically located at a national bibliographical agency—in our case, the Library of Congress or Library and Archives Canada (LAC)—and may or may not be printed on a given serial. If it is printed on the serial, it may or may not be the correct ISSN (but one can hope).

Note that the same ISSN is used for a print serial and any microform or digital reproductions "produced for the purpose of providing surrogates for the original materials."[1] Similarly, a single ISSN is assigned for different file formats (HTML, PDF, etc.) of the same online serial.[2]

The ISSN is tied to the title carried by the serial and when this title changes (or changes sufficiently) the ISSN changes as well. If the title is generic in nature (for example, "Annual Report," "Newsletter," "Proceedings") the name of its issuing body is linked to the title, and similarly when this name changes (or changes sufficiently) the ISSN changes as well. Otherwise, if the title is not unique—even one that has been linked to the name of its issuing body—it is augmented by other data (for example, place of publication, beginning year of publication) to render it unique. Such a unique title is called a key title and is assigned to the serial by the ISSN center along with the ISSN. For more details, the incurably curious are referred to the *ISSN*

*Manual: Cataloguing Part.*[3] See especially section 2.2 giving general rules for ISSN assignment.

If your serial carries an ISSN—an eight-digit number helpfully introduced by the initials "ISSN"—your task will be simply to search the catalog by this ISSN and retrieve the serial, then make sure the serial record retrieved describes the serial you need to catalog. Bibliographic records retrieved via an ISSN search may or may not describe the serial in hand because publishers sometimes change titles without applying for a new ISSN, and sometimes they have only a vague idea as to which title an ISSN belongs.

Finding the ISSN on the serial may also present something of a challenge. Whereas the ISBN typically appears on the back of a book for ease of barcode scanning, the ISSN may appear almost anywhere. While a library journal often displays its ISSN on the cover (for obvious reasons), other publications may hide it away. Book-like serials (annuals and monographic series) may carry the ISSN along with the ISBN in the preliminaries of a given volume. Periodicals, on the other hand, may carry it in the colophon or at the bottom of an inside page with data relating to second-class mailing privileges. Or the ISSN may appear nowhere. Serials catalogers develop a sixth sense about where to look, and when to give up.

## THE ISSN PORTAL

The ISSN Portal (portal.issn.org) is a handy source for clarifying questions relating to ISSN and serials, especially foreign serials, since it is where the authoritative records for ISSN assignments reside. Unfortunately, access costs an arm and a leg. If you are lucky enough to have access, you are blessed, especially if you have a non-unique title that pulled up a bazillion records in your regular cataloging database. Re-approaching that database armed with an ISSN from the Portal almost always makes life easier.

## SEARCHING BY TITLE, ISSUING BODY, OR A COMBINATION OF THESE

If your serial does not carry an ISSN—or if it does carry one but you failed to retrieve the appropriate bibliographic record (or any bibliographic record) by searching under it—you will need to select other attributes to help identify the manifestation so that you can search for it efficiently in the catalog and recognize it if you find it.

Except in the rare case of a truly distinctive title, searching a catalog by title for a serial can be an overwhelming and frustrating experience, especially for the cataloger wishing to find all the necessary records. Still, it must be done because the consequence of failure may be the creation of a duplicate record or the failure to link records for related serials.

How one searches for a serial depends on the nature of the title. The experienced serials cataloger develops a sixth sense about the best method, but here are some helpful rules of thumb:

1. If the item in hand is the first issue, include the date of that issue in the search argument. This will limit the result set to serials that began in that year. However, bear in mind that this is a case where absence of evidence is not evidence of absence. The serial may already be present in the catalog, but the original cataloger did not know when it began and so could not supply a beginning year. Bear in mind also that the beginning year is based on the chronological designation whenever one is present and so will not always correspond to the beginning year of publication.

2. In cases of serials with non-distinctive titles—Statistical Bulletin, Annual Report, Journal, etc.—include as an element in the search argument the name of any corporate body associated with the serial, even if the name of the body is also not distinctive. Bear in mind that in such situations you are grasping at straws. The prospect of having to review thousands of candidate records for "Annual Report" is a daunting one to say the least, and any strategy that will usefully reduce the result set is welcome. One caveat: If the corporate body is unfamiliar, search authority records first for an authorized access point, to ensure that you search under the correct form of name. For example, searching for the Annual Report of the Toyota Motor Corporation under "Toyota Motor Corporation" will produce an invalid result set, because the authorized access point for the corporation is "Toyota Jidōsha Kabushiki Kaisha" (as you surely knew).

3. Search under all titles found on the item, no matter how obscure. A title that is obscure today might have been less so in the past. Conversely, a title that was obscure in the past may be prominent today.

4. If typography suggests a given string of text might or might not be part of the title, search for the title both including the string and excluding it.

5. If you know of a related resource with a more distinctive title, a search for that title may lead you to your target serial via a link that provides a specific identifier (an ISSN, record control number, or other identifier).

This is the extent of the Wisdom of Searching, acquired over decades of machine searching against increasingly dense and opaque files of serial catalog records, searching made more challenging by the need to bear in mind ever more tolerant definitions of minor title change.

This chapter has been short. In contrast, the next chapter—addressing the nitty-gritty of serials cataloging with RDA—will be long, but hopefully not unconscionably so.

**NOTES**

1. *ISSN Manual: Cataloguing Part* (Paris, France: ISSN International Centre, 2009), 28, www.issn.org/files/issn/Documentation/Manuels/ISSN_Manual_ENG_ED_2009.pdf.

2. "ISSN and Electronic Publications," www.issn.org/2-22638-ISSN-and-electronic -publications.php.

3. *ISSN Manual: Cataloguing Part* (Paris, France: ISSN International Centre, 2009), www.issn.org/files/issn/Documentation/Manuels/ISSN_Manual_ENG_ED_2009.pdf.

# CHAPTER 4

# CATALOGING SERIALS AND ONGOING INTEGRATING RESOURCES USING RDA

S NOTED IN CHAPTER 2, UNLIKE RDA TOOLKIT, this manual is not designed for use as an online tool. It is designed for use as a book. Consequently, we have tried to minimize the need to jump around in the text when dealing with a single question. In fact, because this manual focuses on one type of cataloging—the cataloging of serials and ongoing integrating resources—there should be even less jumping around than in the past. Even under AACR2, catalogers had to look in at least three chapters—chapter 1 (general rules), chapter 2 (books, pamphlets, and printed sheets), and chapter 12 (continuing resources)—when describing a printed serial.

Beyond this, we have integrated ISBD, MARC 21, and other formatting instructions into the text. These "record syntaxes" are given separately in RDA, with syntaxes for descriptive data (ISBD and MARC 21) set out in appendix D and those for access point control in appendix E.

Although these record syntaxes are not part of RDA proper, they are, as a practical matter, integral to the cataloging of library resources, at least for the immediate future. The use of ISBD is mandated by principle 5.3 in the Statement of International Cataloguing Principles (and its associated footnote), which declares that "descriptive data should be based on an internationally agreed standard, [which] for the library community [is] the International Standard Bibliographic Description."[1] In the case of MARC 21, its inclusion in the text is simply an acknowledgment of its predominant use in the current online cataloging environment in North America. It must be recognized, however, that while MARC 21 can support RDA in a world of bibliographic and authority records (RDA implementation scenarios 3 and 2), it cannot support RDA implementation scenario 1, a database structure that mirrors the FRBR and FRAD conceptual models.[2] For this reason, work has begun on developing a successor to MARC 21 capable of supporting scenario 1.[3]

For what it's worth, a similar tension prevailed in the early days of AACR2, when the overwhelming majority of libraries still operated in a card catalog environment, though more and more of them were using MARC to produce those catalog cards. The first two editions of Maxwell's classic *Handbook for AACR2* (1980, 1989) were oriented entirely to that environment, with MARC content designation appearing only with the third edition in 1997.[4]

## ORGANIZATION

This chapter is organized as follows:

1. General instructions relating to RDA and MARC 21
2. Attributes of resources (manifestations and items and the works and expressions they embody)

    - Generally organized by ISBD area
    - ISBD-prescribed punctuation integrated into examples
    - MARC 21 coding integrated into examples
    - Notes that relate to a particular element are given with the instructions for that element, not with instructions relating to the Notes area
    - Where RDA provides more instructions covering a class of element (e.g., titles) these are addressed at the point where that element is first encountered
    - Where RDA indicates access may be appropriate for a particular element to support a particular user task, this is noted

3. Relationships between resources
4. Identifying works and expressions (authorized access point for the resource)
5. Identifying related entities (authorized access points for persons, corporate bodies, and other resources related to the resource being described)
6. Special instructions relating to online serials
7. Special instructions relating to ongoing integrating resources

For each element, a brief introductory discussion provides context, followed by guidance on recording the particular element, recording changes to the element over time, recording notes related to the element, and providing structured access to the element when important.

This chapter should be treated as a supplement to RDA, MARC 21, and ISBD. Even as you read it for the first time, it is well on its way to obsolescence. And though there is no need to jump around from place to place as long as you remain within the confines of chapter 4, readers are strongly encouraged to consult the text of RDA, etc., for the latest guidance on any given question(s). RDA being an online tool, it is eminently updatable, and for readers so inclined, there is the added enticement of being able to jump around to their hearts' content.

# 1. GENERAL INSTRUCTIONS RELATING TO SERIALS CATALOGING USING RDA AND MARC 21

## Cataloging Preliminaries: MARC 21 Matters External to RDA

This manual presumes a rudimentary familiarity with the MARC 21 Bibliographic format, at least insofar as it applies to the cataloging of monographs (i.e., books). For this reason, we will typically address MARC elements only to the extent that they are unique to the cataloging of serials or ongoing integrating resources, or have some unusual application within this realm.

When cataloging a serial from scratch, the first step is to request a blank workform or—when the serial being cataloged closely resembles one described by an existing bibliographic record—to request a workform derived from that record. For example, in OCLC one would request a "continuing resources" workform or derive from an existing "continuing resources" record. In terms of "mode of issuance" [RDA 2.13], a "continuing resources" workform accommodates both serials and integrating resources. On these workforms, certain coded elements are typically completed prior to diving into cataloging proper, particularly many of the elements occurring in what MARC-speak calls the leader (or record label) and the control fields (numbered 006 to 008). Elements in these "fixed fields" are defined only by their absolute position (byte) in a given MARC field, whereas in the record displayed to the cataloger they are kindly preceded by mnemonic codes—at least somebody thinks they're mnemonic—at the top of the workform.

For example, in an OCLC "continuing resources" workform, the following elements display, drawn from the leader and control field 008:

| Type | ELvl | Srce | GPub | Ctrl | Lang |
|------|------|------|------|------|------|
| **BLvl** | **Form** | **Conf** | **Freq** | MRec | **Ctry** |
| **S/L** | **Orig** | **EntW** | **Regl** | Alph | |
| **Desc** | **SrTp** | **Cont** | **DtSt** | **Dates** | |

Each of the bolded elements above is treated below in alphabetical order by its OCLC mnemonic, followed in parentheses by the MARC 21 name of the element and its corresponding position in the leader (LDR) or 008 control field. Elements are not listed if they are not applicable to the cataloging of serials or ongoing integrating resources.

**BLvl** (bibliographic level: LDR/07). This is the mode of issuance [RDA 2.13].
   s = serials
   i = integrating resources

**Conf** (conference publication: 008/29).
   1 = content consists of proceedings or collections of papers from conferences
   0 = other

**Cont** (nature of contents: 008/25-27). A series of up to three codes that
   identify types of material constituting a significant portion of the content (as
   evidenced by mention in the title proper, notes, or subject headings. If the
   entire work constitutes a particular type of material, use **EntW** (nature of
   entire work: 008/24) instead.
   #—Not specified
   a—Abstracts/summaries
   b—Bibliographies
   c—Catalogs
   d—Dictionaries
   e—Encyclopedias
   f—Handbooks
   g—Legal articles
   h—Biography
   i—Indexes
   k—Discographies
   1—Legislation
   m—Theses
   n—Surveys of literature in a subject area
   o—Reviews
   p—Programmed texts
   q—Filmographies
   r—Directories
   s—Statistics
   t—Technical reports
   u—Standards/specifications
   v—Legal cases and case notes
   w—Law reports and digests
   y—Yearbooks
   z—Treaties
   5—Calendars
   6—Comics/graphic novels

**Ctry** (country of publication: 008/15-17). A two- or three-character code taken
   from the *MARC Code List for Countries*[5] identifies the country or state/
   province of publication. See the introduction to that publication for more

detailed instructions. It should correspond to the first recorded place of publication in the latest issue consulted.

**Dates** (date 1 [beginning date]: 008/07-10 / date 2 [ending date]: 008/11-14). The beginning and ending years are recorded (based on the *chronological designation* on the first and last serial issues or, in the absence of chronological designations, the dates of publication). This is a different practice from monograph cataloging, where dates of publication are always used. It dates from a time when catalogers did not routinely record dates of publication for serials. If the exact year is unknown, one or more **u**'s are substituted for digits, depending on whether the year, decade, century, or millennium is unknown. If the resource is still being published, date 2 is recorded as "9999." If the publication status is unknown and expected issues have not been received for more than three years, date 2 is recorded as "uuuu." If the first or last issue covers more than one year (say, "Biennial report for 2003-4"), the latest year is recorded (in this case, 2004).

**Desc** (descriptive cataloging form). On RDA records, this code indicates whether or not ISBD punctuation is included.
i = record includes ISBD prescribed punctuation
c = record omits ISBD prescribed punctuation

**DtSt** (type of date/publication status: 008/06).
c = currently published [date 2 contains "9999"]
d = ceased publication (dead)
u = unknown [date 2 contains "uuuu"]

**ELvl** (encoding level: LDR/17). Different systems employ different values to indicate the fullness of the bibliographic information and coding in the record. Consult your local system documentation.

**EntW** (nature of entire work: 008/24). See **Cont** (nature of contents: 008/25-27) above for guidance.

**Form** (form of item: 008/23). This element identifies the physical/digital form of the resource:

# = none of the following
a = microfilm                   f = Braille
b = microfiche                  o = online (remote access electronic)
c = micro-opaque                q = direct access electronic (CD-ROM, etc.)
d = large print                 r = regular print reproduction

**Freq** (frequency: 008/18). This element should be coded with the latest known frequency when the frequency is recorded (see RDA 2.14, below). If no frequency is recorded, record a value of [u] (unknown).

**GPub** (government publication: 008/28). For the official publications of governments and international organizations, this element identifies the level of government:

# = not a government publication

i = international organization      s = state, province, territory

f = national (federal or unitary)      c = multilocal

a = autonomous or semi-autonomous entity    l = local

m = sub-national region      o = other

**Lang** (Language: 008/35-37). A three-character code drawn from the *MARC Code List for Languages*6 identifies the primary language of the publication. See the introduction to that publication for more detailed instructions.

**Orig** (form of original item: 008/23). This element identifies the physical/digital form of the original manifestation when the resource being cataloged is a reproduction:

# = none of the following

a = microfilm      e = newspaper format

b = microfiche      f = Braille

c = micro-opaque      o = online (remote access electronic)

d = large print      q = direct access electronic (CD-ROM, etc.)

**Regl** (regularity : 008/19). This element should be coded when the frequency is recorded (see RDA 2.14). If no frequency is recorded, record a value of [u] (unknown).

**S/L** (entry convention: 008/34). Use [2] for integrating resources and for online serials that do not retain their earlier titles. Use [0] (successive entry) for other serials cataloged using RDA.

**Srce** (cataloging source: 008/39). Use code [c] if the record is being created as part of a cooperative cataloging program such as CONSER; otherwise use code [d].

**SrTp** (type of serial or integrating resource: 008/21). This element indicates whether the serial or integrating resource is of one of the following types:

# = none of the following

m = monographic series      d = updating database

| | |
|---|---|
| n = newspaper | l = updating loose-leaf |
| p = periodical | w = updating website |

**Type** (type of record: LDR/06) Although serials can use a variety of record types, most text-based serials are coded as non-manuscript language materials [value = a].

## Vocabulary [RDA 1.1]

Before diving into RDA, it is helpful to get comfortable with the terminology one will be encountering. Perhaps the most important terms are those that characterize the resource in terms of the four Group 1 entities of the FRBR conceptual model: work, expression, manifestation, and item.

A *work* is a distinct intellectual or artistic creation (the "content" of the resource in the most abstract or conceptual sense). Translations as well as editions of serials that are targeted at specific audiences are treated as expressions.

An *expression* is the realization of a work in a particular pattern of text, sound, movement, etc. (the "content" as experienced by the user). While most serial works are realized in a single expression, some are issued in multiple expressions. They may be issued in special editions—with content (other than advertising) targeting a particular audience—or they may be translated into one or more languages. For example, the *Financial Times* is issued in six editions: Asia, Europe, India, Middle East, UK, and US. Likewise, *Scientific American* is published in fourteen local language editions. Each such targeted edition or translation is considered a separate expression.

A *manifestation* is the physical or digital embodiment of an expression of a work. For example, the online (PDF) version of *The Consumer Price Index,* issued by Statistics Canada, is a manifestation, as is the online (HTML) version.

An *item* is a single exemplar (copy) or instance of a manifestation. That copy of a journal on the shelf over there, for instance, or the one on your desk.

(Readers wishing a more in-depth treatment of FRBR entities are referred to chapter 2 and the resources listed at the end of that chapter.)

A *resource* (as used in RDA chapters 1–4 relating to the elements of bibliographic description) is typically the manifestation, of which the item being cataloged is an exemplar, though for certain RDA elements it can refer to the item itself.

A *serial* is a resource issued in successive parts, usually bearing numbering, that has no predetermined conclusion.

RDA instructions that apply to serials also apply to:

- Reproductions of serials. This includes reproductions issued all at once as well as those issued in successive parts. (For example, a reproduction published in 2010 of a periodical originally published from 1781 to 1789.)

- Resources that exhibit the characteristics of a serial but are of limited duration. (For example, a newsletter published during a conference.)

An *integrating resource* is a resource that is kept up to date by means of parts that are integrated into the resource, such as replacement pages of a manual; additions, changes, and deletions from a database; or edits to a website. Typically the earlier versions of an integrating resource are obliterated, in that, for example, pages are discarded, database records are removed or changed, or the previous version of a website is overwritten. (Note that this manual deals only with *ongoing* integrating resources, those that—like serials—have no predetermined conclusion.) An example of an integrating resource would be the online catalog of the Deutsche National-bibliothek (*Katalog der Deutschen Nationalbibliothek*), or indeed the online catalog of any library, constantly in a state of flux as new records are added, old records are removed, and existing records are changed.

An *authorized access point* is what was called a *heading* under AACR2 and earlier cataloging codes: the formalized access point that represents an entity (person, corporate body, work, etc.) in the catalog. In our current record-based environment, an authorized access point is typically represented in the catalog by its own authority record, identifying the entity and providing access, as necessary, via variant forms of its name. For example, **New South Wales. Ministry for the Status and Advancement of Women** is the authorized access point for the entity that appears in its publications as *Ministry for the Status and Advancement of Women, New South Wales,* and *NSW Ministry for the Status and Advancement of Women.*

A *creator* is a person, family, or corporate body responsible for the creation of a serial, including those jointly responsible for its creation. Most serials have no creators in this sense, but when they do, the authorized access point for the first-named creator is used as the initial part of the *authorized access point* for the serial. For example, Roger Ebert is the creator of *Roger Ebert's Movie Yearbook.* The authorized access point for the Yearbook consists of the authorized access point for Mr. Ebert (Ebert, Roger) followed by its title. Corporate bodies are treated as creators only of certain categories of work set out in RDA 19.2.1.1.1.

## CORE Elements for Describing a Resource [RDA 1.3, 5.3]

Certain elements are considered CORE elements in RDA, or CORE *if* certain circumstances apply. These CORE elements comprise a minimum element set for an RDA record. In this manual, CORE elements are prominently identified as such, but for convenience they are presented here as MARC 21 elements, along with any additional elements that are CORE for the CONSER Standard Record:

- [022] $a ISSN (internationally recognized identifier for the manifestation)
- [245] $a Title proper / $c statement of responsibility relating to title proper (if more than one, only the first recorded is required)

(Note that statement of responsibility is not CORE for CONSER Standard Record.)

- [250] $a Designation of edition, designation of a named revision of an edition
- [362] $a Numeric and/or alphabetic designation of first issue (chronological designation of first issue)—numeric and/or alphabetic designation of last issue (chronological designation of last issue)
- [264] #0 $c Date of production (for a resource in an unpublished form)
- [264] #1 $a First place of publication : $b first publisher's name, $c date of publication
- [264] #2 $a First place of distribution (if place of publication not identified) : $b first distributor's name (if publisher not identified), $c date of distribution (if date of publication not identified)
- [264] #3 $a First place of manufacture (if neither place of publication nor place of distribution identified) : $b first manufacturer's name (if neither publisher nor distributor identified), $c date of manufacture (if neither date of publication, date of distribution, nor copyright date identified)
- [264] #4 $c Copyright date (if neither date of publication nor date of distribution identified)
- [300] $a Extent (if the resource is complete or total extent is known)
- [336] $a Media type [*CORE for CONSER Standard Record*]
- [337] $a Content type
- [338] $a Carrier type
- [490] $a Title proper of series ; $v numbering within series. $a Title proper of subseries ; $v numbering within subseries
- [588] $a Note on Issue, Part, or Iteration Used as the Basis for Identification of the Resource [CORE for CONSER Standard Record]

Note that additional elements should be considered CORE whenever they would be needed to differentiate the manifestation or item being described from other manifestations or items that bear similar identifying information.

## Transcribing Data [RDA 1.4, 1.7]

RDA 1.4 instructs that elements be recorded in the language and script in which they appear on the sources from which they are taken.

However, as long as bibliographic data is being recorded in MARC 21 records, this instruction will be subject to certain limitations. Specifically, if a title or other element to be transcribed employs characters outside the MARC-8 character set or in a non-roman alphabet, the cataloger will need to refer to the Library of Congress-Program for Cooperative Cataloging Policy Statement (LC-PCC PS) relating to RDA 1.4 for specific guidance. This LC-PCC PS includes instructions on the transcription of punctuation, spacing, symbols, etc., as well as the convention of using angle brackets (<>) to indicate that available data is incomplete. Examples employing this convention will be found throughout the examples in this manual, since information about serials and integrating resources is seldom complete.

RDA 1.7 provides default instructions on the *style* employed in transcription. However, agencies are free to apply the style rules from another source (for example, the *Chicago Manual of Style*) or come up with their own. This manual assumes catalogers will be following LC practice in this area, that is, leaving it up to the cataloger whether to take the capitalization as found in the source or to capitalize according to RDA appendix A, but applying RDA 1.7.3–1.7.9 for punctuation, numerals, symbols, abbreviations, etc. A related LC-PCC PS provides expanded guidance in these matters.

Finally, catalogers will be operating within the constraints of the data entry system they are using and, if they are entering data into a cooperative cataloging system, the constraints that apply within that system. For many libraries, one such constraint is the MARC-8 character set.[7] For such libraries, characters that cannot be reproduced within this character set must be represented by a characterization within square brackets. For example, the Greek character Ω would be characterized as "[omega]" or "[Omega]" depending on whether or not its case was significant. The LC-PCC PS for RDA 1.4 contains detailed instructions on transcription in the context of the MARC-8 character set, covering nearly every conceivable situation.

## Changes: When to Create a New Description [RDA 1.6]

RDA 1.6 describes the conditions under which a serial can be said to have sufficiently changed that a new description is required. These are different for serials and ongoing integrating resources.

### SERIALS

Create a new description when:

1. A serial changes to an integrating resource or multipart monograph
2. There is a change in media type (for example, a print serial is discontinued in favor of an online or [more rarely today] microform version)
3. There is a major change in the title proper (more on this below)
4. There is a change in responsibility affecting the identification of the serial (more on this below)
5. There is a change in the edition statement that indicates a change of scope or coverage (more on this below)

### ONGOING INTEGRATING RESOURCES

Create a new description when:

1. An integrating resource changes to a serial or multipart monograph
2. There is a change in media type (for example, a print or microform ongoing integrating resource is discontinued in favor of an online version)
3. There is a change in the edition statement that indicates a change of scope or coverage (more on this below)

## The Nasty Details (Serials):
## Major and Minor Changes in the Title Proper

One of the cardinal rules of publishing is that publishers do no favors for catalogers. Okay, maybe it isn't a cardinal rule, but it would be if publishers were aware of catalogers. This arises from a conflict of interest: publishers are interested in selling their products, while catalogers are interested in helping people find them. Sometimes these interests coincide, but often the business of selling takes place in ignorance of the subsequent need for finding. For serials, this means that there will be title changes. Serial titles change for any number of reasons. Titles may change as the result of a serious and thoughtful process, or they may change for less serious and thoughtful reasons (but reasons nonetheless!), or because the new publisher never liked the old publisher, or even just by accident (in which case the title may get changed back with the next issue), or for a multitude of other reasons, entirely defensible as well as less so. It is up to the cataloger to decide how important the observed change is. To help them, RDA devotes considerable space to the subject of title changes.

It is useful simply to memorize these categories, since doing so can save you a lot of time and pain. It's a lot easier—and much less time-consuming—to add an access point on an existing record than to create a whole new record only to discover afterwards that it was unnecessary.

RDA 2.3.13 distinguishes between *major* and *minor* changes in the titles proper of serials. Such changes occur when the title proper on the latest issue in hand differs from the title proper on an earlier issue or the title proper recorded in field 245 on the existing bibliographic record.

A major change results in the creation of a new record, while a minor change just results in a change to an existing record. In FRBR terms, a major change in title proper signals a new work.

There are three categories of major change:

1. The addition, deletion, change, or reordering of any of the first five words (the first six words if the title begins with an article) unless the change belongs to one or more of the categories listed under *minor changes* (see below)

2. The addition, deletion, or change of any word after the first five words (the first six words if the title begins with an article) that changes the meaning of the title or indicates a different subject matter

3. A change in a corporate body name given anywhere in the title if it represents a different corporate body (including a change of name that results in a new authorized access point for the body)

The second and third categories are fairly straightforward and require little elaboration. If the cataloger would add a new subject heading or a new corporate name heading based on a change in the title proper, then a major change has occurred.

It is the first category that causes the most trouble for serials catalogers, since it sometimes comes down to a matter of judgment and definition, and numerous changes in this category occurring all at once may tempt one to imagine a sort of cumulative effect of minor changes that then amounts to a major change. However, the instruction for handling minor changes is clear: in case of doubt, consider the change to be a minor change.

There are nine categories of minor change:

1. A difference in the representation of a word or words anywhere in the title (e.g., one spelling vs. another; abbreviated word or sign or symbol vs. spelled-out form; arabic numeral vs. roman numeral; number or date vs. spelled-out form; hyphenated word vs. unhyphenated word; one-word compound vs. two-word compound, whether hyphenated or not; an acronym or initialism vs. full form; or a change in grammatical form [e.g., singular vs. plural])

2. The addition, deletion, or change of articles, prepositions, or conjunctions anywhere in the title

3. A difference involving the name of the same corporate body and elements of its hierarchy or their grammatical connection anywhere in the title (e.g., the addition, deletion, or rearrangement of the name of the same corporate body, the substitution of a variant form)

4. The addition, deletion, or change of punctuation, including initialisms and letters with separating punctuation vs. those without separating punctuation, anywhere in the title

5. A different order of titles when the title is given in more than one language on the source of information, provided that the title chosen as title proper still appears as a parallel title proper

6. The addition, deletion, or change of words anywhere in the title that link the title to the numbering

7. Two or more titles proper used on different issues of a serial according to a regular pattern

8. The addition to, deletion from, or change in the order of words in a list anywhere in the title, provided that there is no significant change in the subject matter

9. The addition, deletion, or rearrangement anywhere in the title of words that indicate the type of resource such as "magazine," "journal," or "newsletter" or their equivalent in other languages

These require some explanation.

One broad class of minor change, which encompasses most of category 1 and all of category 4 in the preceding list might be summarized as "changes that do not affect the way the title proper sounds." (For example, "Bibliography on 20th-century U.S., Canadian, and Mexican history" and "Bibliography on twentieth century US, Canadian and Mexican history" both sound identical when read aloud.)

Another broad class, encompassing part of category 1and all of category 2, might be summarized as "minor grammatical variations that would disappear if the title were abbreviated" (singular vs. plural; the addition, deletion, or change of articles, prepositions, or conjunctions).

A third broad class is changes of appearance rather than substance, which encompasses part of category 1 and all of category 3: an abbreviated word vs. a spelled out form, a change in the way the name of a corporate body appears (so long as it does not signal a different corporate body).

The remaining categories (5 through 9) are rather specific:

Changes in category 5 typically occur when the language of the text of a serial changes over time or when a serial is published by a body with more than one official language. Examples of the former are scientific journals that were originally published in German (once the language of science) but are now published in English. Examples of the latter are publications of the European Union, where the title proper may appear in multiple languages, and the one appearing first may change from one issue to the next. Note that changes in this class are minor only so long as the original title proper continues to appear.

Changes in category 6 encompass such linking phrases as "for the calendar year," "for the fiscal year ending," etc. (links consisting simply of articles, prepositions, etc., are already covered by category 2).

Changes in category 7 are recurring changes that follow a predictable pattern. For example, a monthly publication that includes an annual "buying guide" that lacks the title proper of the serial but is integrated into its numbering scheme; a scientific journal where issues (and titles) alternate between one specialization and another; or a daily newspaper with a different name for its Sunday issue (e.g., *The Boston Sunday Globe*).

Changes in category 8 are limited to titles proper that include lists of words, specifically where the inclusion or order of words in the list has changed due to sloppiness or editorial whim, but there has been no change in the subject coverage of the serial.

Finally, changes in category 9 relate to the presence or absence of a "type of resource" word. While this is fairly straightforward, there are always "borderline" words that may cause the cataloger to hesitate. As always, in case of doubt, consider the change to be a minor change.

Note that for the session laws of US states and for US almanacs published prior to 1901, the Library of Congress treats all title changes as minor (LC-PCC PS 2.3.2.13).

## Changes in Responsibility for the Work (Serials) [RDA 6.1.3.2]

Personal and family responsibility for serials is rare and is limited to the situations described in RDA 19.2.1.1.3, where a single person or family is identified as the creator of a serial *as a whole*. A change in personal responsibility for a serial is, by definition then, impossible.

For serials, a change in corporate responsibility means a change in the corporate body involved in the identification of the serial work. A responsible corporate body may be involved in the identification of the serial work because the authorized access point for that body is used to identify the serial work in conjunction with the preferred title of the work [RDA 6.27]—in terms of MARC 21, the corporate body appears in field 110—or as an addition to the preferred title of the work [RDA 6.6.1].

Note that a corporate body is considered responsible for a serial only if the serial falls into one of the categories listed in RDA 19.2.1.1.1 (see the guidelines on identifying the resource, below).

## The Basis of the Bibliographic Description and Sources of Information (Serials) [RDA 2.1–2.2]

When creating the bibliographic description for a serial, two questions arise:

1. Where should I look for the elements I'll be recording?
2. What elements should I record?

The first question is addressed by RDA 2.1 (Basis for Identification of the Resource) and RDA 2.2 (Sources of Information).

RDA treats a serial as a Resource Issued in More Than One Part (even if the publisher loses interest, and only one part is ever issued), and RDA 2.1.2.3 sets out the criteria for selecting the part or parts that will serve as the basis for identifying the serial as a whole:

1. If the issues or parts are numbered sequentially, select the lowest numbered issue or part.
2. If the issues or parts are not numbered, or are not sequentially numbered, then select the issue or part with the earliest date of issue.

If such an issue or part is not the *first* issue or part (because that issue or part was not available), then make a note [MARC 21 588 $a] identifying the issue or part that is being used as the basis for describing the serial. Note that CONSER practice is to *always* make such a note, even when the first issue or part is serving as the basis:

[588] ## $a Description based on: Volume 2, number 4 (autumn 2003)
[588] ## $a Description based on: Tome 1, numéro 1 (hiver 2001) [CONSER practice]

Once an appropriate issue or part has been selected, the next question is what source within that issue or part to prefer as a source of information about the serial. The order of preference is given RDA 2.2.2.2 (Resources Consisting of One or More Pages, Leaves, Sheets, or Cards (or Images of One or More Pages, Leaves, Sheets, or Cards):

1. The title page, defined as "a page at the beginning of a resource bearing the title proper and usually, though not necessarily, the statement of responsibility and the data relating to publication. If this information is given on facing pages or pages on successive leaves, with or without repetition, treat these pages collectively as the title page."

2. If there is no title page, then use one of the following sources, in descending order of preference:

    a. The cover
    b. The caption (the top of the first page of the text, preceding the text itself)
    c. The masthead (a formal statement of title, ownership, editors, etc.)
    d. The colophon (a formal statement at the end of the resource giving the title and/or other publication information)
    e. Another source within the resource that bears a title, preferring a source that presents it *formally* (i.e., distinct from the text)
    f. Another source that forms part of the resource (such as a container), preferring a source that presents information *formally* (i.e., distinct from the text)

(Note that it was once a common practice for libraries to discard the covers and unnumbered pages of issues prior to binding, and add a volume title page and/or index. Although not stated in RDA, when the description is based on such a volume title page, this should be noted, as it falls into category f above.)

RDA 2.20.2.3 directs that the source of information be identified in a note [MARC 21 500 $a] whenever it is other than the title page:

[500] ## $a Title from cover.

When there is more than one preferred source of information (for example, two title pages), generally select the first occurring source, except:

1. If the sources are in different languages or scripts [RDA 2.2.3.1]:

    a. Select the source in the language or script (or predominant language or script) of the content.

    b. If the text occurs in more than one language, then:

        • Select the source in the language or script of the translation (if translation is known to be the main purpose).

- Select the source in the original language (if this is known).

  c. Select the first occurring source.

2. If the resource is a facsimile or reproduction of an original publication, with a preferred source for the reproduction as well as the original, select the preferred source for the reproduction [RDA 2.2.3.3].

When information that would normally be transcribed is taken from a source outside the resource itself, it should be enclosed in square brackets [RDA 2.2.4].

## Numbers Expressed as Numerals or Words [RDA 1.8]

RDA 1.8 applies to numbers in the numbering area [MARC field 362], the dates in the publication, production, distribution, etc., area [MARC field 260 $c], and numbering in the series area [MARC field 490].

Numerals may be transcribed as they appear or recorded in the form preferred by the cataloging agency. Libraries following LC practice should record numerals as they appear [RDA 1.8.2 and related LC-PCC PS]. Substitute numerals for numbers expressed as words.

Years that appear foreshortened in the source should be expanded. For example, "1967-72" should be recorded as "1967-1972" [RDA 1.8.4].

Ordinal numbers are recorded as numerals, following the practice of the language involved, when this can be ascertained (1st, 2nd, 3rd, etc.; 1er, 2e, 3e, etc.); otherwise, 1., 2., 3., etc.

## Treatment of Facsimiles and Reproductions [RDA 1.11]

RDA continues the AACR2 practice of describing the facsimile or reproduction as such.[8]

Under RDA, the reproduction and the original manifestation are treated as related manifestations. Libraries following LC practice should use a structured description for each related manifestation and record the relationship on the bibliographic record for both the original and the reproduction (LC-PCC PS 27.1.1.3):

[245] 04 $a The religious intelligencer.
[264] #1 $a Ann Arbor, Michigan : $b University Microfilms, $c 1951-1974.
[300] ## $a 10 microfilm reels (22 volumes) : $b illustrations ; $c 35 mm

[336] ## $a text $2 rdacontent

[337] ## $a microform $2 rdamedia

[338] ## $a microfilm reel $2 rdacarrier

[362] 1# $a Published issues: Vol. 1, no. 1 (June 1, 1816)-vol. 22, no. 19 (October 7, 1837).

[500] ## $a Several pages are stained, creased, tightly bound or have print faded and show-through with some loss of text. Pagination is irregular. Volume 16, numbers 27-29 and volume 18, numbers 38-39 and 46 are missing. Volumes 21 and 22 lack title page and index.

[776] 08 $i Reproduction of (manifestation): $t Religious intelligencer. $d New-Haven : Nathan Whiting, 1816-1837. $h 22 volumes : illustrations ; 22 cm. $w (OCoLC)1763668

A reciprocal relationship is recorded on the record for the original manifestation:

[776] 08 $i Reproduced as: $t Religious intelligencer. $d Ann Arbor, Michigan : University Microfilms, 1951-1974. $h 10 microfilm reels (22 volumes) : illustrations ; 35 mm $w (OCoLC)6594624

# 2. ATTRIBUTES OF RESOURCES

Manifestations and items and the works and expressions they embody (by ISBD area)

## What Kind of Serial? Content Form and Media Type Area (ISBD Area 0)

### ELEMENTS

- Content type: [RDA 6.9] [MARC 21 336] [CORE]
- Media type: [RDA 3.2] [MARC 21 337] [CORE for CONSER Standard Record]

### CHANGES FROM AACR2

- Content form and media type/GMD:
  - AACR2 (and earlier editions of ISBD): a resource is characterized using a general material designation (GMD) that displays between square brackets following the title proper in the Title and Statement of Responsibility Area (ISBD Area 1). (Example: New scientist [microform].) In AACR2 MARC 21 records, the GMD is recorded in [245] $h.

    ◦ RDA: a resource is characterized using three newly defined elements (with three newly defined MARC 21 fields). These can be used to generate corresponding display constants for a newly defined ISBD Area 0.

## About Content Form and Media Type

The first thing to determine when one has been handed a serial is what kind of serial one has been handed. Is it a printed serial? Is it a microform serial? Is it an electronic serial? (Fortunately, there are few serial works of art [aside from Andy Warhol's Campbell Soup cans] or serial microscope slides, so we will leave the cataloging of those to specialists.)

This section deals with how RDA answers these questions. It requires some explanation, and hopefully that explanation will prove enlightening. The two RDA elements described in this section—content type and media type—along with a third—carrier type—were developed in order to characterize the resources represented by RDA bibliographic records in such a way that they could be usefully exchanged with systems employing ONIX, an exchange format widely employed within the publishing community. At the same time, the publishing community undertook to ensure that resources represented by ONIX records could be so characterized that they could be usefully exchanged with library systems employing RDA. To achieve this purpose, the RDA and ONIX communities cooperatively developed a framework for resource categorization to facilitate the development of conforming community-specific vocabularies (such as the three RDA elements). Those interested in a deeper understanding of this topic are referred to the latest version of the framework.[9]

Area 0 of the ISBD also conforms to the RDA/ONIX framework. Consequently, systems employing ISBD syntax can transform data in the RDA *content type* and *media type* elements into the corresponding display constants for ISBD area 0.

These RDA elements supersede the GMDs employed under AACR2. They may be used by institutions to characterize RDA records in whatever way seems most useful to their users. For example, the formal RDA terms may be suppressed locally in favor of more user-friendly terms or display icons.

## Individual Elements

### CONTENT TYPE [RDA 6.9] [CORE]

*Content type* is a categorization reflecting the fundamental form of communication in which the content is expressed and the human sense through which it is intended to be perceived. The following are the most common content types for serials:

- *Text:* Content expressed through a form of notation for language intended to be perceived visually. The corresponding ISBD content form is *Text*.

- *Spoken word:* Content expressed through language in an audible form. Includes recorded readings, recitations, speeches, interviews, oral histories, computer-generated speech, etc. The corresponding ISBD content form is *Spoken word.*
- *Tactile text:* Content expressed through a form of notation for language intended to be perceived through touch (e.g., Braille). The corresponding ISBD content form and content qualification are *Text (tactile).*

MARC 21 record syntax:

> [336] ## $a content type term $b content type code $2 rdacontent

Give a term and optionally a code for the content type. (Terms are used in the examples below.) When multiple content types are present, give the content type of the predominant part of the serial in the first $a and the content type of any accompanying material in a second $a. Alternatively, use separate [336] fields (see last example below).

A complete list of content terms, along with corresponding MARC codes, will be found in the Term and Code List for RDA Content Types (identified in subfield $2 as rdacontent) on the LC website.[10]

## MEDIA TYPE [RDA 3.2] [LC-PCC CORE]

*Media type* is a categorization reflecting the general type of intermediation device required to view, play, run, etc., the content of a resource. The following are the most common media types for serials:

- *Audio:* Media designed for use with a playback device such as a turntable, audiocassette player, CD player, or MP3 player. Includes media used to store digitally encoded as well as analog sound. The corresponding ISBD media type is *audio.*
- *Computer:* Media designed for use with a computer, whether remotely accessed or accessed directly (from a computer tape or disc, for example). The corresponding ISBD media type is *electronic.*
- *Microform:* Opaque or transparent media carrying reduced-size images and intended to be used with appropriate reading machinery. The corresponding ISBD media type is *microform.*
- *Unmediated:* Media that can be perceived directly through one or more human senses (eye-legible text, for example). No ISBD media type is supplied when the resource is unmediated.

MARC 21 Record Syntax:

> [337] ## $a *media type term* $b *media type code* $2 rdamedia

Give a term and optionally a code for the media type. (Terms are used in the examples below.) When multiple media types are present, give the media type of the predominant part of the serial in the first $a and the media type of any accompanying material in a second $a. Alternatively, use separate [337] fields (see last example, below).

A complete list of media terms, along with corresponding MARC codes (not required) will be found in the Term and Code List for RDA Media Types (identified in subfield $2 as rdamedia) on the LC website.[11]

## FULL EXAMPLES (MARC 21 AND ISBD RECORD SYNTAXES)

### ONLINE JOURNAL

[336] ## $a text $2 rdacontent
[337] ## $a computer $2 rdamedia
ISBD area 0 → Text : electronic

### PRINT JOURNAL

[336] ## $a text $2 rdacontent
[337] ## $a unmediated $2 rdamedia
ISBD area 0 → Text

### BRAILLE JOURNAL

[336] ## $a tactile text $2 rdacontent
[337] ## $a unmediated $2 rdamedia
ISBD area 0 → Text (tactile)

### AUDIO JOURNAL

[336] ## $a spoken word $2 rdacontent
[337] ## $a audio $2 rdamedia
ISBD area 0 → Spoken word : audio

### PRINT JOURNAL WITH ACCOMPANYING CD

[245] 00 $a BBC music magazine.
[300] ## $a volumes + $e audio discs
[336] ## $a text $a performed music $2 rdacontent
[337] ## $a unmediated $a audio $2 rdamedia

*or*

[336] ## $a text $2 rdacontent
[336] ## $a performed music $2 rdacontent
[337] ## $a unmediated $2 rdamedia
[337] ## $a audio $2 rdamedia
ISBD area 0 → Text + Music (performed) : audio

## Titles Borne by the Resource:
## Title and Statement of Responsibility Area (ISBD Area 1)

### ELEMENTS

- Title proper [RDA 2.3.2] [MARC 21 245] [CORE]
- Parallel title proper [RDA 2.3.3] [MARC 21 245/246] [LC-PCC CORE]
- Other title information [RDA 2.3.4] [MARC 21 245] [LC CORE]
- Parallel other title information [RDA 2.3.5] [MARC 21 245]
- Variant title [RDA 2.3.6] [MARC 21 246]
- Earlier title proper of an integrating resource [RDA 2.3.7] [MARC 21 247] [LC CORE]
- Later title proper (minor title changes) [RDA 2.3.8] [MARC 21 246] [LC-PCC CORE unless applying the alternative when the changes are numerous]
- Key title [RDA 2.3.9] [MARC 21 222] [LC CORE]
- Abbreviated title [RDA 2.3.10] [MARC 21 210] [LC CORE]
- Statement of responsibility relating to the title proper [RDA 2.4.2] [MARC 21 245] [CORE]
- Parallel statement of responsibility relating to the title proper [RDA 2.4.3] [MARC 21 245]

### CHANGES FROM AACR2

#### CAPITALIZATION

- AACR2: Capitalization of titles is governed by prescribed style conventions.
- RDA
  - Agencies may opt to apply in-house style conventions for capitalization.
  - Agencies may accept digital data from external sources "as is" with regard to capitalization.

### CORRECTIONS AND OMISSIONS

- AACR2: Errors in titles are signaled by following unexpected text with a bracketed [!] or [sic], by inserting bracketed missing characters in the appropriate place, or by following a known error with a bracketed [i.e.] and the corrected form.
- RDA: Data is simply transcribed "as is."
- The mark of omission is used whenever data is omitted from the title proper, even when the omission occurs at the beginning.

## ABOUT TITLES BORNE BY THE RESOURCE (GENERAL INSTRUCTIONS) [RDA 2.3]

Publishers assign titles to resources (or not) for a variety of reasons: to appeal to a particular market segment, to fulfill some legal or other requirement (in which case the title is likely to be long and sometimes opaque to the uninitiated), to create a desired visual effect, and occasionally to describe the content. For print and online serials and integrating resources, the profusion of confusion is compounded by the ease with which such resources can be produced: anyone can create an online serial or blog and consequently anyone does. In some of these cases, the title may be an afterthought (if any thought went into it at all). For example, the principal audience of a corporate annual report is the shareholders, who generally will receive a copy in the mail. An accompanying cover letter may identify the colorful document as an annual report, but the shareholder will look in vain for anything in the document itself that does so. The primary purpose of the document is to promote the firm, and so its name will figure prominently, but probably nothing else, at least in regard to a title.

Likewise, title changes may occur because of a change of publisher, change of editor, change of fashion, change of heart, and sometimes a change of content. Sometimes the title changes by accident, when an out-of-date template is used for its layout by whatever employee was assigned the task of preparing the issue for publication. Sometimes, after changing the title, the publisher has a change of heart or indeed forgets that they changed the title in the first place, and the old title rises from the dead to resume its duties.

This context often makes the serial cataloger's task a challenge when it comes to identifying titles and especially when it comes to selecting one as the intended title, the *title proper*. This is what separates the true serials cataloger—who relishes such situations—from the mere dilettante.

Typically, a title appears on the resource itself. But in unusual situations it may be taken from accompanying material (perhaps that cover letter to shareholders or the website where articles can be downloaded) or from reference sources. It may be assigned to the resource by an outsider, either a registration agency (for example, a key title assigned by an ISSN center) or, in extraordinary circumstances, by you as the cataloger.

RDA 2.3 deals with titles. But a word of caution: RDA 2.3 deals with *all* titles borne by the resource, including variant titles and, in some circumstances, earlier or later titles. This section will follow the structure of RDA, first addressing matters that apply to all titles, followed by instructions that apply to particular kinds of title: title proper, parallel title proper, etc. Except in cases where the resource carries only a single title (the de facto title proper), your primary task will be to evaluate the titles you encounter in terms of these categories and then to enter them in the catalog record following the applicable instructions.

But first the general instructions . . .

## IRREPRODUCIBLE RESULTS

Sometimes you would like to transcribe something that cannot be transcribed due to limitations of the character set involved. In such cases, follow in-house guidelines or the LC-PCC PSs associated with RDA 1.4 (Language and Script) and RDA 1.7.5 (Symbols):

[245] 00 $a I [love] Santa Fe guidebook.
[246] 1# $a I [heart] Santa Fe guidebook
[500] ## $a On title page and cover "[love]" appears as a heart.

## INACCURACIES

Titles are transcribed as they appear, applying the general instructions in RDA 1.7. However, inaccuracies in a title should not be transcribed if they are corrected on subsequent issues of the serial. In such cases, record the corrected title and make a note giving the uncorrected title. Record the uncorrected title as a variant title if considered important for access [RDA 2.3.1.4 exception]:

[245] 00 $a World report.
[246] 10 $i Misspelled title on issue for 1988: $a Wrold report

## OMISSIONS

If information appears in a title that changes from issue to issue, omit this information and replace it with a mark of omission ( . . . ). Do so even if the omitted information occurs at the beginning of the title proper. Bear in mind that this instruction is interpreted broadly to include any element of the title proper that is subject to change over time (e.g., the name of a government official). This may be clarified in a note [RDA 2.3.1.4 exception].

Note that if the omitted data affects the grammatical case of other words in the title, the original case is retained even though the related data is missing:

[245] 00 $a Frommer's budget travel guide. $p Washington, D.C. . . . on $ . . . a day.
[500] ## $a Each issue has an amount in the title, e.g., '92-'93 has $40
[Title on serial: Frommer's budget travel guide. Washington, D.C. '92-'93 on $40 a day.]
[245] 00 $a . . . annual report
[Title on serial: 1st annual report.]
[245] 00 $a Monumenta. $p Epistolarum . . .
[Title on serial: Monumenta. Epistolarum tomus 1. The authorized access point for the serial would use the case that would be appropriate in the absence of a grammatically linked volume: Monumenta. Epistolae.]

## TITLES THAT MENTION OR ARE GRAMMATICALLY LINKED TO EARLIER TITLES

Any statement relating the current title to an earlier title (for example, Title A, incorporating Title B) should be treated as two elements: a Title A portion, which should be treated as the title of the resource being cataloged, and a Title B portion, which should be treated as the title of a related resource [RDA 2.3.1.4 exception].

### EXAMPLE

On item: International Gas Report, Including World Gas Report
(Latter serial was absorbed in 1988)
[245] 00 $a International gas report.
[780] 05 $t World gas report $g 1988 $x 0143-9766

## USING THE NAME OF AN ISSUING BODY, ETC., AS A SUBSTITUTE FOR THE TITLE

Sometimes a resource lacks a title as such. In these cases, the name of a person, family, or corporate body appearing on the resource may be recorded as the title [RDA 2.3.1.5]. The nature of the publication may be given as a summarization of content [RDA 7.10].

### EXAMPLE

[110] 2# $a Gaz de France
[245] 10 $a Gaz de France.
[520] ## $a Annual report.

## TITLES OF PARTS AND SECTIONS [RDA 2.3.1.7]

*Case 1:* When a serial

- Is a separately issued part or section of another serial,
- Its title consists of a title common to all parts or sections and a designation and/or title unique to that particular part or section, and
- All these elements appear together in the same source

record the title as follows (including punctuation):

Title common to all parts. Designation of part or section, Title of part or section

Depending on the kind of title—title proper, variant title/later title, earlier title—such titles are recorded in MARC 21 field 245, 246, or 247 as follows:

$a Title common to all parts. $n Designation of part or section, $p Title of part or section

Parts and sections can themselves have parts and sections.

**EXAMPLE**

[245] 00 $a Deutsche Nationalbibliographie. $p Wöchentliches Verzeichnis. $n Reihe B, $p Monografien und Periodika ausserhalb des Verlagsbuchhandels

Note that in the preceding example, "ausserhalb" actually appears on the item as "außerhalb" but has been modified in accordance with the LC-PCC PS for RDA 1.4 (Language and Script).

*Case 2:* When a serial

- Is a separately issued part or section of another serial,
- Its title consists of a title common to all parts or sections and a designation and/or title unique to that particular part or section, and
- These elements appear in different sources

record the title common to all parts instead as the title proper of a series (series title) (see RDA 2.12):

[24X] $a Title of part or section
[490] $a Title common to all parts

Whenever the designation and/or title of the part or section are grammatically linked to the title common to all parts or sections, the title is recorded in the normal manner.

## TREATMENT OF SUPPLEMENTS [RDA 2.3.1.7]

When a serial

- Is a supplement to another serial, and
- Its title consists simply of the title of this other serial and a term indicating its status as a supplement

record the title as follows (including punctuation):

Title of the serial. Term indicating a supplement

Depending on the kind of title—title proper, variant title/later title, earlier title—such titles are recorded in MARC 21 fields 245, 246, or 247 as follows:

[24X] $a Title of the serial. $p Term indicating a supplement

However, if the term is grammatically linked to the title of the other serial (e.g., Supplement to. . . ), the title is recorded as a simple title proper.

**EXAMPLE**

[245] 00 $a Supplement to Books on demand.

[730] 0# $a Books on demand: author guide.

Note that *Books on demand: author guide* is the actual title proper of the related resource.

## INDIVIDUAL ELEMENTS

### TITLE PROPER [RDA 2.3.2] [MARC 21 245] [CORE]

The title proper is the chief name of the serial. It includes any alternative titles. Like other titles, it may include the designation and/or title of a part or section or a term indicating that it is a supplement to another resource (see above).

### CHANGE FROM AACR2

- Under AACR2, punctuation that might be mistaken for ISBD punctuation was altered.
- Under RDA, punctuation is transcribed "as is."

### SELECTING THE TITLE PROPER

1. *Selecting a source: Order of preference:*
    a. Title page: A page at the beginning of an issue bearing the title proper and usually, though not necessarily, the statement of responsibility and the data relating to publication. If this information is given on facing pages or pages on successive leaves, with or without repetition, treat these pages collectively as the title page.
    b. Cover: Can include both the inside and the outside of the front and back covers, as well as the spine.
    c. Caption: The beginning of the first page of the text.
    d. Masthead: The section (usually on the editorial page or next to the table of contents) giving information relating to the publication, such as the owner's name, a list of the editors, etc.
    e. Colophon: Data usually occurring at the bottom of a page toward the end of an issue, containing the title, the printer's name, date and place of printing, etc.
    f. Accompanying material

    g. Container

    h. Published description of the serial

    i. Any other source

2. *Preferred sources in different languages or scripts*: If there are preferred sources in different languages or scripts, choose the source in the predominant language and script of the content. If no language predominates, choose the source in the original language. If the original language cannot be determined, choose the first occurring source.
3. *Reproductions*: If cataloging a reproduction with its own title page, choose that source.
4. *Multiple forms of title in the same source*: If the title appears in various forms in the same source, or a given text string can be interpreted in a variety of ways, make your best guess, based on the sequence, layout, and typography of the titles. In case of doubt, favor a title that is also featured elsewhere in the serial, such as the running title or masthead title. If this doesn't work, choose the most comprehensive title.

    *Exception:* If the title appears both as an acronym or initialism and in a fuller form, choose the fuller form and record the acronym or initialism as other title information [RDA 2.3.2.5].

## IDENTIFYING THE BASIS OF THE DESCRIPTION

RDA practice is to make a note *when the title proper is taken from a source other than the title page* [RDA 2.20.2.3], and to identify the issue used as the basis for the description *when it is other than the first* [RDA 2.20.13.3].

CONSER Standard Record practice combines these notes and extends their use to *all* cases:

- Always identify the source of the title proper, *even when it is the title page.*
- Always identify the issue consulted, *even when it is the first.*

[588] ## $a Description based on: 1er (año 2000); title from cover.

Provide additional access to any other titles not chosen as the title proper (see "Variant Title [RDA 2.3.6]" below).

## RECORDING THE TITLE PROPER

The title proper may have a variety of structures:

- Simple title: Sports illustrated
- Title and alternative title: Farmer's museum, or, Lay preacher's gazette
- Common (overarching) title and section or part title: Area wage survey. Washington, D.C.-Md.-Va. Metropolitan area

- Common (overarching) title, with a designation for the section or part: Clinical and experimental hypertension. Part B, Hypertension in pregnancy
- Common (overarching) title, without section or part title: Physical review. A

Record the title proper as you would any other title (see the introduction to this chapter). However, if the serial is divided into parts and bears only the titles proper for these component parts (e.g., Annual report for 1970. Projections for 1971), record the title proper of the first component part as the title proper of the serial, followed by the titles proper of any other component parts, each separated from its predecessor by a space-semicolon-space. Provide an additional access point for the titles of any other component parts.

**EXAMPLE**

[245] 00 $a Annual report for . . . ; $b Projections for. . . .
[730] 0# $a Projections for. . . .

## RECORDING CHANGES IN THE TITLE PROPER (SERIAL)

For the instructions governing changes in the title proper, see "The Nasty Details," earlier in this chapter. Recall that a major title change (as defined there) signals a new serial (and a new description).

## RECORDING CHANGES IN TITLE PROPER (INTEGRATING RESOURCE) [RDA 2.3.2.12.3]

The title proper of an integrating resource is *always* the latest title proper. Retain the earlier title proper *as such* unless the change is felt to be insignificant. If the changes are numerous, make a general note [RDA 2.3.7.3].

**EXAMPLE**

[245] 00 $a Washington State newsstand.
[247] 10 $a Washington newspapers database $f <Oct. 6, 1999>

(See also "7. Ongoing Integrating Resources," below.)

## PARALLEL TITLE PROPER [RDA 2.3.3] [MARC 21 245/246] [LC-PCC CORE]

The title proper may appear in more than one language or script. Such "parallel" titles proper may appear on the issue serving as the basis of the description, or on earlier or later issues. To qualify as a parallel title proper, RDA does not require that a title be a translation of the title proper, or that it appear in the same source as the title proper;

merely that it be "presented as the equivalent of the title proper" somewhere within the resource [RDA 2.3.3.1, RDA 2.3.3.2].

**MARC 21/ISBD RECORD SYNTAX**
Without statement of responsibility:

> [245] 00 $a Title proper = $b Parallel title proper.
> [246] 11 $a Parallel title proper

With common statement of responsibility:

> [245] 00 $a Title proper = $b Parallel title proper / $c statement of responsibility.
> [246] 11 $a Parallel title proper

With related statement of responsibility:

> [245] 00 $a Title proper / $c statement of responsibility = Parallel title proper / parallel statement of responsibility.
> [246] 11 $a Parallel title proper

If taken from a different source than the title proper, this should be noted if important [RDA 2.3.3.3, RDA 2.20.2.4].

**EXAMPLE**

> [500] ## $a French title from cover.

Multiple parallel titles proper should be recorded in the order in which they appear in the resource [RDA 2.3.3.3].

Treat parallel titles proper appearing on earlier or later issues as variant titles [RDA 2.3.3.5.2].

## CHANGES IN PARALLEL TITLE PROPER [RDA 2.3.3.5]
The parallel titles proper of a serial are always whatever appears on the earliest issue available. The parallel titles proper of an integrating resource are always whatever appears on the latest iteration. Record as variant titles any later/earlier parallel titles proper that are felt to be important for identification or access.

Make a note if there is a change in the order of titles proper.

**EXAMPLE**
> [500] ## $a Order of titles varies.

**MARC 21/ISBD RECORD SYNTAX**

A parallel title proper recorded in the title and statement of responsibility area is recorded in field 246 with a second indicator value "1"; earlier/later parallel titles proper are recorded with an introductory note and a second indicator value "#" (blank):

> [245] nn $a title proper = $b parallel title proper
> [246] 11 $a parallel title proper
> [246] 1# $i introductory note: $a earlier/later parallel title proper

**EXAMPLES**

> [245] 00 $a Geographical names of Canada = $b Toponymie du Canada.
>
> [246] 11 $a Toponymie du Canada
>
> [246] 1# $i Former parallel title: $a Site Web des noms géographiques officiels du Canada $f <Feb. 14, 1996>
>
> [245] 00 $a Revista interamericana de bibliografía = $b Review of inter-American bibliography.
>
> [246] 11 $a Review of inter-American bibliography
>
> [246] 1# $i English title, 1952- given as: $a Inter-American review of bibliography
>
> [245] 00 $a Bulletin de l'Institut international de statistique.
>
> [246] 1# $i Issues for 1964- have also English title: $a Bulletin of the International Statistical Institute
>
> [500] ## $a Order of titles varies.

## OTHER TITLE INFORMATION
## [RDA 2.3.4] [MARC 21 245] [LC CORE]

Other title information is information that appears in conjunction with, and is subordinate to, the title proper. It may be indicative of the character, contents, etc., of the serial or the motives or occasion for its publication.

Determining whether text appearing in the same source as the title proper appears "in conjunction with" the title proper is ultimately a judgment call, based on its position relative to the title proper, typography, and cataloger experience with similar resources. As with the title proper, other title information may include an embedded statement of responsibility.

Other title information is not a CORE RDA element. Nor is it required for a CONSER Standard Record. In this context, although RDA 2.3.2.5 instructs that an initialism or acronym of the title appearing in the same source as the title proper be recorded as other title information, this only applies if an agency treats other title information as a local core element. The CONSER Standard Record treats such initialisms and acronyms of the title as variant titles (see "Variant Titles," below).

Having said that, Library of Congress RDA policy is to record other title information. For that reason, I will go into a bit more detail here than I would otherwise.

## CHANGE FROM AACR2

- AACR2 1.1E6 directed that when the title proper needed explanation, a brief addition would be supplied in square brackets as other title information. This is not done under RDA. However, it may be possible to record the addition as a summarization of content. (See under "Notes," below [RDA 7.10].)

Under AACR2, other title information that was felt to be important for identification was typically recorded in a note. However, there were two situations where the serials cataloger routinely transcribed other title information as such:

- The other title information contained an embedded statement of responsibility
- The title proper appeared in the preferred source both in a full form and in the form of an acronym or initialism (the acronym or initialism was recorded as other title information)

These two situations are exemplified below.

### MARC 21/ISBD RECORD SYNTAX

[245] $a title proper : $b other title information

### EXAMPLES

As local CORE element:

[245] 00 $a Catalogue & index : $b periodical of the Library Association Cataloguing and Indexing Group.

[245] 00 $a Linguisitics and language behavior abstracts : $b LLBA.

[246] 30 $a LLBA

In CONSER Standard Record:

[245] 00 $a Linguisitics and language behavior abstracts.

[246] 1# $a LLBA

As a note (AACR2 practice locally carried over to RDA):

[245] 00 $a Montana.

[500] ## $a "A journal of western history."

[245] 00 $a Dialogue.

[500] ## $a "A journal of Mormon thought."

*But:*

> [245] 00 $a Monoclonal antibodies.
>
> [Omitted: "a quarterly publication containing availability of new monoclonal antibodies for all researchers." (because it is not important for identification)]

## VARIANT TITLE [RDA 2.3.6] [MARC 21 246]

A variant title is a title (other than the title proper) associated with the serial. Variant titles include:

- Titles appearing on the serial or integrating resource
  - Added title page title (title appearing on an added title page)
  - Caption title (title appearing at the beginning of the first page of text)
  - Cover title (title appearing on the cover)
  - Distinctive title (title unique and specific to a particular issue)
  - Fluctuating title (title that fluctuates back and forth between issues)
  - Running title (recurring title at the bottom or top of most pages)
  - Spine title (title appearing along the spine of an issue)
  - Other title referring to the serial or integrating resource
- Titles associated with the serial through reference sources
- Cataloger-supplied titles
  - Corrected titles
  - Expanded titles (by spelling out numbers, ampersands, etc.)
  - Something that may be a title
- Access to parts of a title
  - Alternative titles (e.g., "The emerald, or, Miscellany of literature")
  - Section titles
  - Emphasized parts of a title (e.g., presented in a different color, font, case, or orientation)
- Variations on these appearing on earlier or later issues or iterations

### MARC 21 RECORD SYNTAX

A variant title is recorded in field 246 as follows if a note is wanted (important for both identification and access):

> [246] 1# $i introductory text: $a variant title

If a note is wanted but no access point (important for identification but not access), record as follows:

> [246] 2# $i introductory text: $a variant title

If an access point is wanted but no note (important for access but not identification), record as follows:

[246] 3# $a variant title

Note that CONSER Standard Record practice is to use value "1" in all cases.

**EXAMPLES**

Caption title:

[110] 2# $a University of Hong Kong.

[245] 10 $a Report for . . . / $c the University of Hong Kong.

[246] 1# $i Caption title, <1927->: $a Report of the working of the University of Hong Kong for . . .

Spine title:

[245] 00 $a . . . Caprice, Monte Carlo, El Camino service manual.

[246] 1# $i Spine title, <1987->: $a . . . service manual, Caprice, Monte Carlo, El Camino

Corrected title:

[245] 00 $a African seminar series.

[246] 1# $i No. 26 has title misspelled: $a African semminar series

Expanded title:

[245] 00 $a St. Louis directory of. . . .

[246] 3# $a Saint Louis directory of . . .

[245] 00 $a Catalogue & index.

[246] 3# $a Catalogue and index

[245] 00 $a Year-book of made-up examples

[246] 1# $a Year-book of made-up examples

Something that may be a title:

[245] 00 $a Bulletin of the atomic scientists.

[246] 1# $i At head of title: $a Science and public affairs

When the "something" may be part of the title rather than a title in itself:

[245] 00 $a Business review.

[246] 0# $i At head of title: $a International

[246] 3# $a International business review

Alternative titles (provide access to first half when it consists of fewer than five words; provide access to the second half always):

[245] 04 $a The emerald, or, Miscellany of literature.

[246] 1# $a Emerald

[246] 1# $a Miscellany of literature

Section titles (appearing in subfield $p of field 245):

> [245] 00 $a Current housing reports. $n Series H-150, $p Annual housing survey, United States and regions. $n Part A, $p General housing characteristics.
> [246] 1# $a Annual housing survey, United States and regions
> [246] 1# $a General housing characteristics

Emphasized parts of a title:

> On item: Tables showing progress of FEDERAL AID AND ALLIED HIGHWAY PROGRAMS
> [245] 00 $a Tables showing progress of Federal and allied highway programs
> [246] 1# $a Federal and allied highway programs

Other titles:

> [245] 00 $a Serial publications in the British Museum (Natural History) library, on microfiche.
> [246] 1# $i Title on eye-readable header: $a BMNH serials

## EARLIER TITLE PROPER OF AN INTEGRATING RESOURCE [RDA 2.3.7] [MARC 21 247] [LC CORE]

Earlier titles proper are those appearing on earlier iterations of an integrating resource, but no longer appearing. The earlier title proper is recorded along with the date it was viewed. When a record is being revised so that the existing title proper is being changed to an earlier title proper, the date viewed will be the last recorded date viewed (e.g., from a note such as "Title from title bar (viewed October 6, 1999).").

### MARC 21 RECORD SYNTAX

> [247] 10 $a earlier title proper $f <date viewed>

### EXAMPLE

Before:

> [245] 00 $a Washington newspapers database.
> [500] ## $a Title from title bar (viewed October 6, 1999).

After:

> [245] 00 $a Washington State newsstand.
> [247] 10 $a Washington newspapers database $f <October 6, 1999>
> [500] ## $a Title from title bar (viewed December 21, 2003).

Note that the date viewed is recorded as a simple date between angle brackets in subfield $f. (See also "7. Ongoing Integrating Resources," below.)

## LATER TITLE PROPER (MINOR TITLE CHANGES)
## [RDA 2.3.8] [MARC 21 246] [LC-PCC CORE]

Later titles proper are those that result from minor changes to the title proper of a serial. (For a list of minor changes, see "Recording Changes in the Title Proper of a Serial," above.) Record both the later title proper and the related numbering or publication dates. Alternatively, if the changes have been numerous and slight, make a general note.

### MARC 21/ISBD RECORD SYNTAX

[246] 1# $i introductory phrase: $a later title proper

### EXAMPLES

[245] 04 $a The Los Angeles woman.
[246] 1# $i Issues for 3rd quarter 1990- have title: $a LA woman
[245] 00 $a Annual report of pipeline safety.
[246] 1# $i Issues for 1999- have title: $a Annual report on pipeline safety

## KEY TITLE [RDA 2.3.9] [MARC 21 222]
## [LC CORE (FOR ISSN CATALOGERS ONLY)]

A key title is a unique title linked to a particular ISSN. Key titles are devised and assigned by ISSN centers, based on the title proper. When a title proper is not unique, it is augmented by the name of an issuing body (separated from the title proper by a space-dash-space) or a place, year, or other distinguishing attribute (in parentheses). Key titles may be found in the ISSN Register, accessible via subscription to the ISSN Portal.[12]

### MARC 21 RECORD SYNTAX

[222] #n $a key title $b *(qualifying information)* [2nd indicator = non-filing characters]

### EXAMPLE

[222] #0 $a Öffentliche Dienst $b (Köln)

## ABBREVIATED TITLE
## [RDA 2.3.10] [MARC 21 210] [LC CORE (FOR ISSN CATALOGER ONLY)]

Abbreviated titles are assigned by ISSN centers (abbreviated key titles) or by other agencies that maintain formal lists of such abbreviated titles for use in their abstracting and indexing services (such as the National Library of Medicine). Abbreviated key titles may be found in the ISSN Register, accessible via subscription to the ISSN Portal.[13] Abbreviated titles found on the resource itself may also be recorded in this element.

### MARC 21/ISBD RECORD SYNTAX

[210] 0n $a *abbreviated title* $b *(qualifying information)* $2 *source* [2nd indicator = 0 (assigned by ISSN center [abbreviated key title]) or # (other source identified in subfield $2)]

**EXAMPLES**

Example of abbreviated key title:

[210] 0# $a Manage. improve. cost reduct. Goals

Example of abbreviated title assigned by the National Library of Medicine (source code in subfield $2):

[210] 00 $a JAMA $2 dnlm

## ABOUT STATEMENTS OF RESPONSIBILITY [RDA 2.4]

A statement of responsibility identifies or refers to those responsible for creating or contributing to the intellectual or artistic content of a resource. Such information may be embedded in the title proper or other title information, but it is only treated as a discrete element when it is presented separately in the resource.

A statement of responsibility may occur in association with:

- The title proper
- The designation of edition (including a named revision of an edition)
- The title of a series or subseries

Statements of responsibility are recorded as they appear on the serial. Optionally, a statement can be abridged if no loss of "essential information" will result [RDA 2.4.1.4 option], and persons, etc., after the first-named can be omitted and replaced by a bracketed general characterization (e.g., "[and six others]") [RDA 2.4.1.5 option].

Statements of responsibility identifying the editor of a serial are recorded only if felt to be an important means for identifying the serial [RDA 2.4.1.4 exception].

In cases of multiple statements of responsibility, record them in the order indicated by the sequence, layout, or typography on the source of information. In case of doubt, or if such statements are taken from a source other than the source for the related title proper or designation of edition, record them in the order that seems to make the most sense [RDA 2.4.1.6].

If the relationship between the title proper or designation of edition and those named in the statement of responsibility is not clear, add a bracketed word or phrase to clarify this relationship [RDA 2.4.1.7].

If a statement of responsibility is added, deleted, or changed on a subsequent issue of the serial, make a note if considered important for identification or access [RDA 2.4.1.10].

## INDIVIDUAL ELEMENTS

### STATEMENT OF RESPONSIBILITY RELATING TO THE TITLE PROPER [RDA 2.4.2] [MARC 21 245] [CORE]

A statement of responsibility relating to the title proper is taken from the same source as the title proper or, failing that, another source within the issue (or rarely, elsewhere).

A statement of responsibility may or may not indicate the type of responsibility involved. In the absence of an explicit statement such as "Prepared by . . . ," the name of a person or corporate body occurring in close proximity to the title usually qualifies as a statement of responsibility. However, such a name occurring near the foot of a page should be treated as the publisher in the absence of evidence to the contrary.

A person or family is not generally recorded in a statement of responsibility unless they are being treated as the creators of the intellectual or artistic content. Record an editor only if the name will provide a useful means of identifying the serial (e.g., the editor was associated with the serial for all or most of its existence or the editor is better known than the serial) [RDA 2.4.1.4 exception].

#### EXAMPLES

> [245] 04 $a Les temps modernes / $c directeur: Jean-Paul Sartre.
>
> [245] 04 $a The enemy / $c Wyndham Lewis, editor.

Record such an editor in a note if the relationship is not recorded on the same source or the same issue as the title proper.

#### EXAMPLES

> [245] 00 $a The Saturday review.
> [362] 1# $a Issues published: Volume 1, number 1 (August 2, 1924)-volume 34, number 52 (December 29, 1951).
> [500] ## $a Edited by Norman Cousins, 1942-1951.
> [700] 1# $a Cousins, Norman, $e editor.

Take a statement of responsibility relating to the title proper from the same source as the title proper or, failing this, from elsewhere in the serial [RDA 2.4.2.2].

If not all such statements are being recorded, prefer a statement identifying the creator(s) of the intellectual or artistic content or, failing this, the statement given first [RDA 2.4.2.3].

If a statement appears in more than one language or script, prefer the statement in the language or script of the title proper. If this criterion does not apply, record the statement given first [RDA 2.4.2.4].

Secretaria de Communicaciones y Obras Publicas

DIRECCION GENERAL DE
AERONAUTICA CIVIL

## ALMANAQUE
## HONDUREÑO
## 1961

SERVICIO METEOROLOGICO
NACIONAL

Año de la ejecucion del laudo

[245] 00 $a Almanaque hondureño / $c Secretaria de Communicaciones y Obras Publicas, Dirección de Aeronautica Civil.

[260] ## $a Tegucigalpa: $b Servicio Meteorológico Nacional.

REPUBLIC OF THE PHILIPPINES
CONGRESS OF THE PHILIPPINES
SENATE

## Journal of the Senate
FIRST REGULAR SESSION
1987-1988

Prepared by the Journal Division and
Publication and Editorial Division
under the supervision of

SECRETARY
ERIBERTO M. BERNAL

[245] 00 $a Journal of the Senate / $c Republic of the Philippines, Congress of the Philippines, Senate ; prepared by the Journal Division and Publication and Editorial Division.

## SERIAL AS RESPONSIBLE ENTITY

The names of serials present a conundrum in terms of statements of responsibility, in that serials are sometimes both an intellectual or artistic creation and the collective name of the group producing it. In general, the name of the serial should be recorded in a note and a nonspecific relationship [MARC 21 787] may be recorded with the serial.

### EXAMPLE

On item:

> Southern living 1990 garden annual
> by the Garden Department of Southern living magazine
> [245] 00 $a Southern living . . . garden annual.
> [787] 1# $t Southern living $x 0038-4305 $w (DLC) 70000890 $w (OCoLC)2457928

(No note needed: Title of related serial occurs in title proper.)

### EXAMPLE

On item:

> Better homes and gardens
> 1989
> CHRISTMAS CRAFTS
>
> [245] 00 $a Christmas crafts.
> [246] 3# $a Better homes and gardens . . . Christmas crafts
> [500] ## $a At head of title: Better homes and gardens.
> [787] 1# $t Better homes and gardens $x 0006-0151 $w (DLC) 27006944 $w (OCoLC)5902855

(A variant title is recorded since some users might consider "Better homes and gardens" to be part of the title proper. A note explains the reason.)

Note that CONSER Standard Record practice since June 2007 has been not to require a statement of responsibility when the related access point was represented by an authority record. Library of Congress RDA policy is to record the statement of responsibility when present. However, if more than one statement of responsibility is present, only the first is required.

### MARC 21/ISBD RECORD SYNTAX

> [245] title proper / $c statement of responsibility relating to the title proper ; subsequent statement of responsibility relating to the title proper.
> [245] title proper = $b parallel title proper / $c statement of responsibility relating to the title proper.

## CHANGES IN STATEMENT OF RESPONSIBILITY [RDA 2.4.1.10.2]

Make a note if the body, etc., named in the statement of responsibility changes, unless a new description is required (see "Changes: When to Create a New Description," above). If the responsible entity is important for access, provide an authorized access point for the entity.

### MARC 21 RECORD SYNTAX

[550] ## $a [Relationship]: [name of body or bodies], [dates of relationship]; [name of body or bodies], [dates of relationship]; [etc.]

### EXAMPLE

[245] 00 $a Journal of Brucian philosophy / $c Walamaloo Normal School, Department of Philosophy.

[550] ## $a Issued by: Walamaloo State College, Department of Philosophy, <April 1957-January 1972>; Walamaloo State University, Department of Philosophy, <April 1985-January 1992>

[710] 2# $a Walamaloo Normal School. $b Department of Philosophy, $i issuing body.

[710] 2# $a Walamaloo State College. $b Department of Philosophy, $i issuing body.

[710] 2# $a Walamaloo State University. $b Department of Philosophy, $i issuing body.

## PARALLEL STATEMENT OF RESPONSIBILITY RELATING TO THE TITLE PROPER [RDA 2.4.3] [MARC 21 245]

A parallel statement of responsibility may relate to the title proper or to a parallel title proper. It should be taken from the same source as the title proper to which it relates.

Note that CONSER Standard Record practice since June 2007 has been not to require a statement of responsibility when the related access point is represented by an authority record. (This practice is currently under review for RDA.)

### MARC 21/ISBD RECORD SYNTAX

Parallel statements of responsibility relating to the title proper appear in the same subfield as the statement of responsibility.

[245] $a title proper / $c statement of responsibility relating to the title proper = parallel statement of responsibility relating to the title proper.

### EXAMPLE

[245] 00 $a Blah! / $c International Union of the Undead = Union internationale des morts-vivants.

Parallel statements of responsibility relating to a parallel title proper appear in the same subfield as the parallel title proper.

> [245] $a title proper / $c statement of responsibility relating to the title proper = parallel title proper / parallel statement of responsibility relating to the title proper.

**EXAMPLE**
> [245] 00 $a Narcotic drugs / $c International Narcotics Control Board, Vienna = Stupéfiants / Organe international de contrôle des stupéfiants, Vienne.

## IDENTIFYING RESPONSIBLE PERSONS, FAMILIES, AND CORPORATE BODIES

If the name of a responsible person, family, or corporate body is important for access, add an authorized access point (see "5. Identifying Related Entities," below.)

## Edition area (ISBD Area 2)

### ELEMENTS
- Designation of Edition [RDA 2.5.2] [CORE] [MARC 21 250 $a]
- Parallel Designation of Edition [RDA 2.5.3] [MARC 21 250 $b]

While RDA defines other elements in this area, they are seldom if ever used with serials or ongoing integrating resources.

### CHANGES FROM AACR2
Transcription:

- AACR2 (and ISBD): Arabic numerals are substituted for numbers expressed in other ways (including spelled out), unless this might result in confusion. Any terms listed in AACR2 Appendix B are abbreviated according to the instructions given there.
- RDA: Elements of the edition statement are transcribed exactly as they appear in the source, without substitution or abbreviation.

Terminal punctuation:

- AACR2: Edition area ends with a single period.
- RDA (revised ISBD): Edition area ends with two periods whenever the last element in the area ends in a period (for example, an abbreviation).

## ABOUT EDITIONS

An edition is a version of a work aimed at a particular audience. This audience may be those interested in the latest version of a work (much as the principal audience for most newspapers and popular magazines consists of those interested in the latest issue) or it may be those comprising a particular demographic slice (for example, persons living in a particular region, persons belonging to a particular profession, or persons interested in obtaining the work in a particular physical or digital format).

While the version may be explicitly identified on the resource, this is not necessary so long as the version is known to meet the requirements of an edition. When present, this identification will usually occur as a discrete statement, but alternatively, it may be "embedded" in another statement, such as the title or other title information. Only when it occurs as a separate statement or needs to be supplied by the cataloger is this information recorded in an "edition statement" in terms of RDA. Consequently, computer algorithms cannot use the presence or absence of an edition statement as a reliable means of identifying all the versions of a given work.

While edition statements may be signaled by the presence of the word "edition" (or its analog in another language) on the resource—First edition, CD-ROM edition, etc.—this is not necessary, and often the challenge for the cataloger is determining whether a given term is referring to a version of a work or to a subunit of that work.

For serials cataloging, editions that represent revisions or successive iterations of a work—those aimed at an audience principally interested in the latest version—are recorded as numbering. In this case, the designation of the edition—1st edition, 2006 edition, etc.—is treated as the designation of the issue [RDA 2.5.2.5]. (For guidance on recording numbering, see the discussion of "Editions as Numbering," below.)

Only editions that aim at an audience representing a particular demographic—and that pertain to the serial as a whole—are recorded in serial edition statements. (See "Designation of Edition," below.)

## INDIVIDUAL ELEMENTS

### DESIGNATION OF EDITION [RDA 2.5.2] [CORE]

In general, take the designation of edition from the resource itself, preferring the same source as the title proper. If taken from a source outside the resource, enclose the designation in square brackets [RDA 2.5.2.2, RDA 2.2.4].

If the designation appears in more than one language or script, record the designation in the same language and script as the title proper or, failing this, the one that appears first in the source from which the designation is taken [RDA 2.5.2.4]. The rejected designation may be recorded as a parallel designation of edition. (See RDA 2.5.3, below.)

#### MARC 21/ISBD RECORD SYNTAX

[250] ## $a designation of edition.

Examples of editions aimed at particular demographics are geographic editions, special interest editions, special format or presentation editions, and language editions. The statement appearing on the resource is recorded as a designation of the edition.

**EXAMPLES**

> [245] 00 $a Motor freight directory.
> [250] ## $a Ohio edition.
> [245] 04 $a The weight control digest.
> [250] ## $a Professional edition.
> [245] 00 $a Nutri-topics.
> [250] ## $a Educator.
> [*Nutri-topics* is also issued in editions designated "Health professional/researcher"
> and "Consumer" that represent versions of a common work]
> [245] 00 $a Adult Bible studies.
> [250] ## $a Large print edition.

Occasionally an edition may be named on the resource without explicitly including the word "edition" or an analogous term. In such cases, it is important to determine whether the word or phrase identifies an intended audience or a subunit of the content.

This is not always clear-cut. After all, a serial may both be aimed at a particular regional audience and coincidentally cover that region exactly. In such cases, the nature of the content is often a guide. If the serial contains "reference" content—statistics, a directory, etc.—it is likely a part or section of a larger serial rather than an edition. In the end, you must exercise judgment.

**EXAMPLE**

> [245] 00 $a Fishing & hunting news.
> [250] ## $a Western Washington.
> ["Western Washington" refers to the geographic area of the intended audience]
> [245] 00 $a Directory of North American military aviation communications, VHF/
> UHF. $p Northeastern.
> ["Northeastern" refers to the geographic area (subunit of North America) covered
> by the content]

If a designation of edition is an integral part of, or grammatically linked to, the title proper, other title information, etc., it is recorded as part of the title proper, etc., and is not recorded as a separate edition statement. Fortunately, this is rare [RDA 2.5.2.6].

**EXAMPLE**

> [245] 00 $a Chicago journal of commerce edition of the Wall Street journal.
> [no edition statement recorded]

## PARALLEL DESIGNATION OF EDITION [RDA 2.5.3]

One or more parallel designations of edition may be recorded if required by the cataloging agency (e.g., an agency operating in a country with more than one official language). They are recorded in the order indicated by the sequence, layout, or typography on the source(s). The sources for a parallel designation of edition are the same as those for a designation of edition.

### MARC 21/ISBD RECORD SYNTAX

[250] ## $a designation of edition = $b parallel designation of edition.

The other elements given in RDA as elements of the edition statement [RDA 2.5.4–2.5.9] virtually never occur in connection with serials. In fact, no examples have been found. Should you come upon an example, please contact the author, and he will revise the text accordingly.

## SPECIAL SITUATIONS

### EDITIONS AS NUMBERING

When individual issues of a serial are designated as successively numbered or dated "editions," the individual edition statements (First edition, 2011 edition, etc.) are treated as numbering, and recorded following the provisions of RDA 2.6 (see "Numbering (Serials) Area," below).

### EXAMPLE

[362] 0# $a 1st edition-32nd edition

[recorded as numbering of serials rather than an edition statement]

When individual numbers are themselves issued in revised editions, as is sometimes the case with monographic series, this fact is recorded in a note. However, if an individual number is designated as "first edition" (or something analogous), this should be ignored and no note made unless there is evidence that subsequent editions were also published.

### EXAMPLE

[515] ## $a Some numbers issued in revised editions.

When a specific issue, or a specific recurring issue, is designated as an "edition" of a special type, having a specific target audience (such as collectors or people with money to spend), this fact is recorded in a note.

### EXAMPLES

[515] ## $a Volume 1, number 1 called "Special collector's edition."

[515] ## $a December issue each year called Special buyer's guide edition.

When editions are treated as numbering, statements of frequency of revised editions are recorded as notes on frequency [RDA 2.14].

## ACCOMMODATING MULTIPLE EDITIONS WITH MINOR DIFFERENCES

RDA does not address the problem that arises when the differences between distinct editions are not significant in terms of the typical user. Such editions may differ only in advertising (the audience aimed at in this case being defined by the economic characteristics of the residents of a given postal code). In such cases, this fact may be recorded in a note.

### EXAMPLE

[515] ## $a Issued in numerous editions that differ only in advertising.

Occasionally, differences between distinct editions may be *very* significant in terms of the typical user but not in terms of the typical library. In such cases, this fact may be recorded in a note.

### EXAMPLE

[245] 00 TV guide.

[515] ## $a Issued in numerous editions.

[On the other hand, a library specializing in the history of broadcast media might choose to catalog the individual local editions.]

## CHANGES IN EDITION STATEMENT

Designations of editions may change over time. When these do not indicate a change in scope, this fact is recorded in a note [RDA 2.20.4.5.2].

Recall that for a serial, the edition statement represents the edition on the earliest issue, while for an ongoing integrating resource it represents the edition on the latest iteration.

### EXAMPLE (SERIAL)

[250] ## $a International edition in English.

[500] ## $a Edition statement varies: International edition, 1998-

### EXAMPLE (INTEGRATING RESOURCE)

[250] ## $a International edition.

[500] ## $a Edition statement varies: International edition in English, 1993-1997.

## Numbering (Serials) Area (ISBD Area 3)

### ELEMENTS

- It's complicated (see below).

### CHANGES FROM AACR2

Transcription

- AACR2 (and ISBD): Arabic numerals are substituted for numbers expressed in other ways (including spelled out), unless this might result in confusion. Any terms listed in AACR2 Appendix B are abbreviated according to the instructions given there.
- RDA: Numbering of serials is transcribed exactly as it appears in the source, with only limited substitutions. However, numerals continue to be substituted for numbers that are spelled out in the source.

### ABOUT THE NUMBERING OF SERIALS

The numbering of serials can be complicated. The designations that identify a particular issue—be they alphabetic, numeric, chronological, or a combination of these—can present a challenge to the serials cataloger. The systems devised by publishers are fascinating in their seemingly infinite variety. But so long as the resulting designations identify individual issues, catalogers must record them without comment, keeping to themselves any malevolent thoughts.

The numbering of serials can begin and stop repeatedly, with new numbering schemes introduced seemingly at random. The numbers may skip or they may be repeated. Sometimes they will be repeated and then skip in order to get back in step. Occasionally, there may be no explicit numbering at all, in which case it is up to the cataloger to adapt some other element, such as the date of publication or a coverage statement extracted from the text, to serve this purpose. In the absence of a serviceable designation, a resource cannot be cataloged as a serial.

When numbering changes (other than merely a change in an associated term, such as from "number" to "issue"), it is treated as a new sequence, regardless of whether the numbering starts over at "1."

RDA defines numbering as "the identification of each of the issues or parts of a serial," that is, the designation carried on each part that enables that part to be distinguished from other parts. Parts may be distinguished from one another by a number, a letter, or some other character, or some combination, with various levels of hierarchy (series, volumes, issues, etc.). These numeric and/or alphabetic designations may be accompanied by chronological designations (or these chronological designations may occur alone) and may include captions (volume, number, tome, Jahrgang, etc.).

While a numeric and/or alphabetic designation must distinguish one issue or part from another, a chronological designation must do so only when it is the only designation present or the numeric and/or alphabetic designation alone does not identify the issue or part.

A serial may also use an alternative numbering scheme (for example, continuous numbering as well as hierarchical numbering).

Numbering is transcribed in sequences, each sequence consisting of the designation(s) of the first issue or part in a sequence and the designation(s) of the last issue or part.

Since all numbering must be accommodated as a single MARC 21 element ([362] $a), these designations must be distinguished from one another by employing ISBD prescribed punctuation:

- - follows the designation of the first issue or part and precedes the designation of the last issue or part in a sequence.
- ( ) surrounds a chronological designation (including any alternative chronological designation) following a numeric and/or alphabetic designation
- , precedes a level of hierarchy other than the first (comma-space)
- ; precedes a sequence other than the first (space-semicolon-space)
- = precedes an alternative designation (space-equals sign-space)

Numbering of serials may include a numeral, a letter, any other character, or the combination of these with or without an accompanying caption (volume, number, etc.) and/or a chronological designation.

Alternatively, one can routinely record numbering details informally as a note [RDA 2.20.5.3]. This technique is favored by the CONSER Program. RDA provides this technique as an alternative for each element, but provides no examples of such notes. The CONSER application combines these separate RDA alternative instructions into a single note.

## CONSER EXAMPLES

[362] 1# $a Began with August/September 1970; ceased with March 1972.

[362] 1# $a Began with Volume 1, number 1 (January 1995).

[515] ## $a Volume numbering ended with Volume 4, Number 12 (December 1998). Issues for January 1999- not numbered.

[362] 1# $a Began in 1943. Original numbering ended with Vol. 10, No. 12 (June 1952). None published July 1952-June 1974. New numbering began with No. 1 (July 1974). Ceased in 1975.

[362] 1# $a Began and ceased with: 1918.

Whether the numbering is recorded formally, following the RDA instructions, or informally as a note, it is recorded in subfield $a of MARC 21 field 362 (with the indicator set to "0" for a formal statement and "1" for an informal note).

### MARC 21/ISBD RECORD SYNTAX

[362] 0# $a *numbering of serials* [coded for formal display]

[362] 1# $a *numbering of serials* [coded for display as a note]

In the early days of AACR2, numeric and chronological designations were required to "identify" individual issues. Designations that by themselves were insufficient to identify issues were relegated to notes or ignored. Later this practice was relaxed, and designations are now recorded as they appear, just so long as one of them manages to identify the issue, for example:

*Issues:*

| | |
|---|---|
| Volume 1, June 2000 | [362] 1# $a Published issues: Volume 1 (June 2000) |
| Volume 1, July 2000 | *[chronological designations identify issues]* |
| Volume 1, August 2000 | |

*Issues:*

| | |
|---|---|
| Volume 1, number 1, 2000 | [362] 1# $a Published issues: Volume 1, number 1 (2000)- |
| Volume 1, number 2, 2000 | *[numeric designations identify issues]* |
| Volume 1, number 3, 2000 | |

For a cataloging manual aimed at a North American audience, the numbering of serials presents something of a challenge. This is not just because the numbering of serials presents a challenge in and of itself, but also because the CONSER Program recommends recording this numbering in the form of a note rather than using the complex structures of RDA (and of AACR2 before it). Confronted with these two alternative ways of recording numbering, and given his longtime love for the universality of ISBD, the author has decided to adopt a hybrid approach in this manual, applying the alternative of recording the numbering in the form of a note, but incorporating—when constructing that note—the somewhat complex superstructure of RDA elements and the corresponding ISBD punctuation. In combining the best of both worlds, it is hoped that this approach will minimize the drawbacks of each while adhering to the letter as well as the spirit of RDA.

The numbering of serials is governed by the general instructions for recording numerals expressed as words or numerals at RDA 1.8. Numerals are recorded in the form preferred by the agency—LC policy is to transcribe numerals as they appear—except in certain situations:

- Numbers expressed as words are converted to numerals [RDA 1.8.3].
- Inclusive numbers are given in full, even if foreshortened in the source. A slash may be substituted for a hyphen for clarity [RDA 1.8.4, RDA 2.6.1.4 exception].

| | |
|---|---|
| On source: 1961-63 | [362] 1# $a Began with: 1961/1963 |
| On source: Numbers 23-24 | [362] 1# $a Began with: Numbers 23/24 |

- Ordinal numbers are recorded as numerals, using the practice of the particular language, unless the practice is unknown (special rules apply for Chinese, Japanese, and Korean) [RDA 1.8.5].

> On source: Troisième
>
> Shorten to: 3e

Otherwise, designations are recorded as they appear.

### EXAMPLES

> [362] 1# $a Began with: Volume XVI, number 1.
> [362] 1# $a Began with: 1989 through 1990.
> [362] 1# $a Began with: '90.
> [362] 1# $a Began with: Academic year 1990.
> [362] 1# $a Began with: 24th Congress, 1st session.
> [362] 1# $a Began with: Case study 1.

Numbering is recorded in *sequences*. While most serials have a single numbering sequence, it is not uncommon to have several (typically distinguished from one another by a designation such as "new series," "second series," etc.). When such a designation is found, it should be used to introduce the new sequence, preceded by a space-semicolon-space and followed by a comma. If the numbering simply begins over without identifying a new series, supply an appropriate designation in square brackets:

> No 1 (janvier 2003)-no 36 (décembre 2005) ; [nouvelle série], no 1 (janvier 2006)-no 36 (décembre 2008)

It is also possible for a serial to carry two or more sequences in parallel, these latter comprising *alternative designations*. For example, a serial that is the product of a merger between two serials may continue the numbering of both, in a sense traveling both roads but being one traveler. Or a serial may carry both continuous issue numbering and numbering that starts over with each new volume. Each of these constitutes a distinct *alternative* sequence. The instructions in RDA 2.6 apply to elements within any sequence, but those in RDA 2.6.6 to 2.6.9 apply exclusively to alternative designations. Fortunately for our purposes, they are pretty much the regular instructions for designations, just applied to alternative designations.

Sometimes volumes in a monographic series will carry one set of numbering that pertains to the series as a whole and another that pertains to a subseries. Sometimes with a sufficient number of subseries, such schemes can descend several levels. Record only the numbering that pertains to the resource that is being described. If it is the series, record the numbering that pertains to the series; if it is one of the subseries, record the numbering that pertains to that subseries. For more guidance, see the instructions relating to series at RDA 2.12.

When a single issue is published in two or more parts, as may happen when an issue is unusually large, do not include the designations of the parts in the issue numbering (since these do not identify the issue as a whole). Instead, make a note:

[515] ## $a Some numbers issued in parts.

## INDIVIDUAL ELEMENTS

As noted above, individual elements are discussed in terms of sequences. For example, the element called "numeric and/or alphabetic designation of first issue or part of sequence" (phew!) relates to the first issue of the serial and also, if applicable, the first issue of any later sequence (such as "new series, volume 1, number 1").

## NUMERIC AND/OR ALPHABETIC DESIGNATION OF FIRST ISSUE OR PART OF SEQUENCE [RDA 2.6.2]

- [CORE for first or only sequence]
- Source (order of preference):
  - Same source as title proper in the first issue
  - Some other source in the first issue
  - Some other source

If the first issue lacks a designation but subsequent issues carry one, construct a designation for the first issue based on the pattern on subsequent issues, recording it in square brackets. Likewise, if the first issue is not available but its designation can be ascertained, record it in square brackets.

### EXAMPLE

First issue: no designation
Second issue: Volume 1, issue 2
Third issue: Volume 1, issue 3
[362] 1# Began with: [Volume 1, issue 1].

If the designation appears in more than one language or script, record the designation in the language and script of the title proper or, failing that, the designation appearing first [RDA 2.6.2.4].

If the designation consists of different levels (e.g., volumes and numbers) and the levels are not distinguished or linked by punctuation in the source, the levels are recorded separated by commas. If a higher level follows a lower level, these are recorded rearranged in descending order (e.g., "1-1998" would be recorded as "1998-1").

Always record all designations, even if they are unnecessary to identify the issues.

**EXAMPLE**

*Issues:*

Anno 1, v. 1, n. 1

Anno 1, v. 1, n. 2

Anno 2, v. 2, n. 1

["Anno" and "v." are just different ways of representing the same level]

[362] 1# $a Published issues: Anno 1, v. 1, n. 1-

*Issues:*

Vol. 35, no. 162

Vol. 35, no. 163

Vol. 36, no. 164

[The volume designations are unnecessary to identify the issues]

[362] 1# $a Published issues: Vol. 35, no. 162-

If there is a sequence of numbering after the first, record any designation such as "new series" that is associated with this subsequent sequence as a whole. If no such designation is present, supply one in square brackets [RDA 2.6.3, RDA 2.2.4].

If the numeric and/or alphabetic designation of the first issue in a sequence is the only designation present for that issue, follow it by a hyphen. However, if it is the only issue published, follow it by a stop (period).

## CHRONOLOGICAL DESIGNATION OF FIRST ISSUE OR PART OF SEQUENCE [RDA 2.6.3]

- [CORE for first or only sequence]
- Source (order of preference):
  - Same source as title proper in the first issue
  - Some other source in the first issue
  - Some other source

When a numeric and/or alphabetic designation and a chronological designation are given on an issue, record the chronological designation in parentheses following the numeric and/or alphabetic designation.

The numeric and/or alphabetic designation and the chronological designations may be taken from different sources within the same issue. The important thing is to record all applicable designations.

If the form of the chronological designation varies in different sources, choose the source that occurs first in the order of preference above.

**EXAMPLE**

On cover (source for title proper): January/February 1988

On table of contents page (numeric designation, with different chronological designation): Vol. 1, No. 1, February 1988

[362] 1# $a Began with: Vol. 1, no. 1 (January/February 1988).

When a date is given in a non-Gregorian calendar, prefer a date in the Gregorian calendar, if present. Otherwise, record the date in the non-Gregorian calendar, after which you may supply a date in the Gregorian calendar in square brackets.

**EXAMPLES**

On source: Rajab 1395 / Yūliyū 1975

[362] 1# $a Began with: Yūliyū 1975.

On source: Rajab 1395

[362] 1# $a Began with: Rajab 1395 [Yūliyū 1975].

If the first issue lacks a designation but subsequent issues carry one, construct a designation for the first issue based on the pattern on subsequent issues, recording it in square brackets. Likewise, if the first issue is not available but its designation can be ascertained, record it in square brackets.

If the designation appears in more than one language or script, record the designation in the language and script of the title proper or, failing that, the designation appearing first [RDA 2.6.2.4].

Follow the chronological designation of the first issue in a sequence (including any parentheses) by a hyphen. However, if it is the only issue published, follow it by a stop (period).

## NUMERIC AND/OR ALPHABETIC DESIGNATION OF LAST ISSUE OR PART OF SEQUENCE [RDA 2.6.4]

- [CORE for last or only sequence]
- Source (order of preference):
  - Same source as title proper in the last issue
  - Some other source in the last issue
  - Some other source

The other instructions are identical to those for the corresponding designation for the first issue in a sequence (see above). If no designation is recorded for the first issue in a sequence, precede the designation of the last issue with a hyphen.

## CHRONOLOGICAL DESIGNATION OF LAST ISSUE OR PART OF SEQUENCE [RDA 2.6.5]

- [CORE for last or only sequence]
- Source (order of preference):
    - Same source as title proper in the last issue
    - Some other source in the last issue
    - Some other source

The other instructions are identical to those for the corresponding designation for the first issue in a sequence (see above). If the chronological designation is the only designation on the last issue in a sequence, and no designation is recorded for the first issue in a sequence, precede the designation of the last issue with a hyphen.

## ALTERNATIVE SEQUENCES [RDA 2.6.6-2.6.9]

The instructions for recording designations in alternative sequences are identical to those for recording designations in other sequences. When applying ISBD conventions, an alternative designation or sequence is preceded by a space-equals sign-space:

[362] 1# $a Published issues: No 188 (22 oct. 1796 = 1er brum. an 5)-no 500 (4 sept. 1797 = 18 fruct. an 5).

[362] 1# $a Published issues: Bd. 1, Nr. 1 (Frühling 1970)-Bd. 6, Nr. 3 (Winter 1975) = Nr. 1-Nr. 24.

## NOTES ON THE NUMBERING OF SERIALS [RDA 2.20.5]

Aside from notes relating to when a serial begins and ceases (dealt with above), notes on the numbering of serials typically relate to complex or irregular numbering needing explanation [RDA 2.20.5.4] and the period covered [RDA 2.20.5.5].

### MARC 21/ISBD RECORD SYNTAX

In MARC 21, any oddities in the numbering of serials are recorded in [515] $a (numbering peculiarities note):

[515] ## $a numbering peculiarity

### EXAMPLES

[515] ## $a Some volumes issued in revised editions.

[515] ## $a Issues for Aug. 1973-Dec. 1974 also called v. 1, no. 7-v. 2, no. 12.

[515] ## $a Volume numbering irregular: v. 15-18 omitted, v. 20-21 repeated.

[515] ## $a Numbering begins each year with v. 1.

[515] ## $a Numbering irregular; some numbers repeated or omitted.

[515] ## $a Volumes published <1996-1998> lack designation.

[515] ## $a Volumes 5-6 incorrectly called v. 4-5.

[515] ## $a Issues for 1996 are only available as individual articles, organized topically.

[515] ## $a Articles are continually added to each annual volume.

[515] ## $a Report year ends June 30.

[515] ## $a Report year varies.

[515] ## $a Each issue covers: Apr. 1-Mar. 31.

[515] ## $a Each issue since 1961-1962 covers two years.

## Special Situations

### PILOT OR SAMPLE ISSUES

Make notes about pilot or sample issues. Do not record them as the first issue of the serial, unless the designation of the next issue implies a predecessor.

#### EXAMPLES

Sequence of issues: Premier issue, Number 1, Number 2, . . .

[362] 1# $a Began with: Number 1.

[515] ## $a No. 1 preceded by an issue called "premier issue."

Sequence of issues: Premier issue, Number 2, Number 3, . . .

[362] 1# $a Began with: [Number 1].

[515] ## $a First issue called "premier issue."

### ISSUES IN MULTIPLE PARTS

If individual issues are in multiple parts, this is noted. For example, an alphabetical directory issued in an A-K volume and an L-Z volume, or proceedings of a recurring conference where the proceedings of each conference occupy two or more volumes.

#### EXAMPLE

[515] ## $a Issued in parts.

### FULL EXAMPLES (MARC 21 AND ISBD RECORD SYNTAXES)

Because RDA treats each element of numbering separately, but MARC 21 requires that they be recorded as a single data element, sample notes are given below, to demonstrate the appropriate ISBD punctuation and order of elements:

[362] 1# $a Published issues: Volume 1, number 1 (January 5, 1993)-volume 10, #52.

[362] 1# $a Published issues: Volume 1, number 1 (January 5, 1993)-

[362] 1# $a Began with: Volume 1, number 1 (January 5, 1993).

[362] 1# $a Published issues: -volume 10, #52.

[362] 1# $a Ceased with: Volume 10, #52.

## Publication, Production, Distribution, etc., Area (ISBD Area 4)

The ISBD Publication, production, distribution, etc., area corresponds in RDA to four multi-element statements—production statement, publication statement, distribution statement, and manufacture statement—as well as an independent element (copyright date). After reviewing general changes from AACR2, and related changes in MARC 21, this section will look at each of these in turn.

### CHANGES FROM AACR2

Functions (publication, production, distribution, manufacture) and copyright date:

- AACR2 and ISBD: Record as a single area. In the MARC 21 format, record in a single [260] field.
- RDA Record each function (publication, production, distribution, manufacture) and copyright date as discrete statements. In the MARC 21 format, record in repeatable [264] fields with the type of data signaled by the second indicator value.

No place or publisher, distributor, etc.:

- AACR2: When no place of publication, etc., is identified, record "[S.1.]"; when no publisher, etc., is identified, record "[s.n.]"; if neither is identified, record "[S.1. : s.n.]" in a single pair of square brackets. (ISBD now records each within its own pair of square brackets.)
- RDA: When no place of publication, etc., is identified, record "[Place of publication not identified]," etc., in its place; when no publisher, etc., is identified, record "[publisher not identified]" in its place; record each within its own pair of square brackets.

Name of publisher, distributor, etc.:

- AACR2: Give in the shortest form in which it can be understood and identified internationally.
- RDA: Transcribe in the form in which it appears in the source. No cataloger-initiated abbreviations or omissions (optional omission: levels in a corporate hierarchy that are not required to identify the publisher, distributor, etc [generally not applied by those following CONSER practice]).

## REPRODUCTIONS

As under AACR2, reproductions are described as such. Record in publication, etc., statements details relating to the publication, etc., of the reproduction, not the original. The original publication is described as a related manifestation (see "3. Relationships Between Resources," below). Note: Unlike under AACR2, the Library of Congress will be adhering to this part of RDA (see LC-PCC PS 27.1.1.3).

## OVERVIEW OF CHANGES FROM FORMER PRACTICES

The change from the description-based structure of AACR2 to the element-based structure of RDA is most evident in ISBD area 4 (Publication, distribution, etc., area). Under AACR2, information relating to publication, distribution, etc., is recorded in a single area of the bibliographic description, and MARC 21 provided a single field for encoding the data. This practice continued as the first MARC 21 records were created using RDA.

However, RDA provides discrete instructions for each functional area covered by ISBD area 4: production, publication, distribution, and manufacturing. To keep the corresponding encoded data discrete, MARC 21 Bibliographic was amended in 2011 by introducing a new field—[264]—that can be used repeatedly to discretely identify data relating to each functional area.

This section of the manual uses this new approach, using MARC 21 field [264] and addressing each functional area in turn:

- Production statement (CORE for unpublished materials; rare in serials cataloging)
- Publication statement (CORE for the first instance of each constituent element)
- Distribution statement (CORE for a given element if the corresponding element is "not identified" in the publication statement)
- Manufacture statement (CORE for a given element if the corresponding element is "not identified" in either the publication statement or the distribution statement)
- Copyright date (CORE if neither a date of publication or distribution is identified)

## PRODUCTION STATEMENTS

"Production" relates only to unpublished resources such as manuscripts. While not unknown, manuscripts meeting the RDA definition of a serial are more likely to be cataloged as manuscript collections than serials.

## DATE OF PRODUCTION
## [RDA 2.7.6] [CORE FOR UNPUBLISHED MATERIALS]

Date of production is taken from the first and, if the material is no longer being produced, the last issue. If the date is the same for both, record a single date. If the issues are undated and dates are available from other sources, record these in square brackets. If an exact date is unknown, supply an approximate date if available. (See general instructions at RDA 1.9.2.) If one or both dates are unavailable or cannot be approximated, supply the bracketed text "[date of production not identified]" [RDA 2.7.6.6].

### MARC 21/ISBD RECORD SYNTAX

[264] second indicator = 0
[264] $c *date of production.*

### EXAMPLES

[264] #0 $c 1999-
Currently published or last issue not available.
[264] #0 $c 1982-2001.
[264] #0 $c-[2002].
First issue not available.
[264] #0 1967.
First and last issues produced in same year.
[264] #0 $c [date of production not identified]-2002.


## PUBLICATION STATEMENTS
## [ELEMENTS ARE CORE FOR THE FIRST INSTANCE OF EACH]

"Publication" relates to the formal publishing of a resource. There are a variety of ways in which a resource may be published. For example, it may be published by Publisher A or it may be co-published by Publishers A, B, etc. It may be published by publisher A for or on behalf of Organization B, which has no publishing facilities of its own. Older resources may be published by a bookseller or printer. All such arrangements are recorded in the publication statement, though sponsorship arrangements are not. Some publishers may not issue resources under their own name but rather under one or more imprints used for marketing purposes. For purposes of publication statements, such imprints are treated as publisher names.

The publication statement consists of one or more places of publication, the names of one or more publishers, and the date(s) of publication. A single publisher may have one or more associated places.

While RDA provides for recording parallel places of publication and publishers (i.e., in a different language or script), these are not typically recorded by catalogers other than those operating in a multilingual environment. The instructions for recording parallel places of publication and publishers are the same as those for recording the place of publication and publisher. They are preceded by the corresponding element followed by a space-equals sign-space.

## CHANGES IN THE PUBLICATION STATEMENT

When changes in the publication statement take place over time, and these changes are felt to be important for identification or access, they may be recorded as notes [RDA 2.8.1.5.2].

### EXAMPLES

[264] #1 $a Paris ; $a New York : $b Vogue, $c 1964-
[264] 21 $3 1980-May 1993 $a London : $b Voguett
[264] 31 $3 June 1993- $a London : $b Elle

### POSSIBLE NOTE GENERATED FROM THE PRECEDING

Volumes for 1980-May 1993 published: London : Vogue; June 1993- : London : Elle. [Note: In an ISBD display, the data in the first [264] field would display in area 4. The note generated from the other [264] fields would display with other notes in area 7.]

## PLACE OF PUBLICATION
## [RDA 2.8.2] [CORE (FIRST OR ONLY PLACE)]

The place of publication is a place associated with the publisher's name. It typically appears in the same location as the name of the publisher, though it may appear in another location such as the verso of the title page. In the event of a conflict, prefer the place of publication appearing in the same location.

On title page: ROUTLEDGE, Taylor & Francis Group, London and New York
On verso of title page: First published 2009 by Routledge, 2 Park Square, Milton Park, Abingdon, Oxon OX14 4RN; simultaneously published in the USA and Canada by Routledge, 270 Madison Avenue, New York, NY 10016
[264] #1 $a London : $b Routledge, Taylor & Francis Group

The place of publication is transcribed as it appears in the resource, without abbreviation. If it is known to be fictitious, or is ambiguous, a clarification can be provided in a note. Optionally, the name of a larger jurisdiction can be added in brackets if felt to be important for identification or access [RDA 2.8.2.3, RDA 2.20.7.3].

### EXAMPLES

[264] #1 $a Lanham, Maryland
[264] #1 $a Harrow, Middlesex
[264] #1 $a London
[500] ## $a Published in: London, Ontario.
*or, optionally,*
[264] #1 $a London [Ontario]

If recording multiple places of publication, record them in the order indicated by the sequence, layout, or typography on the source of information [RDA 2.8.2.4]. (Only the first place of publication is a CORE element.)

If the place of publication is given in more than one language and/or script, record the form that is in the same language and/or script as the title proper or, failing that, the one that appears first [RDA 2.8.2.5].

If the place of publication is not identified on the serial, and cannot be surmised or approximated, record "[Place of publication not identified]." However, if the place of publication is known, supply it in square brackets. If the exact place is unknown but can be approximated, supply the name of the smallest known jurisdiction in square brackets. In cases of uncertainty, follow any surmised data with a question mark [RDA 2.8.2.6].

### MARC 21/ISBD RECORD SYNTAX
[264] second indicator = 1

[264] $a place of publication

[264] $a place of publication ; $a subsequent place of publication

[264] $a place of publication : $b publisher ; $a subsequent place of publication : $b subsequent publisher

### EXAMPLES
[264] #1 $a [Place of publication not identified]

[264] #1 $a [Hobbiton?] : $b Bilbo Baggins

[264] #1 $a [California]

[264] #1 $a V Praze

## PUBLISHER'S NAME
## [RDA 2.8.4] [CORE (FIRST OR ONLY PUBLISHER)]

The publisher name follows its associated place(s) of publication.

For serials published in the centuries before the emergence of a specialized publisher role, treat printers and booksellers as publishers (i.e., as fulfilling the publisher's role) [RDA 2.8.4.1].

Take the publisher's name from the same source as the title proper, or, failing this, some other source in the serial (see RDA 2.2.4 for additional sources) [RDA 2.8.4.2].

In book-like serials, the name of the publisher will typically appear at the bottom of the title page, in the "imprint position," or it may appear on the verso of the title page. In serials published by societies, institutions, or government agencies rather than by commercial publishers, the place of publication may appear alone in the imprint position, with the name of the organization or agency (implicitly the publisher) appearing at the top of the title page. In magazines, journals, and newspapers, the place of publication and publisher's name may appear in the masthead (the formal statement of publishing and editorial details appearing somewhere inside) or in the colophon on (or near) the last page.

The publisher's name is transcribed as it appears in the resource, without abbreviation or augmentation. However, levels of corporate hierarchy may be omitted if desired [RDA 2.8.1.4 option—generally not applied by those following CONSER practice]. If the name is known to be fictitious, or is ambiguous, a clarification can be provided in a note [RDA 2.8.4.3, RDA 2.20.7.3].

In cases of more than one publisher, record the names in the order indicated by the sequence, layout, or typography on the source of information [RDA 2.8.4.5].

If the publisher's name is given in more than one language and/or script, record the form that is in the same language and/or script as the title proper or, failing that, the one that appears first [RDA 2.8.4.6].

If the publisher is not identified on the serial, and cannot be supplied, record "[publisher not identified]." However, if the publisher is known, supply it in square brackets [RDA 2.8.4.7].

### MARC 21/ISBD RECORD SYNTAX

[264] $b publisher, $c date of publication

[264] $b publisher : $b subsequent publisher

### EXAMPLES

[264] #1 $a Washington, D.C. : $b The World Bank

[264] #1 $a Washington, D.C. : $b Association of Jesuit Colleges and Universities : $b Jesuit Secondary Education Association

## DATE OF PUBLICATION [RDA 2.8.6] [CORE]

A date of publication is more common on book-like serials than periodicals, which are more likely to carry a chronological designation and possibly a copyright date, but no discrete publication date. In such cases, the chronological designation and/or copyright date may be used to infer a date of publication, if the result is not implausible (as when the item is in hand but the copyright year still lies in the future, or the chronological designation refers to a period several years in the past but the issue is known from other evidence to have been published more recently).

If a date of publication is not present and cannot be surmised, or if the first and/ or last issue is not available, supply an approximate date if possible or, if not, do not record a date of publication [RDA 2.8.6.5]. Apply the rule for constructing such a date given in RDA 1.9.2.

### EXAMPLES (FROM RDA 1.9.2)

Actual year known: [2003]

Either of two consecutive years: [2003 or 2004]

Probable year known: [2003?]

Probable range of years: [between 2002 and 2004]

Earliest and/or latest possible date known:
[not before January 1, 2003]
[not after December 31, 2003]
[between December 31, 2002 and March 31, 2003]

Use a hyphen to separate the date of publication of the first issue from that of the last issue. If the last issue has not yet been published, follow the hyphen with a blank.

## DISTRIBUTION STATEMENTS [RDA 2.9] [ELEMENTS ARE CORE IF CORRESPONDING ELEMENTS IN PUBLICATION STATEMENT "NOT IDENTIFIED"]

It is necessary to record elements in the distribution statement only if the corresponding element of the publication statement contains a "not identified" value (such as "[publisher not identified]"). In such cases, only a single value needs to be recorded (the first, if there is more than one to choose from).

The instructions that apply to distribution statements and their elements are identical to those that apply to publication statements and their elements.

Optionally, if the distributor's function is not clear from the distribution statement, record the distributor's name followed by "[distributor]" in square brackets [RDA 2.9.4.4 optional addition]. (Note, however, that the second indicator value in MARC field [264] renders this addition superfluous.)

### EXAMPLES

[264] #1 $a [Place of publication not identified] : $b [publisher not identified], $c [1272?]-

[264] #2 $a Xanadu : $b Distributed by Kublai Khan, $c 1272-

[264] #1 $a Ipswich : $b [publisher not identified], $c [2003]-

[264] #2 $a Notlob : $b Notlob Parrot Mortuary [distributor]

## MANUFACTURE STATEMENTS [RDA 2.9] [ELEMENTS CORE IF CORRESPONDING ELEMENTS IN PUBLICATION AND DISTRIBUTION STATEMENTS "NOT IDENTIFIED"]

It is necessary to record elements in the manufacture statement only if the corresponding element of the publication statement contains a "not identified" value (such as "[publisher not identified]") and there is no distribution statement or the corresponding element likewise contains a "not identified" value. In such cases, only a single value needs to be recorded (the first value, if there is more than one to choose from).

The instructions that apply to manufacture statements and their elements are identical to those that apply to publication statements and their elements.

**EXAMPLE**

[264] #1 $a [Place of publication not identified] : $b [publisher not identified], $c [1888?]-

[264] #3 $a Willoughby : $b Printed by Gart Williams, $c 1888-

## CHANGES IN STATEMENTS RELATING TO PRODUCTION, PUBLICATION, DISTRIBUTION, AND/OR MANUFACTURE

If changes occur on later issues of a serial, and these changes are felt to be important, record them as notes. Notes can be generated from MARC field 264 with appropriate first indicator values.

## COPYRIGHT DATE [RDA 2.11]

### ABOUT THE COPYRIGHT OR PHONOGRAM DATE

Copyright—the claim of intellectual property rights in a resource—is asserted by the presence on the resource of the copyright symbol © followed by a year or, for sound recordings, the phonogram symbol ℗ followed by a year.

The copyright date is a CORE element only if no date of publication or distribution is identified.

## COPYRIGHT DATE [RDA 2.11] [CORE IF PRESENT AND NEITHER DATE OF PUBLICATION NOR DISTRIBUTION IDENTIFIED]

Copyright dates, if present, are transcribed from anywhere in the first and/or last issues of the serial, connected by a hyphen. If the appropriate symbol cannot be reproduced, then it may be spelled out as "copyright" or "phonogram," respectively. If the first or last issue lacks a copyright date, record only the hyphen and the copyright date from the other issue. If multiple copyright dates appear in a single issue, select the latest date.

Note that LC practice (LC-PCC PS 2.11) is not to record copyright dates for serials. Whenever a copyright date is present but a date of publication is absent, the copyright date and/or chronological designation can be used to surmise a date of publication.

### MARC 21/ISBD RECORD SYNTAX

### MARC 21

[264] #4 $c copyright date(s)

**EXAMPLES**

Library of Congress Practice

> [264] #1 $a Cambridge : $b Cambridge University Press, $c 1965-[1975]
>
> On last issue: ©1975 [no date of publication]

Pure RDA Practice

> [264] #1 $a [Place of publication not identified] : $b [publisher not identified], $c [2000?-2011]
>
> [264] #2 $a Boston : $b Distributed by the American Distribution Society
>
> [264] #4 $c ©2001-©2012
>
> [362] 1# $a Published issues: Volume I-volume XII
>
> [Issue ©2012 received in 2011]

## NOTES RELATING TO PUBLISHERS, DISTRIBUTORS, ETC.

Record notes relating to changes in publishers, distributors, etc., using the syntax provided by MARC 21 field [264], if at all possible (see under "Changes in the Publication Statement," above). Such use maximizes use, reuse, and display of the data in the environment envisaged in RDA implementation scenario 1.

Record other notes (such as notes to correct inaccuracies) in field [500] or [550] as appropriate [RDA 2.20.7].

## IDENTIFYING PUBLISHERS, DISTRIBUTORS, ETC. (SUPPLYING AUTHORIZED ACCESS POINTS)

(See "5. Identifying Related Entities," below.)

## Physical Description Area (ISBD Area 5)

### CHANGES FROM AACR2

Recording

- AACR2 and ISBD: The physical description area is recorded as a single sequence.
- RDA: The elements comprising this area are split into those that pertain to the physical or digital container and those that pertain to the intellectual or artistic content (e.g., illustrative matter). In MARC 21, these latter are now recorded in their own discrete fields when they pertain to sound characteristics [344], video characteristics [346], or digital file characteristics [347].

Controlled vocabularies

- RDA: Controlled vocabularies are used to specify the media and carrier types (see "Content Form and Media Type," above, for instructions relating to media type).

Metric units (dimensions)

- AACR2: Metric units are recorded as abbreviations ending in periods.
- RDA: Metric units are recorded as symbols (cm, mm, etc.), without periods.

## ELEMENTS

- Carrier type [RDA 3.3]
- Extent [RDA 3.4]
- Illustrative content [RDA 7.15]
- Color content [RDA 7.17]
- Dimensions [RDA 3.5]

## CARRIER TYPE [RDA 3.3] [CORE]

Carrier type is a categorization reflecting the format of the storage medium and housing of a carrier in combination with the type of intermediation device required to view, play, run, etc., the content of a resource. The following are the most common for serials:

- *Audio* carriers
    Audio disc
- *Microform* carriers
    Microfiche
    Microfilm reel
    Microopaque
- *Unmediated* carriers
    Volume

### MARC 21 RECORD SYNTAX

[338] ## $a carrier type term $b carrier type code $2 rdacarrier

When multiple carrier types are present, give the carrier type of the predominant part of the serial in the first $a and the carrier type of any accompanying material in a second $a. Repeat this for the content type and media type if appropriate. (See example below.)

A complete list of carrier terms, along with corresponding MARC 007/01 codes will be found in the Term and Code List for RDA Carrier Types (identified in subfield $2 as rdacarrier) on the LC website.[14]

**EXAMPLE**

[245] 00 $a BBC music magazine.

[336] ## $a text $a performed music $a rdacontent

[337] ## $a unmediated $a audio $2 rdamedia

[338] ## $a volume $a audio disc $2 rdacarrier

[Each issue is accompanied by a music CD.]

## EXTENT [RDA 3.4] [CORE IF THE RESOURCE IS COMPLETE OR ITS TOTAL EXTENT IS KNOWN]

Typically, the extent of the resource consists of a number followed by an RDA carrier type. For printed serials, the number represents the number of bibliographic volumes encompassed in the numbering borne by the serial. (For example, if the first issue is volume 14, no. 1, and the last is volume 19, no. 12, then the extent is 6 volumes.) This element cannot be recorded for printed serials if either the beginning or ending designation is unknown.

**MARC 21/ISBD RECORD SYNTAX**

[300] ## $a *extent*

**EXAMPLES**

[300] ## $a 15 volumes

[338] ## $a volume $2 rdacarrier

[300] ## $a 213 microfilm reels

[338] ## $a microfilm reel $2 rdacarrier

[300] ## $a 1 online resource

[338] ## $a online resource $2 rdacarrier

## ILLUSTRATIVE CONTENT [RDA 7.15]

Indicate the presence of illustrative content by recording the term "illustrations" in [300] $b.

**MARC 21/ISBD RECORD SYNTAX**

[300] ## preceding element : $b illustrative and color content

**EXAMPLE**

[300] ## $a volumes : $b illustrations ; $c 26 cm

## COLOR CONTENT [RDA 7.17]

Depending on common usage in your country, indicate the presence of color illustrative content (colors other than black, white, and shades of gray) by recording the phrase "color illustrations" or "colour illustrations" (if all illustrations are color) or "illustrations (some color)" or "illustrations (some colour)" if only some illustrations are in color.

### MARC 21/ISBD RECORD SYNTAX

[300] ## preceding element : $b color content

### EXAMPLES

[300] ## $a 16 volumes : $b color illustrations ; $c *26 cm*
[300] ## $a 3 volumes : $b illustrations (some color) ; $c *26 cm*


## DIMENSIONS [RDA 3.5]

If dimensions are recorded, record the height and, if its width exceeds its height, the width of the resource in cm. For microfilm reels, record the diameter in mm.

### MARC 21/ISBD RECORD SYNTAX

[300] ## *preceding element* ; $c *dimensions* [followed by period if followed by a series] [490]

### EXAMPLES

[300] ## $a 25 microfilm reels ; $c 35 mm
[300] ## $a 1,250 microfiches : $b color illustrations ; $c 11 x 15 cm.
[490] 0# $a Publications of the Society for Microfiche Studies

Note: Formerly the dimensions of microfiches were given only when they were not standard A6 (105 x 148 mm). The period following "cm" is required whenever a series statement is present, in order to generate an appropriate ISBD display.


## ACCOMPANYING MATERIAL

Apply the above instructions when recording elements for any accompanying material, using the record syntax below to add them to a MARC 21/ISBD record.

### MARC 21/ISBD RECORD SYNTAX

[300] ## preceding element + $e accompanying material (extent : illustrative and color content ; dimensions)

## Series Area (ISBD Area 6) [RDA 2.12] [CORE]

### ELEMENTS

- Title proper of series [RDA 2.12.2] [CORE]
- Other title information of series [RDA 2.12.4]
- Statement of responsibility relating to series [RDA 2.12.6]
- ISSN of series [RDA 2.12.8]
- Numbering within series [RDA 2.12.9]
- Title proper of subseries [RDA 2.12.10] [CORE]
- Other title information of subseries [RDA 2.12.12]
- Statement of responsibility relating to subseries [RDA 2.12.14]
- ISSN of subseries [RDA 2.12.16]
- Numbering within subseries [RDA 2.12.17]

### ABOUT SERIES

A series statement identifies the series to which a serial belongs, if any, and may include a subseries. One serial in its lifetime may belong to many series.

Because all series are in fact serials, it is easiest to view a series as a larger serial of which the serial being cataloged is a component part, either for its entire existence or for a specified period. As such, the rules for recording the title proper of a series are generally those for recording the title proper of a serial, those for recording a statement of responsibility relating to a series are generally those for recording a statement of responsibility relating to a serial, and so on.

For example, when viewed as a serial in itself, the preferred source for the title proper of a printed series is the source that would be preferred if it were itself being cataloged as a serial, that is, the title page for the series (if any) rather than the title page for the serial, though the two are frequently the same.

### MARC 21/ISBD RECORD SYNTAX

[490] 0# $3 materials specified: $a Title proper of series / statement of responsibility relating to series, $x ISSN of series ; $v numbering within series. $a Title proper of subseries / statement of responsibility relating to subseries, $x ISSN of subseries ; $v numbering within subseries

(Note: If an authorized access point is also being supplied for the series, set the first indicator value to "1.")

## INDIVIDUAL ELEMENTS

### TITLE PROPER OF SERIES [RDA 2.12.2] [CORE]

In general follow the instructions given on recording titles at 2.3.1, though be more critical of whether a given phrase in fact qualifies as a title. The LC-PCC PS for RDA 2.12 offers some guidance in this regard, suggesting certain types of phrase that should be recorded as a quoted note, if at all:

- An *unnumbered* statement of the name of the body responsible for the serial (for example, "An American Astronomical Society publication")
- An *unnumbered* word or phrase indicating a subject category to which the serial is assigned by the publisher
- A string of numbers and/or letters that appears to be assigned to every publication of the body (for example, "UC-13," "CRN 780206-00050," or "SP-MN") unless the string is elsewhere associated with a word or phrase that would be considered a series (for example, "NASA SP" on the title page is associated with "Special Publications" in a list of "NASA scientific and technical publications" and so should be recorded as a series)

When evaluating a series title page, evaluate it as though you were cataloging the series rather than the serial.

### STATEMENT OF RESPONSIBILITY RELATING TO SERIES [RDA 2.12.6]

In general follow the instructions given on recording statements of responsibility in general at RDA 2.4.1. Record a statement of responsibility only if it occurs in close proximity to the title proper of the series and is obviously intended to be understood in connection with that title proper.

### EXAMPLE

[490] 0# $a Technical bulletin / Northern Territory, Department of Primary Education, Economics Section

## ISSN OF SERIES [RDA 2.12.8]

Record the ISSN of the series if present on the serial issue.

### MARC 21/ISBD RECORD SYNTAX

[490] 0# preceding element, $x ISSN of series (format: nnnn-nnnn)

### EXAMPLE

[490] 0# $a LUMIS-Schriften, $x 0177-1388

### NUMBERING WITHIN SERIES [RDA 2.12.9] [CORE]

For serials and ongoing integrating resources, record numbering within a series only if each issue of the serial carries the exact same number. Otherwise, omit any series numbering carried on individual issues.

#### MARC 21/ISBD RECORD SYNTAX

[490] 0# preceding element ; $v numbering

#### EXAMPLE

[490] 0# $a Department of State publication ; $v 7894
[Every issue of the serial bears the Department of State publication number *7894.*]

### SUBSERIES

#### MARC 21/ISBD RECORD SYNTAX

The MARC 21/ISBD record syntax for subseries is identical to that for series.

### TITLE PROPER OF SUBSERIES [RDA 2.12.10] [CORE]

The title proper of the subseries includes (1) section designations and/or section titles, and (2) dependent titles (such as "Supplement").

### ISSN OF SUBSERIES [RDA 2.12.12]

Record the ISSN of the subseries if present on the serial issue. Occasionally, both the series and subseries will carry their own ISSN.

#### EXAMPLE

[490] 0# $a Lund studies in geography, $x 1400-1144. $a Ser. B, Human geography, $x 0076-1478

### CHANGES IN SERIES
### (SERIAL OR INTEGRATING RESOURCE) [RDA 2.8.1.5.3]

When there are changes in the series to which a serial belongs (including a change in the corporate body identified in the statement of responsibility that would result in a different authoritative access point), record each separately, along with the range of issues associated with the series.

#### MARC 21/ISBD RECORD SYNTAX

[490] 0# $3 materials specified: $a series, $x ISSN

**EXAMPLE**

[490] 0# $3 <1967/68->: $a Elementary and secondary education

[490] 0# $3 <1928->: $a Bulletin / U.S. Department of the Interior, Office of
Education

[490] 0# $3 1917/1918-1925/1926: $a Bulletin / Department of the Interior, Bureau
of Education

## Note Area (ISBD Area 7)

Notes are used to provide information that cannot be conveyed through the formal
structure of the catalog record. In catalog codes prior to RDA, notes tended to be
dealt with as a group, reflecting their placement following the other elements of a
formal bibliographic description. In an element-based code such as RDA, however,
notes are generally dealt with under the element to which they relate, and this practice has been followed in this handbook. For example, notes relating to a body that
would normally be recorded in a statement of responsibility are dealt with under the
Statement of Responsibility element (in ISBD Area 1), while notes dealing with numbering peculiarities are dealt with under the numbering area (ISBD Area 3).

Notes that reference related resources are dealt with separately under "Relationships." Notes dealt with below are those that do not relate to a particular ISBD element.

### A GENERAL NOTE ABOUT THE GENERAL NOTE
### (MARC 21 FIELD 500)

MARC 21, like its antecedents, provides field 500 for "general notes." Use this field
sparingly, since it does not resolve to any particular FRBR Group 1 entity—a given
general note may relate to the work, expression, manifestation, or item—and does
not relate to any particular element. Its job description is the MARC equivalent of
"other duties as assigned."

Elements
- Frequency
- Summarization of content
- Language and script of content

### FREQUENCY [RDA 2.14]

MARC 21 provides a structured means of recording notes relating to frequency (see
example below).

**RECORD SYNTAX**

[310] ## $a current frequency, $b associated dates

[321] ## $a former frequency, $b associated dates

RDA 2.14 provides a list of the most common terms used to indicate the frequency of release of successive issues or parts of a serial or the frequency of updates to an integrating resource. These are given in the table below, along with the corresponding code for the **Freq** (current frequency: MARC 21 008/18) element:

| RDA 2.14 TERM | MARC 21 008/18 VALUE |
| --- | --- |
| Daily | d |
| Three times a week | I |
| Semiweekly | c |
| Weekly | w |
| Three times a month | j |
| Biweekly | e |
| Semimonthly | s |
| Monthly | m |
| Bimonthly | b |
| Quarterly | q |
| Three times a year | t |
| Semiannual | f |
| Annual | a |
| Biennial | g |
| Triennial | h |

When none of the terms above describes the frequency, supply a term of your own and use the closest MARC 21 008/18 value. (See MARC 21 Bibliographic for detailed instructions.)

The **Freq** and **Regl** elements are coded for the current frequency in tandem as follows:

When the current frequency is regular, one of the terms above is used, along with the corresponding **Freq** value and a **Regl** value of [r].

When the current frequency is irregular (for example, Six issues yearly [i.e., six issues published randomly over the course of a year]), use the closest **Freq** value (in this case, [b]) and a **Regl** value of [x]. If the current frequency is completely irregular, then use a **Freq** value of [blank] and a **Regl** value of [x].

When the current frequency is irregular but follows a *predictable* pattern (for example, Monthly (except August)), use the closest **Freq** value (in this case, [m]) and a **Regl** value of [n].

For integrating resources that are continuously updated, use the **Freq** value of [k] and the **Regl** value [r].

Record changes in frequency with the associated dates.

[310] ## $a Monthly, $b May 1992-

[321] ## $a Bimonthly, $b Nov./Dec. 1980-Mar./Apr. 1992

## SUMMARIZATION OF THE CONTENT [RDA 7.10]

Typically, bibliographic records for serials have not included summarizations of the content. However, in an online environment this information is often readily available for commercial publications, and its inclusion in the bibliographic record can serve to enhance its chances of inclusion in a result set when a user searches for relevant publications using a keyword search. Such summarizations can often be cut and pasted from the publication website, abbreviated as necessary to remove purely commercial aspects. In such cases, place the summarization in quotation marks, followed by a dash and the source from which the summarization was taken.

### EXAMPLE

[520] // $a "Launched in 1924, the Journal of Chemical Education is the world's premier chemical education journal. The journal publishes peer-reviewed articles and related information as a resource to those in the field of chemical education and to those institutions that serve them. JCE typically addresses chemical content, activities, laboratory experiments, instructional methods, and pedagogies. The Journal serves as a means of communication among people across the world who are interested in the teaching and learning of chemistry. This includes instructors of chemistry from middle school through graduate school, professional staff that support these teaching activities, as well as some scientists in commerce, industry, and government."—Journal website.

## SPECIAL CASE: TITLES THAT MAY LEAD TO CONFUSION

Whenever the name of a person, body, or corporate body appearing on the chief source of the publication is selected as the title of the resource, provide a summarization of the content to characterize the publication.

### EXAMPLE

[100] 2# $a Very Big Corporation.

[245] 1# $a Very Big Corporation.

[520] ## $a Annual report on the activities of the corporation.

## LANGUAGE AND SCRIPT OF CONTENT [RDA 7.12–7.13]

While most serials are monolingual, many are not. The same serial may include different articles in different languages. Serials may be published simultaneously in two or more languages, either as separate serials or as single serials with parallel text. Examples of these are serials issued by international organizations and serials targeting a readership where two or more languages may be in common use. Likewise, important serials published in less commonly used languages may be translated into a more commonly used language in order to increase their potential readership. Finally, even serials publishing articles in a single language may provide summaries in two or more languages. When these conditions apply to separate serials, the bibliographic records should be linked according to the instructions under "3. Relationships between Resources," below. When these conditions apply solely to the serial being described, they should be recorded in the bibliographic record, both in coded form (to support machine retrieval and manipulation [field 041]) and in textual form (to support user interpretation of the record [field 546]).

### RECORD SYNTAX

[546] ## $a Language note
[546] ## $a Language $b Script

When a resource has text in more than one language, give the names of those languages.

### EXAMPLE

[041] 0# $a dan $a dut $a eng $a fre $a ger $a ita
[245] 00 $a Eisen und Stahl = $b Sidérurgie.
[260] ## $a Luxemburg : $b Statistisches Amt der Europäischen Gemeinschaften, $c 1962-1975.
[546] ## $a Text in Danish, Dutch, English, French, German, and Italian.

In cases where some text is in one language and some in another, give the predominant language first, if known.

### EXAMPLE

[041] 0# $a fre $a eng
[245] 00 $a Revue française d'automatique, informatique, recherche opérationnelle, sommaire. $p Analyse numérique.
[546] ## $a Text in French or English.

When summaries are provided in languages other than the language(s) of the text, give the name(s) of the language(s).

**EXAMPLE**

> [041] 0# $a eng $a fre $b dan $b dut $b ger $b ita.
> [245] 00 $a Iron and Steel = $b Sidérurgie.
> [546] ## $a Text in English and French, with summaries in Danish, Dutch, German, and Italian.

Record the script used to express the language content when that is not predictable. Record the language in [546] $a and its script in $b.

**EXAMPLE**

> [546] ## $a Serbian $b Latin.
> [546] ## $a Serbian $b Cyrillic.

## SPECIAL CASE

When the language of the text is not apparent from the title, give the name of the language.

**EXAMPLE**

> [245] 00 $a Elle.
> [260] ## $a Mumbai : $b Published by Nirja Shah for Ogaan Publications
> [546] ## $a Text in English.

## Resource Identifier and Terms of Availability Area (ISBD Area 8)

### ELEMENTS
- Identifier for the Manifestation [RDA 2.15] [CORE] [MARC 21 022]
- Terms of availability [RDA 4.2]

### CHANGES FROM AACR2
- None

### INDIVIDUAL ELEMENTS

### Identifier for the Manifestation [RDA 2.15]

### ABOUT THE ISSN

ISSNs are eight-digit identifiers assigned to serials and ongoing integrating resources by national ISSN centers or the international center in Paris. The first four digits are separated from the last four by a hyphen. The last digit is a check digit whose value comes from a calculation performed on the preceding seven digits. This calculation uses a modulus 11, which can result in a remainder of 10, represented by the roman numeral X in an ISSN.

ISSNs are usually transcribed from the serial or integrating resource, though they may also be taken from an authoritative source such as the ISSN Register.

In general, the resource identified by the ISSN corresponds to the FRBR manifestation. An ISSN is assigned to a particular serial or ongoing integrating resource in a particular medium (print, CD-ROM, microfiche, etc.). However, reproductions—whether in microform or digital form—are not assigned their own ISSNs. A reproduction uses the ISSN of the original because it consists entirely of images of the pages, etc., of that original.

Like the ISBN, the ISSN has been borrowed from another context to serve as a useful identifier for bibliographic resources in the library context. Whereas the ISBN was borrowed from the publisher community (where it is typically used for inventory control), the ISSN was borrowed from the indexing and abstracting community, where it was originally developed as a standardized way of representing serials in bibliographic citations.

Authoritative ISSN can be found in the ISSN Portal, http://portal.issn.org (subscription required), and often in the online catalog of the national library of the country involved.

An incorrect ISSN ($y) is one that contains an error or has been incorrectly associated with the serial. Subfields $z (canceled ISSN), $1 (linking ISSN), and $m (canceled linking ISSN) are assigned by ISSN centers.

### MARC 21/ISBD RECORD SYNTAX

[022] ## $a International Standard Serial Number (ISSN) $y incorrect ISSN

### EXAMPLE

[022] ## $a 0046-225X $y 0046-2254

## ABOUT THE CODEN

CODEN are six-character codes assigned to serials by the Chemical Abstract Service. All alphabetic characters are uppercase.

CODEN can be found in the CAS Source Index (CASSI) Search Tool, http://cassi.cas.org/search.jsp.

### MARC 21/ISBD RECORD SYNTAX

[030] ## $a CODEN $z incorrect/invalid CODEN

### EXAMPLE

[030] ## $a ASIRAF $y ASTAF

**Terms of Availability [RDA 4.2]**

Terms of availability are seldom supplied for serials because they are subject to change from year to year and the terms on which a serial is made available to an individual institution can vary wildly depending on the circumstances. Once upon a time this element served a useful purpose. No more.

## 3. RELATIONSHIPS BETWEEN RESOURCES

The FRBR conceptual model is an entity-relationship model. In addition to describing entities—works, expressions, persons, corporate bodies, etc.—and the attributes that characterize them, an entity-relationship model defines the relationships between these entities. One of the major differences between RDA and its predecessors is the emphasis placed upon these relationships.

In the AACR2 environment (and all cataloging environments that preceded it) relationships between entities were handled in two ways: via a note displayed as part of the catalog record for the resource and, for the more important relationships, an index entry under the access point for the related entity. The index entry increases the likelihood that a user searching for the related entity will find the catalog record for the resource. This is how the world will continue to operate under RDA scenario 3: separate bibliographic and authority records generating index entries for related entities, but without explicit links between the records.

Under RDA scenario 2, explicit links between related entities will be provided, much as they are provided on the Web, where clicking on a particular hyperlinked term will take you to a new page containing relevant information. In RDA scenario 2, clicking on the term will take the user to the record for the related entity, perhaps offering further linking possibilities on arrival (because that record will likely be linked in turn to other records).

The relationships themselves are set out in four RDA sections:

- Section 5 (the so-called *primary* relationships): Relationships *among* the entities represented in the resource being cataloged: work, expression, manifestation, item. (These relationships are not part of implementation scenario 3.)
- Section 6: Relationships between the resource being cataloged—technically the entities (work, etc.) represented in it—and the persons, families, and corporate bodies involved in its creation, etc.
- Section 7: Relationships between the work contained in the resource being cataloged and subject terms and classifications. (These relationships are not yet part of RDA.)
- Section 8: Relationships between the resource being cataloged and other resources. (Technically, between the entities [work, etc.] represented in these resources.)

In scenario 3, we will be concerned only with the relationships set out in sections 6 and 8.

Relationships are by no means new to serials cataloging—in some ways, they are its very essence—but as noted above, they have customarily been presented to the user in one of two ways: in a note or as an access point. In a card catalog, these were distinct methods of presenting relationships. The former simply informed the user of the existence of the relationship—the related resource might or might not be available—while the latter led those interested in the related resource to the corresponding catalog record, in the belief that it might also be of interest. Since filing cards was a labor-intensive process, the latter method was reserved only for very important relationships.

This got a bit muddied during the 1970s with the creation of the ISDS, ancestor to today's ISSN Network. ISDS required modifications to the US MARC serials format to accommodate what were termed "linking entries" for the key titles and ISSN of related serials. In the US MARC serials format (and in today's successor MARC 21 format), these were recorded in fields 760–787. The linking entry fields could be used both to generate notes and, if desired, to provide access via the related title and/or ISSN, though this latter function was never incorporated in the catalog code. In this ambiguity, the linking entry fields anticipated the more robust functionality characteristic of RDA. An element can be a note or it can provide access, as suits the need of the particular user community.

Relationships in RDA are used to link a resource to related entities, in the form of a representation of the related entity. This link is typically in the form of an authorized access point, but in implementation scenario 2 it will include an identifier such as a uniform resource identifier (URI). In MARC 21, such links are available only in those fields set aside for headings. The relationships recorded in fields 760–787 are manifestation-to-manifestation relationships and are in the form of a formal or informal description.

Relationships between manifestations are described below under "Referencing Related Manifestations." Relationships with other entities are described under "5. Identifying Related Entities."

## Referencing Related Manifestations [RDA 27] [MARC 21 760–787]

Related manifestations are the life-blood of traditional serials cataloging, the basis of those family trees recording those myriad relationships: A begat B, and B begat C and D, and their progeny were plentiful, etc. They are also a nightmare for catalogers because such relationships tend to be *reciprocal,* meaning that if you record a relationship between A and B on the record for A, you must do so on the record for B. On the record for A, you must note that it's continued by B, and on the record for B, you must note that it continues A.

Note that although we catalog manifestations, and although the linking entries we record in our MARC records refer to other manifestations (and their identifiers, known as record control numbers in various databases), in RDA there is no such thing as an authorized access point for a manifestation. Authorized access points apply only to works and expressions.

Having said that, given that we are living in a world of bibliographic records, with each representing simultaneously four FRBR entities, CONSER practice will be to continue referring to related manifestations. This is done by referring to the related manifestation using its catalog entry—essentially, the authorized access point for the work/expression embodied in the related manifestation, coded without its full panoply of content designation. Likewise, CONSER will continue to employ this manifestation-level linking technique even when referring to the works and expressions embodied in these manifestations. (For example, when a major title change occurs or when a serial is related to an integrating resource.) Non-CONSER institutions are free to apply RDA 24.4.1 and 24.4.3, recording the identifier of the related manifestation (which includes both key title and ISSN) or an abbreviated ISBD description of the related serial and referring to related works and expressions as such.

The following guidelines relate to recording manifestation-to-manifestation relationships in MARC 21 fields 760–787.

## Guidelines for Referencing Related Manifestations

RDA section 8 (chapters 24–28) deals with relationships between the resource you are cataloging and related works (chapter 25), expressions (chapter 26), manifestations (chapter 27), and items (chapter 28). Chapter 24 deals with the elements that are routinely recorded in authority records for resources (including some new elements).

The relationship designators to be used when recording these relationships are set out in detail in RDA appendix J. Note that use of these designators is optional. The coding in MARC linking entry fields can be used to generate their own relationship designators in most cases.

Relationships between resources are not CORE elements in RDA. However, for CONSER standard records all except [773]/[774] (used for the relationship between a component part and the resource that contains it) are mandatory when applicable.

References to related manifestations consist of:

1. The authorized access point for the work/expression

    a. The authorized access point for the creator, if any
    b. The preferred title of the work/expression

2. The title proper of the manifestation (if different from the preferred title of the work/expression)
3. The designation of edition, if any (unless already present in the preferred title of the work/expression)

## MARC 21 RECORD SYNTAX (CODING OF REFERENCES TO RELATED MANIFESTATIONS)

References to related manifestations are coded in fields 760–787 as follows:

$a [authorized access point for creator]
$s [preferred title of work/expression (when subfield $a is present)]
$t [title proper of manifestation] or [preferred title of work/expression (when subfield $a is not present), followed by title proper of manifestation]
$b [designation of edition (if not part of preferred title of work/expression)]

This structure, rather chaotic in terms of linking data, exists to support text formatting. Recording data in subfield $s allows this data to be displayed in square brackets if so desired, as under AACR2. For title indexing purposes, a receiving system can combine the contents of subfields $s and $t into a single title index string, if desired.

While RDA defines these relationships within the context of the FRBR model, with a particular relationship belonging to a particular FRBR Group 1 entity (work, expression, manifestation, or item), CONSER records are linked by identifiers (LC and/or OCLC control numbers) to bibliographic records for manifestations, with the associated ISSN when available. (It should be noted that the resource identified by an ISSN does not correspond exactly to any FRBR entity, potentially encompassing some, but not all, manifestations belonging to a given expression.)

RDA provides four methods for relating resources (works, expressions, manifestations, items):

1. Identifier
2. Authorized access point
3. Formal description
4. Informal description

In RDA implementation scenario 3, related works and expressions are identified by their authorized access points. Related manifestations are identified by formal descriptions. This has the additional advantage of being consistent with former (AACR2) practice. When the authorized access point for a related resource is not known, an informal description may be used.

The MARC 21 linking entry fields, being designed within the context of the ISSN system, are language-independent. Consequently, there is typically a one-to-one correspondence between a given relationship designator in RDA appendix J and a given linking entry field in MARC 21, or a given second indicator value in the case of sequential relationships (preceding and succeeding entries). The following table sets out the correspondences:

| RDA RELATIONSHIP DESIGNATOR | MARC 21 FIELD |
|---|---|
| *Sequential work relationships (see below)* | |
| Preceded by (work) | 780 |
| Succeeded by (work) | 785 |
| *Whole-part work relationships* | |
| In series (work) | 760 |
| Series contains (work) | 762 |
| *Accompanying work relationships* | |
| Supplement (work) | 770 |
| Supplement to (work) | 772 |
| *Derivative expression relationships* | |
| Translation of (expression) | 765 |
| Translated as (expression) | 767 |
| *Equivalent manifestation relationships* | |
| Reproduction (same carrier type)* | 775 |
| Reproduction (different carrier type)* | 776 |
| *Accompanying manifestation relationships* | |
| Issued with | 777 |

| RDA RELATIONSHIP DESIGNATOR | 780/785 2ND INDICATOR |
|---|---|
| Preceded by (work) | |
| Absorbed (work) | 780: 5 |
| Absorbed in part (work) | 780: 6 |
| Continues (work) | 780: 0 |
| Continues in part (work) | 780: 1 |
| Merger of (work) | 780: 4 |
| Separated from (work) | 780: 7 |

| Succeeded by (work) | |
|---|---|
| Absorbed by (work) | 785: 4 |
| Absorbed in part by (work) | 785: 5 |
| Continued by (work) | 785: 0 |
| Continued in part by (work) | 785: 1 |
| Merged with . . . to form (work) | 785: 7 |
| Split into (work) | 785: 6 |

* See "Special Instructions for Reproductions" below.

Note: Relationship designators qualified by "(work)" may also be used with expressions when appropriate.

In each of the examples below, MARC 21 coded data is followed by a note that might be generated from that data for catalog displays.

In the examples, record control numbers (e.g., Library of Congress control numbers, OCLC control numbers) are not included. These are recorded in subfield $w with the control number preceded by the MARC Organization Code of the agency responsible for the control number scheme in parentheses. See *MARC 21 Bibliographic* for detailed instructions.[15]

### EXAMPLES

[780] 00 $t Jane's intelligence review pointer $x 1352-8491
*Continues:* Jane's intelligence review pointer, ISSN 1352-8491.
[780] 01 $t Journal of youth services in libraries $x 0894-2498

*Continues in part:* Journal of youth services in libraries, ISSN 0894-2498.

[780] 00 $t Top of the news $x 0040-9286
[785] 06 $t Children & libraries $x 1542-9806
[785] 06 $t Young adult library services $x 1541-4302
*Continues:* Top of the news, ISSN 0040-9286.
*Split into:* Children & libraries, ISSN 1542-9806.
*Split into:* Young adult library services, ISSN 1541-4302.

This is an RDA example. There is nothing to prevent systems combining repeated iterations of a single linking field into one note (see alternative example below).

[780] 07 $t International authors' and writers' who's who $x 0143-8263
*Separated from:* International authors' and writers' who's who, ISSN 0143-8263.

Note that when a note is complex, or when more than one related serial is involved in a relationship, the note is recorded explicitly in field 580 and the data in the related linking entry field(s) (760–787) is suppressed from display by setting the value of the first indicator(s) to "1." Otherwise, the coding of the linking entry fields can be used to generate an appropriate note.

**[RESOURCE DESCRIBED: PHYSICIANS' DESK REFERENCE FOR OPHTHALMIC MEDICINES]**

*Volumes for 2001-2005 complemented by:* Physicians' desk reference companion guide; *2006-by:* PDR guide to drug interactions, side effects, and indications.

[580] ## $a Volumes for 2001-2005 complemented by: Physicians' desk reference companion guide; 2006-by: PDR guide to drug interactions, side effects, and indications

[787] 1# $t Physicians' desk reference companion guide $x 1099-5285

[787] 1# $t PDR guide to drug interactions, side effects, and indications $x 1933-706X

**[RESOURCE DESCRIBED: JOURNAL OF APPLIED CHEMISTRY]**

*Merger of:* British abstracts. B I, Chemical engineering, fuels, metallurgy, applied electrochemistry, and industrial inorganic chemistry; *and:* British abstracts. B II, Industrial organic chemistry

[580] ## $a Merger of: British abstracts. B I, Chemical engineering, fuels, metallurgy, applied electrochemistry, and industrial inorganic chemistry; and: British abstracts. B II, Industrial organic chemistry.

[780] 15 $t British abstracts. B I, Chemical engineering, fuels, metallurgy, applied electrochemistry, and industrial inorganic chemistry $x 0365-8740

[780] 15 $t British abstracts. B II, Industrial organic chemistry $x 0365-8929

**[RESOURCE DESCRIBED: JOURNAL OF SMALL AND EMERGING BUSINESS LAW]**

*Merged with:* International legal perspectives, *to form:* Lewis & Clark law review

[580] ## $a Merged with: International legal perspectives, *to form*: Lewis & Clark law review.

[785] 17 $t International legal perspectives $x 1520-4618

[785] 17 $t Lewis & Clark law review $x1557-6582

**[RESOURCE DESCRIBED: JOURNAL OF YOUTH SERVICES IN LIBRARIES]**

*Split into:* Children & libraries; *and:* Young adult library services.

[580] ## $a Split into: Children & libraries; and: Young adult library services.

[780] 00 $t Top of the news $x 0040-9286

[785] 16 $t Children & libraries $x 1542-9806

[785] 16 $t Young adult library services $x 1541-4302

[RESOURCE DESCRIBED: RUSA UPDATE / REFERENCE AND USER SERVICES
ASSOCIATION, A DIVISION OF THE AMERICAN LIBRARY ASSOCIATION. A
QUARTERLY PERIODICAL ABSORBED BY REFERENCE & USER SERVICES
QUARTERLY IN 2002]

> *Absorbed in 2002 by*: Reference & user services quarterly.
> [580] ## $a Absorbed in 2002 by: Reference & user services quarterly.
> [785] 14 $t Reference & user services quarterly $x 1094-9054
> [Resource described: Journal of medical ethics]
>
> *Continued in part by*: Medical humanities, which split off in June 2000 and assumed
> volume numbering beginning with volume 26
> [580] ## $a Continued in part by: Medical humanities, which split off in June 2000
> and assumed volume numbering beginning with volume 26.
> [785] 11 $a Medical humanities $x 1468-215X

In a few cases RDA appendix J lists relationship designators that have no coded
equivalents in MARC 21. These should be explicitly recorded in subfield $i of the
appropriate linking entry field. If no linking entry field is appropriate, use field 787
(other relationship entry).

**EXAMPLE**

> [787] 08 $i Index (work): $t Palmer's index to the Times newspaper

If none of the terms listed in appendix J is appropriate or sufficiently specific, use a
term designating the nature of the relationship as concisely as possible [RDA 24.5.1.3].
In MARC 21, explicitly record such a designation in subfield $i of the appropriate
linking entry field.

**EXAMPLE**

> [776] 1\ $i Issued online as: $t Science (New York, N.Y.) $x 1095-9203

## PROBLEM: TITLE CHANGES OUT OF SYNC (TRANSLATIONS AND ORIGINALS)

Since the authorized access point of an expression is based on the authorized access
point of the work, it follows that when the authorized access point for the work
changes, so does the authorized access point for any expression, even when the title
proper of a manifestation embodying that expression has not changed. While not
required by RDA, LC practice in such situations is to include the title proper of the
manifestation when referencing the related manifestation, LC-PCC PS 6.1.3.2).

**EXAMPLE (TITLE OF ORIGINAL CHANGES; TITLE OF TRANSLATION STAYS THE SAME)**

[130] 0# $a Inzhenernyĭ zhurnal. Mekhanika tverdogo tela. $1 English.

[245] 10 $a Mechanics of solids.

[785] 00 $t Izvestia͡. Mekhanika tverdogo tela. English. Mechanics of solids

[130] 0# $a Izvestia͡. Mekhanika tverdogo tela. $1 English.

[245] 10 $a Mechanics of solids.

[780] 00 $t Inzhenernyĭ zhurnal. Mekhanika tverdogo tela. English. Mechanics of solids

## SPECIAL INSTRUCTIONS FOR REPRODUCTIONS

If you are cataloging a reproduction (microfilm, etc.), LC-PCC PS 27.1.1.3 requires using a structured description to record the details of the original publication.

For serials, this practice is reversed when cataloging the original.

In terms of MARC 21 fields, [775] is used when both original and reproduction use the same carrier type, and [776] is used when the carrier types differ.

## RECORD FOR REPRODUCTION (DIFFERENT CARRIER TYPE)

[245] 00 $a UU world.

[260] ## $a Ann Arbor, Michigan : $b University Microfilms International, $c 2001-

[776] 08 $i Reproduction of (manifestation): $t UU world. $d Boston : Unitarian Universalist Association, 2000- $w (DLC) 00213104 $w (OCoLC)45123880

## RECORD FOR ORIGINAL

[245] 00 $a UU world.

[260] ## $a Boston : $b Unitarian Universalist Association, $c 2000-

[776] 08 $i Reproduced as: $t UU world. $d Ann Arbor, Michigan : University Microfilms International, 2001- $w (DLC) 2003206250 $w (OCoLC)48539513

## FYI

While this manual follows the CONSER practice of identifying related resources by the catalog entry for the manifestation, RDA also supports the ISSN Network practice of recording just the key title and ISSN. (Both are considered acceptable identifiers for manifestations.)

**CONSER PRACTICE**

[776] 08 $i Issued also online: $t Euscorpius $x 1536-9307

[Catalog entry for online version]

[780] 00 $a Freedonia. Ministry of War. $t Annual report

[785] 00 $a Freedonia. Ministry of Defence. $t Annual report

[Catalog entries for earlier/later titles]

[776] 0# $t Euscorpius $c (Online) $x 1536-9307

[Key title of online version]


[780] 00 $t Annual report—Freedonia Ministry of War $x 5678-431X

[785] 00 $t Annual report—Freedonia Ministry of Defence $x 5678-4925

[Catalog entries for earlier/later titles]


# 4. IDENTIFYING WORKS AND EXPRESSIONS [RDA 6]

This section focuses on identifying the work and expression embodied in the resource being cataloged. The same principles apply to identifying related works and expressions. Since this manual is devoted to serials cataloging, it deals with these matters only to the extent that they affect authorized access points on bibliographic records. Readers interested in the construction of authority records for the entities represented by these access points should consult the appropriate chapters of Robert Maxwell's *Handbook for RDA*.

## Outline

- About identifying works and expressions
- Form of the authorized access point in *MARC 21 Bibliographic*
- Creators: Whose work is it, anyway?
- Preferred titles
- Constructing the authorized access point:
    - Works
    - Expressions

## About Identifying Works and Expressions

Under RDA implementation scenario 3—the initial implementation scenario for RDA—works and expressions are *identified* by authorized access points; that is, the authorized access point for the work or expression must be unique within the catalog in order to present the various expressions, manifestations, etc., in a reasonable order (for example, in a "browse" display).

The authorized access point for a work consists of a *preferred title,* possibly augmented and possibly preceded by the authorized access point for a creator.

The preferred title is the title by which a work has come to be known through its use in resources embodying the work or in reference sources [RDA 6.2.2.4]. For serials, it is rare that this needs to be determined. Serials generally appear once (aside from reproductions) and are known by the title under which they appear.

To render the authorized access point for a work unique in the catalog, it may be necessary to augment the preferred title with other elements [RDA 6.3–6.6].

The authorized access point for an expression consists of the authorized access point for a work augmented to identify the expression. For serials, translation into one or more languages is the most common cause for different expressions of a work, in which case the language of the translation is usually sufficient to distinguish expressions.

Under RDA scenarios 2 and 3—linked bibliographic/authority records and entity-relationship or object-oriented databases, respectively—authorized access points will not necessarily need to be unique, so long as the identifier for the work [RDA 6.8] or expression [RDA 6.13] is itself unique. This identifier may or may not be displayed to the user, but it will ensure that apparently identical authorized access points will in practice be able to distinguish among different entities (different John Smiths or different *Sun-Heralds,* for example).

Identifying a work requires answering three questions:

1. Does the work have a creator?
2. Do different manifestations of the work carry different titles proper?
3. Is the title proper or preferred title, in combination with the authorized access point for the creator (if any), unique within the catalog?

These questions are dealt with below after a brief overview of how works and expressions are represented using the *MARC 21 Bibliographic* format.

In reviewing the following cases, bear in mind that when a work has a creator, the authorized access point for the work consists of the authorized access point for the creator followed by the preferred title of the work [RDA 6.27.1.2]. In the *MARC 21 Bibliographic* format, this translates into a [1XX] field for the creator followed by a [240] or [245] field for the preferred title. (When a *MARC 21 Authorities* record exists for the work, the preferred title of the work will be found along with the creator in the [1XX] field or the authority record.)

Note also that the title proper or preferred title of a serial may include designations ($n) and titles ($p) of parts or sections (including supplements), if the serial was cataloged as a part or section. Depending on the complexity of the serial, there may be several levels of parts. (This is especially common with statistical series published as serials.)

## Form of the Authorized Access Point in *MARC 21 Bibliographic*

### CASE 1: WORK WITH A CREATOR

[1XX] Authorized access point for creator.
[245] Title proper (if [1XX] + [245] are unique in the catalog) [default preferred title]

[1XX] Authorized access point for creator.
[240] Preferred title (if [1XX] + [245] are not unique in the catalog)

To identify a related work:
[7XX] Authorized access point for creator. $t Preferred title.

## CASE 2: WORK WITHOUT A CREATOR

[245] Title proper (if unique in the catalog) [default preferred title]
[130] Preferred title (if [245] is not unique in the catalog)

To identify a related work:
[730] Preferred title.

## CASE 3: EXPRESSION OF A WORK WITH A CREATOR (TRANSLATION)

[1XX] Authorized access point for creator.
[240] Preferred title of work. $1 Language of expression

To identify a related work:
[7XX] Authorized access point for creator. $t Preferred title of work. $1 Language of expression.

## CASE 4: EXPRESSION OF A WORK WITHOUT A CREATOR (TRANSLATION)

[130] Preferred title of work. $1 Language of expression

To identify a related expression:
[730] Preferred title of work. $1 Language of expression.

## CASE 5: EXPRESSION OF A WORK WITHOUT A CREATOR (REGIONAL EDITION)

(Note that in this case, our current practice does not enable the MARC record syntax to identify this as an expression of a work. The edition statement from the expression is recorded in parentheses in the same subfield as the last element of the preferred title of the work.)

[130] Preferred title of work (Edition statement)

To identify a related expression:
[730] Preferred title of work (Edition statement)

## Whose Work Is It, Anyway?

A serial work, like any work, may have what RDA calls a creator. However, whereas creators are fairly common in monograph cataloging they are much less common in serials cataloging. This is because responsibility for serials tends to be diffuse. An individual can write a book. It is much harder to write a serial. In 2010, roughly 20 percent of the serials recorded in the CONSER database had what RDA would call a creator. Persons were creators only 0.2 percent of the time, and corporate bodies roughly 20 percent of the time. The remaining 80 percent of serials were entered under title. Since the CONSER database includes pre-AACR2 records—roughly 1/8 of the 1.2 million serial records present in 2010—and given that entry under corporate names was more common prior to AACR 2 (see the history of serials cataloging in chapter 2), these numbers probably underestimate the percentage of serials entered under title following AACR2 (and prospectively RDA).[16]

### PERSONS OR FAMILIES AS CREATORS

Persons, like serials, do not typically have predetermined conclusions. On the other hand, they don't live forever, so it is rare to regard a person as the creator of a serial in the same way that a person can be the creator of a book. It does happen, but it's rare. Families, on the other hand, seldom agree on anything, so it is hard to see them carrying on a joint enterprise such as a serial over any length of time.

RDA 19.2.1.1.3 governs the conditions under which a person or family can be considered to be the creator of a serial, and offers "indications" that can help make a determination:

- The name or part of the name of the person is in the title proper
- The person or family is publisher of the serial
- Content consists of personal opinions, etc.
- Lack of another person, another family, or a corporate body involved with the serial

For a person to be considered the creator of a serial, we set a rather high bar, at least in practice. It's a no-brainer only when:

- The person is unequivocally responsible for the content of the serial as a whole
- Different issues are unlikely to be created by different persons or families
- The serial is unlikely to continue without that person's or family's responsibility

Examples of serials that fail this test are the many travel guides written by individuals but known by their title and/or sponsor/franchise rather than by the author's name. In these cases, the author's name does not typically appear on the cover and may not even appear on the title page. The author is contracted to produce a product conforming to a given style and format, and when that author leaves, then another will be found to take their place and produce a similar product. The reader will usually be oblivious.

**EXAMPLE**
[130] 0# $a San Diego (DK eyewitness top 10 travel guides)

In this case, DK Publishing issues a variety of travel guide series, each conforming to a style and format aimed at satisfying the needs of a particular class of consumer. Guides in the Top 10 series are aimed at the traveler with little time but a strong desire to see the "top" attractions of a specific place. So the guide to San Diego conforms to the format prescribed by DK for its Top 10 guides, with a focus on San Diego attractions. While the acknowledgments section in the 2011 guide identifies Pamela Barrus as its author, her name does not appear on the cover or in the book's publicity material. The structure of the guide is imposed by the publisher, and the copyright is held by the publisher. By this evidence, Ms. Barrus is deemed to have failed the test for "creatorship" of this serial. The user is much more likely to seek this resource by the title, publisher, or series than by the name of the person who put together the 2011 edition of the guide.

Having said that, there are serials that are unequivocally works of personal authorship, even invoking the strict interpretation given above, and in such cases the authorized access point for the work duly includes the authorized access point for the author. (In general, blogs fall into this category.)

**EXAMPLES**
[100] 1# $a Ebert, Roger
[245] 10 $a Roger Ebert's movie yearbook.
[Note: An annual compilation of Roger Ebert's film reviews and interviews.]

[100] 1# $a Stone, I. F. $q (Isidor Feinstein), $d 1907-1989
[245] 10 $a I.F. Stone's weekly.
[Note: Stone was also the publisher.]

[100] 1# $a Bolles, Richard Nelson
[245] 10 $a What color is your parachute?
[Note: An annual publication of Bolles's career advice.]

[100] 1# $a Lehrer, Jonah
[245] 10 $a Frontal cortex.
[Note: A blog.]

The key here is to take the perspective of the user. If you believe the user is likely to approach the serial using the name of the person involved, there is an argument for treating that person as the creator, but not otherwise. If you think you have a serial that is a work of personal authorship, regard it with skepticism, but if it passes muster, by all means go ahead and treat it as such.

Users of this manual are presumed to be fluent in the cataloging of works of personal authorship, so detailed instructions on selecting a particular name or form of name to serve as the basis for an authorized access point are not provided here. Users are referred to RDA chapter 9 and related policy statements for further guidance.

In the extremely rare case that more than one person is considered the creator, treat the person with principal responsibility for the content as the creator or, if this is not indicated, the person named first [RDA 6.27.1.3].

## FAMILIES AS CREATORS

There is an example under RDA 9.2.1.3 of a family as creator: Barner (Family) as the creators of *The Barner Family Newsletter,* and this typifies the sort of publication that may have a family as its creator. Family blogs and websites are other examples.

## CORPORATE BODIES AS CREATORS [RDA 19.1.1.1]

Corporate bodies have a greater chance of being considered the creators of serial works than do individuals or families, but the criteria for making this determination are rather complex.

Note that if these criteria are satisfied, the corporate body is considered to be the creator even in cases of collaboration between one or more corporate bodies and one or more persons [RDA 6.27.1.3 exception].

First, the corporate body must originate the work, issue it, or cause it to be issued. What does this mean? Fortunately, there's an LC-PCC PS for that. The LC-PCC PS clarifies that when RDA (and AACR2 before it) says "issues" it really means what the rest of us mean by "publishes." It also usefully provides examples of each combination of originating and issuing:

- *Originating and issuing:* Body A originates the content and publishes it.
- *Originating and causing to be issued:* Body A originates the content and contracts with Body B (who couldn't care less about the content) to publish it. Sometimes this is indicated explicitly, e.g., "Published for the Historical Association by Routledge & Paul." Sometimes it is inferred: "The Historical Association" appears on the item above the title, while "Routledge & Paul" appears in the customary "publisher" position at the bottom.
- *Originating but not issuing:* Body A is a consultant to Body B, which actually publishes the work. Body A is the originator of the work, i.e., the content originates with Body A. This is unusual with serials.

Once we have established that a corporate body has originated the work, issued it, or caused it to be issued, we must determine whether it falls into one of six categories (actually many more than six, but they're consolidated into six so as not to frighten off the faint of heart). Here they are, with examples:

- Works of an administrative nature dealing with any of the following aspects of the body itself:
    - Its internal policies, procedures, finances, and/or operations
    - Its officers, staff, and/or membership (e.g., directories)
    - Its resources (e.g., catalogues, inventories)

**EXAMPLES**

[110] 2# $a Klowa Indian Tribe of Oklahoma
[245] 10 $a Annual report / $c Klowa Tribe of Oklahoma.

[110] 1# $a Maine
[245] 10 $a Maine.gov : $b official Web site of the state of Maine.

[110] 2# $a American Bar Association. $b Section of Intellectual Property Law
[245] 10 $a Membership directory / $c American Bar Association, Section of Intellectual Property Law.

[110] 1# $a California. $a Legislature. $b Senate. $b Committee on Transportation and Housing
[245] 10 $a Legislative bill summary / $c California Legislature, Senate Transportation and Housing Committee.

- Works that record the collective thought of the body (e.g., reports of commissions, committees; official statements of position on external policies, standards)

**EXAMPLE**

[110] 1# $a United States. $b Congress. $b House. $b Committee on Un-American Activities.
[245] 10 $a Annual report for the year . . . / $c Committee on Un-American Activities.

- Works that report the collective activity of
    - A conference (e.g., proceedings, collected papers)
    - An expedition (e.g., results of exploration, investigation)
    - An event (e.g., an exhibition, fair, festival) falling within the definition of a corporate body [RDA 18.1.2]

provided that the conference, expedition, or event is named in the resource being described. (Note: RDA, like AACR2, includes as a second definition of conference: "A meeting of representatives of a corporate body that constitutes its legislative or governing body." Hence, this category applies to national parliaments, state and provincial assemblies, etc., and, by extension, to their committees, etc.)

**EXAMPLES**

[111] 2# $a Annual Workshop on Sea Turtle Biology and Conservation

[245] 10 $a Proceedings of the . . . Annual Workshop on Sea Turtle Biology and Conservation.

[110] 1# $a Swaziland. $b Parliament. $b Senate

[245] 10 $a Official verbatim report (Hansard) of the . . . session of the . . . Parliament / $c Swaziland Senate.

[110] 1# $a Canada. $b Parliament. $b Senate. $b Special Committee on Aging

[245] 10 $a Proceedings of the Special Senate Committee on Aging = $b Délibérations du Comité sénatorial spécial sur le vieillissement.

- Works that result from the collective activity of a performing group as a whole where the responsibility of the group goes beyond that of mere performance, execution, etc.

**EXAMPLE (BELIEVE IT OR NOT)**

[110] 2# $a Barnhouse Jazz Ensemble

[245] 10 $a Barnhouse Jazz Ensemble.

[annual recordings of performances on audiocassettes]

- Cartographic works originating with a corporate body other than a body that is merely responsible for their publication or distribution.

**EXAMPLES**

[110] 2# $a Rand McNally and Company

[245] 10 $a Rand McNally commercial atlas.

- Legal works of the following types:
    - Laws of a political jurisdiction
    - Decrees of a head of state, chief executive, or ruling executive body
    - Bills and drafts of legislation
    - Administrative regulations, etc.
    - Constitutions, charters, etc.
    - Court rules
    - Treaties, international agreements, etc.
    - Charges to juries, indictments, court proceedings, and court decisions

**EXAMPLES**

[110] 1# $a Canada. $b Federal Court

[245] 10 $a Canada Federal Court reports = $b Recueil des arrêts de la Cour fédérale du Canada.

Beyond this, there are government and religious officials considered to be creators [RDA 19.2.1.1.2]. They are considered to be creators of the following types of official communications:

- Official communications by heads of state, heads of government, heads of dependent or occupied territories, or heads of international bodies (e.g., messages to legislatures, proclamations, executive orders).
- Official communications from popes, patriarchs, bishops, etc. (e.g., orders, decrees, pastoral letters, bulls, encyclicals; official messages to councils, synods).

**EXAMPLES**

[110] 1# $a United States. $b President.
[245] 10 $a Economic report of the President transmitted to the Congress.

[110] 1# $a United States. $b President.
[245] 10 $a Public papers of the Presidents of the United States.

If more than one corporate body is considered the creator, use the authorized access point for the corporate body with principal responsibility or, if principal responsibility is not indicated, the corporate body named first [RDA 6.27.1.3]. To expedite conversion to an FRBR-based bibliographic framework, it is helpful in such instances to add to each authorized access point an appropriate relationship designator from RDA Appendix I.

## Preferred Title for Work [RDA 6.2.2] [CORE]

**EXAMPLES**

[110] 2# $a Canadian Botanical Association
[245] 10 $a Directory of the Canadian Botanical Association & Canadian Society of Plant Physiologists.
[710] 2# $a Canadian Society of Plant Physiologists

RDA 6.0 gives five purposes for identifying works and expressions:

a. To bring together descriptions when works or expressions have appeared under different titles
b. To identify a work when the title proper differs from the title by which it is known
c. To differentiate works that have the same title
d. To support hierarchical displays of the expressions of a work
e. To refer from one work or expression to another

Purposes (a) and (b) seldom apply to modern serials, since serials are seldom re-issued under different titles or published with one title in one country and a different title in another. (There is no known serial equivalent to *Harry Potter and the [Philosopher's/Sorcerer's] Stone*.) However, the remaining purposes are equally valid for serials and monographs.

These purposes are achieved by first constructing an authorized access point for the work, based on a preferred title.

(More specific uses of preferred titles for legal works are discussed below, but those remote regions are best explored only by the most agile law catalogers.)

## ADDITIONS TO PREFERRED TITLES

The basis for the preferred title is the title proper (see instructions for selecting the title proper under "Title and Statement of Responsibility," above). Note that although RDA 6.2.1.7 instructs to retain any initial article, CONSER practice is to apply the alternative instruction and omit an initial article unless the title is to be accessed under that article (e.g., *Los Angeles Times*).

If the title proper—either by itself or in combination with the authorized access point for the creator—uniquely identifies the work, then it can be used as the preferred title for the work alone, without any additions.

### EXAMPLES

[245] 00 $a Journal of research in superfluidity.
[Title proper is unique.]

[110] 2# $a International Society for Research in Superfluidity.
[245] 10 $a Annual report / $c International Society for Research in Superfluidity.
[Title proper is unique in combination with the authorized access point for the society.]

If the title proper—either by itself or in combination with the authorized access point for the creator—does not uniquely identify the work, then it will need to be augmented by adding in parentheses one or more of the elements specified in RDA chapter 6. When more than one addition is made, separate them from one another by a space-colon-space.

Choice of appropriate elements is left to the discretion of the cataloger, though preference should be given to elements that will be meaningful to the user. LC-PCC PS 6.27.1.9 provides some more detailed guidance, stating that when the preferred title is not unique and is generic in nature, that is, it consists simply of a term indicating a type of publication—Bulletin, Journal, Newsletter, Monograph, etc.—and/or a term indicating frequency, then the issuing body should be added in preference to other additions. LC-PCC PS 6.27.1.9 further states that such an addition should be in the form of the authorized access point for the issuing body.

In these cases, when the name of the issuing body changes (or a different issuing body becomes responsible), a new description must be created under a preferred title qualified by the authorized access point representing the new name or body.

RDA is silent regarding the form of geographic name to use in those cases where the place of publication is an appropriate qualifying term, but the place has changed its name. However, LC-PCC PS 6.27.1.9 stipulates "the name the place had at the time the first/earliest issue was published" in the form it would have as an authorized access point.

**EXAMPLE**

> [130] 0# $a Nieuw Amsterdamer (New Amsterdam, N.Y.)
> *not*
> [130] 0# $a Nieuw Amsterdamer (New York, N.Y.)

In other cases, when the term serving as the basis for the addition to a preferred title changes, do not change the preferred title.

## FORM OF WORK
## [RDA 6.3] [CORE IF NEEDED TO DIFFERENTIATE]

**EXAMPLES**

> [130] 0# $a Scottish History Society (Series)
> [Title is the name of the society.]

> [130] 0# $a McCall's (Pattern book)
> [A journal of the same title is issued by the same publisher.]

## DATE OF WORK
## [RDA 6.4] [CORE IF NEEDED TO DIFFERENTIATE]

**EXAMPLES**

> [130] 0# $a Dublin magazine (1762)
> [A journal of the same title was published beginning in 1965.]

## PLACE OF ORIGIN OF WORK
## (RDA 6.5) [CORE IF NEEDED TO DIFFERENTIATE]

The place of origin should be recorded in the form prescribed in RDA chapter 16. The instructions are basically unchanged from AACR2.

**EXAMPLES**

> [130] 0# $a Advocate (Boise, Idaho)
> [A journal of the same title is published in Nairobi.]

> [130] 0# $a Libération (Paris, France : 1944)
> [A newspaper of the same title was published in Paris beginning in 1973.]

## OTHER DISTINGUISHING CHARACTERISTICS OF WORK [RDA 6.6] [CORE IF NEEDED TO DIFFERENTIATE]

RDA 6.6.1.3 leaves the choice of distinguishing characteristic up to the cataloger, but ideally it will be an element that will be meaningful to the user and enable them to recognize the work. Finding such a meaningful characteristic may not always be possible, but it should be a goal even if we fall short.

**EXAMPLES**

Distinguishing characteristic: Authorized access point for the issuing body

> [130] 0# $a Bulletin (Geological Survey (South Africa))
> [130] 0# $a Bulletin (New York State Museum)

## EXCEPTIONAL PRACTICES FOR SOME LEGAL WORKS [RDA 6.19.2] [CORE]

RDA 6.19.2 contains special instructions for legal works that need to be borne in mind when cataloging such materials. These are summarized below insofar as they apply to serial publications. (RDA 6.29 provides instructions for constructing the access points.) Recall that legal works of the types listed under RDA 19.2.1.1.1 are considered to have corporate bodies as creators.

### SPECIFIC TYPES OF LEGAL WORKS

#### COMPILATIONS OF LAWS, ETC.

RDA 6.19.2.5.1 directs that compilations of laws are entered under the conventional collective title "Laws, etc." unless a compilation on a particular subject has a citation title (an official short title, e.g., "§1. Title and divisions of act. This Act shall be known as THE PENAL CODE OF CALIFORNIA, and is divided into four parts . . ."). (Note: These are *documents* in the sense used in RDA A.18 and so the title should be capitalized as per that instruction rather than following the normal instructions for capitalization.)

**EXAMPLE**

> [110] 1# $a California.
> [240] 1# $a Penal Code of California
> [245] 10 $a Penal Code : $b including penal provisions of other codes : including

enactments through the end of the . . . regular session of the legislature.
[citation title: Penal Code of California]

## ET IN ARCANIA EGO . . .

The LC-PCC PS for RDA 6.29.1.32 calls for applying this instruction to compilations of laws of the US states, session laws of the US states, and codes of the US states. For compilations of laws from jurisdictions other than the US states, the LC-PCC PS calls for using the conventional collective title "Laws, etc." followed in parentheses by an appropriate designation—usually the title proper—to identify the compilation. For guidance on the handling of state compilations—be warned that in some cases California, Louisiana, and Texas receive different treatment than the other states—readers are referred to the LC-PCC PS. Good luck.

### EXAMPLES

[110] 1# $a United States.
[240] 1# $a Laws, etc. (U.S. code annotated)
[245] 10 $a United States code annotated.

[110] 1# $a Ohio.
[240] 10 $a Laws, etc. (Session laws: 1803- )
[245] 10 $a Acts of the state of Ohio.
[246] 3# $a Acts of a general nature passed by the General Assembly of the State of Ohio
[246] 3# $a Acts passed at the session of the General Assembly of the State of Ohio
[246] 3# $a General and local acts passed and joint resolutions adopted by the General Assembly
[etc.]
*[See LC-PCC PS 6.29.1.32 for further guidance.]*

## COMPILATIONS OF TREATIES, ETC. [RDA 6.19.2.8]

RDA 6.1.9.2.8 calls for use of the conventional collective title "Treaties, etc."

### EXAMPLES

[110] 1# $a United States.
[240] 1# $a Treaties, etc. (United States treaties and other international agreements)
[245] 10 $a United States treaties and other international agreements.

## Constructing Authorized Access Points for Works

The authorized access point for a work consists of the authorized access point for the person or corporate body selected as the creator or preferred creator (if applicable) followed by the preferred title for the work [RDA 6.27.1.2].

## Constructing Authorized Access Points for Expressions

For serials, expressions other than translations, while somewhat rare, are not unknown. Typically, these are editions aimed at a particular audience or geographic area.

The authorized access point for a translation consists of the authorized access point for the work, augmented by a term indicating the language of a translation [RDA 6.27.3]. Take the term from the current edition of the *MARC Code List for Languages.*[17]

**EXAMPLES**

[130] 0# $a Kolloidnyĭ zhurnal. $1 English
[245] 10 $a Colloid journal of the Russian Academy of Sciences = $b Kolloidnyĭ zhurnal.

[110] 2# $a Fellowship of the Ring.
[240] 1# $a Hîr nín ú dollen i Rîw Anírach. $p Gwaith. $1 English
[245] 10 $a Official journal of the Fellowship of the Ring. $p Debates.

### CASE 1: PERSON AS CREATOR OR PREFERRED CREATOR

Authorized access point for the work of a personal author:

[100]  Authorized access point for the author
[245]  Title proper.

or (if title proper is not unique in combination with the author):

[100]  Authorized access point for the author
[240]  Title proper (Distinguishing characteristics)

or (if a translation):

Authorized access point for an expression of such a work (translation):

[100]  Authorized access point for the author
[240]  Authorized access point for the title of the work. $l Language of the expression.

[Note: The title in fields [245] and [240] may include designations ($n) and titles ($p) of parts or sections if these parts or sections are cataloged as individual serials.]

## CASE 2: CORPORATE BODY AS CREATOR OR PREFERRED CREATOR

Authorized access point for the work of a corporate body:

[110] Authorized access point for the corporate body
[245] Title proper.

or (if title proper is not unique in combination with the corporate body):

[110] Authorized access point for the corporate body
[240] Title proper (Distinguishing characteristics)

or (if a translation):

Authorized access point for an expression of such a work (translation):

[110] Authorized access point for the corporate body
[240] Authorized access point for the title of the work. $l Language of the expression.

[Note: The title in fields [245] and [240] may include designations ($n) and titles ($p) of parts or sections if these parts or sections are cataloged as individual serials.]

## CASE 3: NO CREATOR OR PREFERRED CREATOR

Authorized access point for a work if no creator:

[245] Title proper

or (if title proper is not unique):

[130] Title proper (Distinguishing characteristics)

or (if a translation):

Authorized access point for an expression of such a work (translation):

[130] Authorized access point for the work. $l Language of the expression.

Or (if a regional or other specialized edition):

[130] Authorized access point for the work (Edition statement)

[Note: The title in fields [245] and [130] may include designations ($n) and titles ($p) of parts or sections if these parts or sections are cataloged as individual serials.]

### IDENTIFIER FOR THE WORK [RDA 6.8] [CORE]

An identifier for the work is a character string uniquely associated with the work itself or with a surrogate for the work, such as an authority record.

The Library of Congress will not begin supplying identifiers for works until it can do so by machine, at which time they will appear in subfield $0 of the relevant MARC 21 field (see record syntax below).

Note: Serial works represented on most current bibliographic records do not have corresponding authority records.

#### MARC 21 RECORD SYNTAX

[130] $0 [when the authorized access point begins with the preferred title for the work]

[240] $0 [when the authorized access point begins with the authorized access point for a person, family, or corporate body]

The identifier is preceded by the related MARC organization code enclosed in parentheses.

#### EXAMPLE

[110] 1# $a United States

[240] 10 $a Laws, etc. (United States statutes at large) $0 (DLC)no 98065388

### IDENTIFIER FOR THE EXPRESSION [RDA 6.13] [CORE]

An identifier for the expression is a character string uniquely associated with the expression itself or with a surrogate for the expression, such as an authority record.

The Library of Congress will not begin supplying identifiers for expressions until it can do so by machine, at which time they will appear in subfield $0 of the relevant MARC 21 field (see record syntax, above).

Note: Serial expressions represented on most current bibliographic records do not have corresponding authority records.

#### MARC 21 RECORD SYNTAX

[130] $0 [when the authorized access point begins with the preferred title for the work]

[240] $0 [when the authorized access point begins with the authorized access point for a person, family, or corporate body]

The identifier is preceded by the related MARC organization code enclosed in parentheses.

#### EXAMPLE

[130] #0 $a Sbornik zadach po obshchemu kursu fiziki. $1 English $0 (DLC)n 85803596

## OTHER PERSON, FAMILY, OR CORPORATE BODY ASSOCIATED WITH A WORK [RDA 19.3] [CORE IF USED IN THE AUTHORIZED ACCESS POINT FOR THE WORK]

Record any person, family, or corporate body associated with the work if considered important for access. Make a note if the relationship of the person, etc., to the serial is not apparent.

### MARC 21 RECORD SYNTAX

[700] Authorized access point for a person or family associated with a work

[710] Authorized access point for a corporate body (other than a conference entered under its own name) associated with a work

[711] Authorized access point for a conference entered under its own name

### EXAMPLES

[245] 10 $a Directory of Canadian ornithologists = $b Répertoire des ornithologistes canadiens.

[550] ## $a "Compiled for the Migratory Birds Conservation Division of the Canadian Wildlife Service, with assistance from the Society of Canadian Ornithologists."—English home page.

[710] 2# $a Canadian Wildlife Service. $b Migratory Birds Conservation Division.

[710] 2# $a Society of Canadian Ornithologists.

[245] 00 $a Japan travel view / $c prepared by the Research Department of the Travel Industry Association of America.

[710] 2# $a Travel Industry Association of America. $b Research Department.

[130] #0 $a Treaty series (United Nations)

[245] 10 $a Treaty series : $b treaties and international agreements registered or filed and recorded with the Secretariat of the United Nations.

[710] 2# $a United Nations. $b Secretariat.

[245] 00 $a Occasional papers of the California Academy of Sciences.

[710] 2# $a California Academy of Sciences.

[130] 0# $a Acorn (Charleston, Ill.)

[245] 14 $a The acorn.

[264] 21 $3 1986-1990 $a Charleston, IL : $b Philosophy Department., Eastern Illinois University, $c 1986-

[264] 23 $3 1990- $a Saint Bonaventure, N.Y. : $b St. Bonaventure University, Philosophy Department

[550] ## $a Issued by the Gandhi-King Society.

[710] 2# $a Gandhi-King Society.

[245] 00 $a Zoological parks and aquariums in the Americas.

[550] ## $a Volumes for 1978/79-1993/94 issued by: American Association of Zoological Parks and Aquariums; volumes for 1994/95-1996/97 issued by: American Zoo and Aquarium Association.

[710] 2# $a American Association of Zoological Parks and Aquariums.

[710] 2# $a American Zoo and Aquarium Association.

[245] 00 $a Digestive and liver diseases : $b official journal of the Italian Society of Gastroenterology and the Italian Association for the Study of the Liver.

[710] 2# $a Società italiana di gastroenterologia.

[710] 2# $a Associazione italiana per lo studio del fegato.

[130] 0# $a Guidelines for newspapers (Oceania. Ministry of Truth)

[245] 101 $a Guidelines for newspapers / $c Minitrue.

[710] 1# $a Oceania. $b Ministry of Truth.

# 5. IDENTIFYING RELATED ENTITIES

**Authorized access points for persons, corporate bodies, and other resources related to the resource being described**

## Identifying Related Works and Expressions (Authorized Access Points)

It is rare that a serial will require an authorized access point for a related work or expression. This is most common when one serial supplements the other, and the title proper of the supplement does not begin with the title proper of the related serial.

When the authorized access point consists of a title alone, it is recorded in the MARC [730] field.

When the authorized access point encompasses both a creator and a title, it is recorded in the MARC field appropriate to the creator (with the title beginning in subfield $t rather than $a):

- [700] for a person or family
- [710] for a corporate body
- [711] for a conference (unless subordinate to a corporate body)

The relationship is also explicitly recorded in the appropriate [760–787] field (see "3. Relationships between Resources," above).

### EXAMPLE

[245] 00 $a Supplement to the Journal of the American Oriental Society.

[772] 1# $t Journal of the American Oriental Society $x 0003-0279 $w (DLC) 12032032 $w (OCoLC)1480509

[730] 0# $a Journal of the American Oriental Society.

## Identifying Related Persons, Families, and Corporate Bodies

Relationships with persons, families, and corporate bodies—the FRBR Group 2 entities—are generally discussed under the appropriate element. For example, relationships with editors are discussed under the statement of responsibility.

RDA provides two methods for identifying related persons, families, and corporate bodies:

- Authorized access point ("headings" in the old lingo)
- Identifier (e.g., authority record control number)[18]

This section deals with authorized access points.

### IDENTIFYING RELATED PERSONS AND FAMILIES

Because authorized access points for persons and families are seldom needed in serials cataloging, detailed instructions on the selection of preferred names and construction of authorized access points are omitted here. It is assumed that catalogers using this manual are already familiar with such instructions through their routine application in monograph cataloging. If not, catalogers are referred to RDA chapters 9, "Identifying Persons," and 10, "Identifying Families," and the related parts of *Maxwell's Handbook for RDA* for detailed guidance.

If needed as part of the authorized access point for the work, authorized access points for persons and families are recorded in MARC field [100]; otherwise, they are recorded in field [700]. Record a relationship designator from RDA appendix I to indicate the specific relationship between the person and the resource (e.g., editor) in subfield $e of field [100] or [700] whenever this is likely to be useful.

Note that if an authorized access point is needed for the editor of a serial, the appropriate relationship term from appendix I is *editor of compilation.*

### IDENTIFYING RELATED CORPORATE BODIES

It is perhaps fitting for something as challenging as serials cataloging that the FRBR Group 2 entity most often associated with it—the corporate body—is equally challenging. These challenges are dealt with in detail in RDA chapter 11 ("Identifying Corporate Bodies").

Like serials, corporate bodies are susceptible to change. And like serials, there are changes and there are *changes.* Once upon a time—before Lubetzky's reforms—cataloging rules identified corporate bodies by the latest name, much as they identified serials by the latest title. And when a corporate body changed its name, all the existing catalog records associated with that body would be pulled from the catalog, the name would be changed, and they would be returned to the catalog under the new name. This could produce some interesting results. For example, a serial associated with a corporate body might be linked to a name—the body's latest name—that did not yet exist when the serial was published! Needless to say, this could make using the catalog something of a challenge for the uninitiated.

With Lubetzky's reforms, changes in the name of a corporate body, like changes in the name of a serial, were handled successively, and a resource would be associated with whatever name the body bore when that resource was issued.

A corporate body can be somewhat remiss in consistently presenting its name, and it becomes the task of the cataloger—usually a serials cataloger (who is presumably used to this sort of treatment)—to determine when a changed name represents a real change and when it merely represents carelessness, or a desire for a particular momentary effect on a particular resource, or an experimental marketing ploy. It can get tricky.

RDA, like its predecessors, talks about changes of name and variant names. Distinguishing one from the other requires skill and detective work. If there is an explicit statement—"Esso is changing its name to Exxon"—or Old Name appears on every issue up to December 2005, while New Name appears on every issue afterward, there is little doubt that a change has taken place (though there is always the possibility that New Name represents a different body rather than a later name of the same body). In case of doubt, perform detective work. With the Web this work has become much easier than in the past, since most bodies with the resources to issue a serial have the resources to maintain a Web presence. A corporate website will often provide all the information you need to ascertain that, yes, a deliberate name change has taken place. When a corporate website is absent or provides insufficient background to make a determination, it may be helpful to consult Wikipedia or a similar reference source, where fans of the body may have provided more complete information.

When Name A persists, we have a problem and must determine whether it persists for nostalgic reasons or because the change of name is only apparent. This determination is made based on the instructions for selecting among variant names, and the process is analogous to that used for selecting among variant titles (see "Selecting the Preferred Name of a Corporate Body," below).

What follows are the more important RDA instructions for selecting and recording the name of a corporate body. For detailed guidance, the reader is referred to the text of RDA.

## WHAT IS A CORPORATE BODY?

According to RDA 11.0, "a body is considered to be a corporate body only if it is identified by a particular name (i.e., if the words referring to it are a specific appellation rather than a general description)." In languages such as English, this is often signaled by capitalization and/or the use of the definite article ("the Workshop on Serials Cataloging in These Trying Times" is a particular name; " a workshop on serials cataloging in these trying times" is not). In other languages, sorting this out may present more of a challenge.

Ad hoc events (fairs, expeditions, sporting events, etc.) are corporate bodies, as are vessels such as ships and spacecraft.

**EXAMPLE**

[110] 2# $a Enterprise (Starship)
[245] 10 $a Captain's log / $c Starship Enterprise.

## RECORDING THE NAME OF A CORPORATE BODY [RDA 11.2.1]

Record the name of a corporate body using the general guidelines on capitalization, numbers, accents, etc., found at RDA 8.5. This means transcribing the name as it appears, but capitalizing according to the instructions in appendix A, adding accents when integral to the name, and eliminating spaces when they occur between the letters (or letters followed by stops) of an initialism, etc.

**EXAMPLE**

In source: B. B. C. Symphony Orchestra
Record as: B.B.C. Symphony Orchestra

## SELECTING THE PREFERRED NAME OF A CORPORATE BODY [RDA 11.2.2]

The preferred name of a corporate body is based on the form of name appearing in (in this order):

1. Preferred sources of information in resources associated with the body
2. Elsewhere in resources associated with the body
3. Anywhere else

If this results in different forms of the same name being equally valid, choose (in this order):

1. The form that is *formally* presented in the source (i.e., the form that appears on its own rather than in the text)
2. The most common form
3. A brief form that would differentiate the name from others
4. The name found in reference sources
5. The official name

If the name appears using variant spellings, choose the spelling on the first resource received. However, if the difference is the result of orthographic reform, choose the spelling that reflects the current orthography (LC-PCC PS 11.2.2.5.1).

If the name appears in different languages, choose (in this order):

1. The name in the official language of the body
2. The name in the language preferred by the cataloging agency
3. The name used most often in the body's publications

In case of doubt, use the form that appears first in the first resource received. For international bodies, choose the name in the language preferred by the cataloging agency when this is used in the body's publications.

### EXCEPTIONS

Having said this, there are peculiar categories of body that have special instructions in subsections of RDA 11.2.2 (religious bodies, fraternal and knightly orders, church councils, diplomatic conferences, autocephalous patriarchates, diocese, etc., of the Eastern Church, religious orders and societies, local places of worship). Only the most commonly occurring of these—governments and conferences—are discussed below.

*Governments.* Use the name of the area governed (France rather than République française; Kensington and Chelsea rather than Royal London Borough of Kensington and Chelsea).

*Conferences.* Prefer the form of name that includes the name or abbreviation of the name of an associated body (unless the authorized access point for the conference would begin with the authorized access point for that body; see "Subordinate Bodies," below).

### CHANGE OF NAME [RDA 11.2.2.6]

Like serials, corporate bodies change their names. Consider the new name to represent a new body.

#### EXAMPLE

1849-1933: New Britain Normal School
1933-1959: Teachers College of Connecticut
1959-1983: Central Connecticut State College
1983- : Central Connecticut State University

### OMISSIONS [RDA 11.2.2.7–11.2.2.10]

- Initial articles, unless the intent is to access the name under the article (i.e., apply the alternative instruction under RDA 11.2.2.8)
- Full stops (periods) after initials, unless this is the most common form
- Citations of honor awarded to the body
- Terms of incorporation, etc., unless integral to the name or needed to show that the name represents a corporate body. (If such a term is retained and occurs at the beginning of the name, transpose it to the end.)
- An initial word or phrase indicating the private nature of a body (Asian languages only), unless integral to the name
- Abbreviations (USS, HMCS, etc.) occurring at the beginning of the name of a ship

**EXAMPLES**

> Amis de la terre (not Les amis de la terre)
>
> *but* Los Angeles
>
> Royal Ulster Constabulary (not Royal Ulster Constabulary GC [the body was awarded the George Cross])
>
> Zhongguo yin hang (not Zhongguo yin hang gu fen you xian gong si)
>
> *but* Monsters, Inc.
>
> Forstprojektierun Potsdam, VEB (not VEB Forstprojektierun Potsdam)
>
> Surprise (not HMS Surprise)

## TRANSLITERATION [RDA 11.2.2.12]

Transliterate any name written in a nonroman script, using the ALA-LC Romanization Tables: Transliteration Schemes for Nonroman Scripts.

## SUBORDINATE AND RELATED BODIES [RDA 11.2.2.13]

[Note: The instructions in RDA dealing with subordinate non-government, government, and religious bodies (RDA 11.2.2.13-20) will be merged and/or reorganized (but not changed in substance) in the July 2013 update to RDA Toolkit. The following reflects the pre-July 2013 arrangement.]

Special instructions may apply when one body is subordinate or related to another body. If the name of such a body falls into one of the types listed below and under RDA 11.2.2.14, its name is recorded as a subdivision of the other body. Special instructions apply for governmental and religious bodies and are set out in RDA 11.2.2.18 and 11.2.2.30, respectively.

For names that fall into one of these types and include the name (or an abbreviation of the name) of the other body, omit that name or abbreviation when recording the name.

**EXAMPLE**

> Harvard University. Press *not* Harvard University. Harvard University Press

If the name of a body falls into one of the types listed under RDA 11.2.2.14 and so is treated as a subdivision of a higher body, see "Direct or Indirect Subdivision," below, for instructions on

1. Which higher body to select from a hierarchy of potential higher bodies
2. When to retain an intermediate level in such a hierarchy of higher bodies

*Type 1:* A name containing a term that by definition implies that the body is part of another (e.g., Department, Division, Section, Branch).

**EXAMPLES**

> University of Woolloomooloo. Philosophy Department
>
> Zhongguo yi qi yi biao xue hui. Jing mi ji xie fen hui.
>
> [Note: It was common practice under AACR2 to abbreviate "Department" to "Dept." This is no longer the case.]

*Type 2:* A name containing a word that normally implies administrative subordination (e.g., Committee, Commission) provided that the name of the higher body is required for the identification of the subordinate body.

### EXAMPLES

Fundación Terram. Dirección de Estudios
[Name as it appears in source: Fundación Terram, Dirección de Estudios]
Musée Rodin. Cabinet des dessins
[Name as it appears in source: Musée Rodin, Cabinet des dessins]
*but*
Hereford Diocesan Board of Education
UW-Madison Campus Planning Committee
National Commission on United Methodist Higher Education

*Type 3:* A name that is general in nature or that does no more than indicate a geographic, chronological, or numbered or lettered subdivision of a parent body. (However, in case of doubt, record the body directly under its name.)

### EXAMPLES

American Dental Association. Research Institute
[Name as it appears in source: Research Institute, American Dental Association
Health Foundation (see also "Type 6" and "Direct or Indirect Subdivision," below)]
Jean and Alexander Heard Library. Friends of the Library
[Name as it appears in source: The Friends of the Library, The Jean and Alexander
Heard Library, Vanderbilt University]
Hawaii Macadamia Nut Association. Annual Meeting
[Name as it appears in source: Hawaii Macadamia Nut Association, Annual
Meeting]
[Note: under AACR2, the frequency term would not have been treated as part of the
name]
Costume Society of America. Region II
[Name as it appears in source: CSA Region II / Costume Society of America]
Dartmouth College. Class of 1957
[Name as it appears in source: Dartmouth Class of 1957 / Dartmouth College]
*but* (case of doubt)
Human Resources Center
[Name changed from: Human Resources Corporation]

*Type 4:* A name that does not convey the idea of a corporate body.

### EXAMPLES

British Library. Science, Technology, and Industry
[Name as it appears in source: Science, Technology, and Industry, British Library]

University of Washington, Bothell. Human Resources

[Name as it appears in source: University of Washington, Bothell, Human Resources]

*Type 5:* A name of a university faculty, school, college, institute, laboratory, etc., that simply indicates a particular field of study.

**EXAMPLES**

Princeton University. Bureau of Urban Research

[Name as it appears in source: Bureau of Urban Research, Princeton University]

Universidad Autónoma de Nuevo León. Facultad de Ciencias Forestales

[Name as it appears in source: Facultad de Ciencias Forestales / Universidad Autónoma de Nuevo León]

*but* (because of presence of additional distinctive word(s))

Australian Centre for Child Protection

[Name as it appears in source: Australian Centre for Child Protection, University of South Australia]

Harvard Law School

[Name as it appears in source: Harvard Law School]

[Note: The Harvard Law School is part of Harvard University]

*Type 6:* A name that includes the entire name of the higher or related body.

**EXAMPLES**

American Dental Association. Health Foundation

[Name: American Dental Association Health Foundation]

Dunedin Botanic Garden. Friends

[Name: Friends of the Dunedin Botanic Garden]

Harvard University. Press

[Name: Harvard University Press]

## Joint Committees [RDA 11.2.2.16]

A special case. The handling of such committees varies, depending on what they are joint committees *of.* See RDA 11.2.2.16 for further guidance.

## Local Units of US Political Parties [RDA 11.2.2.17]

A special case. See RDA 11.2.2.17 for further guidance.

## DIRECT OR INDIRECT SUBDIVISION [RDA 11.2.2.15, RDA 11.2.2.20]

If the name of a body falls into one of the types listed under RDA 11.2.2.14 or 11.2.2.19 and is treated as a subdivision of a higher body, and there is a hierarchy of bodies involved:

1. Select as the higher body the lowest body in the hierarchy that is recorded directly under its own name.
2. If the higher body selected in step 1 may have more than one subordinate unit with this same name farther down its hierarchy, retain the lowest intermediate body or bodies in the hierarchy that will meaningfully distinguish this body from its namesake.

### EXAMPLES

Public Library Association. Audiovisual Committee
[Hierarchy: American Library Association, Public Library Association, Audiovisual Committee]
American Library Association. Reference and Adult Services Division. History Section. Bibliography and Indexes Committee
[Note: more than one division may have a History Section; more than one section may have a Bibliography and Indexes Committee]
California. Department of Corrections. Research Division
[Hierarchy: California, Health and Welfare Agency, Department of Corrections, Research Division] [Note: while more than one department may have a Research Division, it is unlikely more than one agency will have a Department of Corrections]

## GOVERNMENTAL BODIES [RDA 11.2.2.18]

[Note: The instructions for governmental bodies are being combined with those for non-governmental bodies in the July 2013 update to RDA Toolkit.] A governmental body may be recorded:

1. Under its own name
2. As a subdivision of a higher governmental body (if it falls under one of the RDA 11.2.2.13 types above)
3. As a subdivision of the government (if it falls under one of the RDA 11.2.2.19 types below)

## SUBORDINATE AND RELATED GOVERNMENTAL BODIES
## [RDA 11.2.2.19]

[Note: The instructions for governmental bodies are being combined with those for non-governmental bodies in the July 2013 update to RDA Toolkit.] If the name of a government body falls into one of the types listed below, record its name as a subdivision of the government. See "Direct or Indirect Subdivision," above, for instructions on:

1. Which higher body to select from a hierarchy of potential higher bodies
2. When to retain an intermediate level in such a hierarchy of higher bodies

*Type 1:* An agency with a name containing a term that by definition implies that the body is part of another (e.g., Department, Division, Section, Branch).

*Type 2:* An agency with a name containing a word that normally implies administrative subordination in the terminology of the government concerned (e.g., Committee, Commission), provided that the name of the government is required for the identification of the agency.

*Type 3:* An agency with a name that is general in nature or that does no more than indicate a geographic, chronological, or numbered or lettered subdivision of the government or of one of its agencies recorded subordinately.

*Type 4:* An agency with a name that does not convey the idea of a corporate body and does not contain the name of the government.

*Type 5:* An agency that is a ministry or similar major executive agency (i.e., one that has no other agency above it) as defined by official publications of the government in question.

*Type 6:* A legislative body (see RDA 11.2.2.22 for detailed instructions on these bodies and their committees, etc.).

*Type 7:* A court (see RDA 11.2.2.24 for detailed instructions).

*Type 8:* A principal service of the armed forces of a government (see RDA 11.2.2.25 for detailed instructions).

*Type 9:* A head of state or head of government (see RDA 11.2.2.21 for detailed instructions, including juntas).

*Type 10:* An embassy, consulate, etc. (see RDA 11.2.2.26 for detailed instructions).

## ADDITIONS TO CORPORATE NAMES

Make additions to corporate names whenever necessary to distinguish two otherwise identical names, or when such an identifier is helpful in identifying the body.

### PLACE [RDA 11.3]

What RDA 11.3.3 calls "location of headquarters" is more helpfully thought of under the broader phrase "place associated with the corporate body." If the body has a character that is national, provincial, etc., then this place will be the name of the associated nation, province, etc., unless this name is insufficient or inappropriate to the context. In all other cases, this will be the local place (which may be as specific as a neighborhood, if such fine distinctions are appropriate). The names of certain places are abbreviated according the instructions in RDA appendix B.11. If the name of the place changes during the time of the body's existence, use the latest place name.

Add the name of the place in parentheses following the name of the corporate body.

#### EXAMPLES

Republican Party (N.Y.)

Sociedad Nacional de Agricultura (Chile)

Fawlty Towers (Torquay, England)

St. John's Church (Lafayette Square, Washington, D.C.)

Petropavlovskaia krepost' (Saint Petersburg, Russia)

*or:* Петропа́вловская крѣпость (Saint Petersburg, Russia)

*not:* Petropavlovskaia krepost (Leningrad, Russia)

### DATE [RDA 11.4]

Conferences associated with serials tend to be of the ongoing variety, for obvious reasons. Consequently, the date of a conference [RDA 11.4.2] does not typically apply in serials cataloging. The date of establishment and/or termination [RDA 11.4.3–11.4.4] may apply, however, particularly when two or more bodies with identical names are established in the same place.

Add the date in parentheses following the name of the corporate body.

#### EXAMPLES

Cincinnati Medical Society (1819)

Cincinnati Medical Society (1831-1858)

Cincinnati Medical Society (1874-1894)

Cincinnati Medical Society (1925- )

### ASSOCIATED INSTITUTION [RDA 11.5]

When a corporate body is entered under its own name rather than the name of a higher or related body as specified in RDA 11.2.2.13 and 11.2.2.19, the name of the higher or related body may nonetheless put in an appearance as a means of distinguishing the body from another of the same name. This is appropriate whenever the name of the higher or related body provides a better identification than place or date, or if place or date are unavailable or insufficient as means of differentiation.

Add the name (in its form as an authorized access point) in parentheses following the name of the corporate body.

### EXAMPLES

Institut geologii (Akademiia nauk SSSR. Karel'skii nauchnyi tsentr)
Institut geologii (Akademiia nauk SSSR. Komi nauchnyi tsentr)

## OTHER DESIGNATION ASSOCIATED WITH THE CORPORATE BODY [RDA 11.7]

Whenever the name of a corporate body does not convey the sense of a corporate body (e.g., Bartholomew), add a suitable term to clarify this, in the language and orthography of the agency creating the record.

Add the term in parentheses following the name of the corporate body, with its first letter capitalized. If such a term alone is insufficient to distinguish one body from another, follow it with a space-colon-space and a place or date(s), whichever is most appropriate.

### EXAMPLES

Bartholomew (Firm)
Gingerbread Wales (Organisation)
Elks (Musical group)
Elks (Fraternal order)
KGB (Musical group)
KGB (Radio station)
Fusion (Organization : Brighton, England)
Fusion (Organization : Chichester, England)

To distinguish between jurisdictions other than cities or towns, use a term for the type of jurisdiction in the language and orthography of the agency creating the record or, in case of doubt, the language of the jurisdiction.

Add the term in parentheses following the name of the corporate body, with its first letter capitalized. If the jurisdiction is already distinguished by a place, separate the place from a following term by a space-colon-space.

### EXAMPLES

Cork (Ireland : County)
[The authorized access point for the city of Cork is: Cork (Ireland)]
New York (State)
[The authorized access point for the city of New York is: New York (N.Y.)]
Darmstadt (Germany : Regierungsbezirk)
Darmstadt (Germany : Landkreis)

When none of these situations applies, choose a term in the language and orthography of the cataloging agency that makes an appropriate distinction.

**EXAMPLES**

> Korea (North)
> Congo (Democratic Republic)

When two or more authorities claim jurisdiction over the same territory, use an appropriate description. If the jurisdiction is of limited duration, follow this by a comma-space and the beginning and ending years (separated by a hyphen) [RDA 11.4.3.3, RDA 11.4.4.3, RDA 11.7.1.6].

**EXAMPLES**

> Michigan (British military government, 1812-1814)
> Germany (Territory under allied occupation, 1945-1949)

## Complete Record Examples

### PRINTED TEXT

[LDR] 02147cas a2200469 i 450
[001] 16272557
[005] 20120131070809.0
[007] t|
[008] 100608c20119999pauqr p 0 a0eng
[010] ## $a 2010203152
[022] 0# $a 2155-6989 $2 1
[035] ## $a (OCoLC)ocn639264065
[037] ## $a IGI Global, 701 E. Chocolate Ave., Hershey, PA 17033 $c $545.00 (1 yr., institutions)
[040] ## $a DLC $b eng $c DLC $d DLC $e rda
[042] ## $a pcc $a nsdp
[050] 00 $a TA1634 $b .I644
[082] 10 $a 006 $2 14
[210] 0# $a Int. j. comput. vis. image process. $b (Print)
[222] #0 $a International journal of computer vision and image processing $b (Print)
[245] 00 $a International journal of computer vision and image processing / $c an official publication of the Information Resources Management Association.
[246] 1# $a Computer vision and image processing
[246] 1# $a IJCVIP
[260] ## $a [Hershey, PA] : $b IGI Publishing, $c [2011]-
[300] ## $a volumes : $b illustrations ; $c 26 cm
[310] ## $a Quarterly

[336] ## $a text $2 rdacontent

[337] ## $a unmediated $2 rdamedia

[338] ## $a volume $2 rdacarrier

[362] 1# $a Began with: Vol. 1, No. 1 (January-March 2011).

[588] ## $a Description based on: Vol. 1, No. 1 (January-March 2011); title from cover.

[588] ## $a Latest issue consulted: Vol. 1, No. 1 (January-March 2011).

[650] #0 $a Computer vision $v Periodicals.

[650] #0 $a Image processing $v Periodicals.

[710] 2# $a Information Resources Management Association.

[776] 08 $a Online version: $t International journal of computer vision and image processing $x 2155-6997 $w (DLC) 2010203153 $w (OCoLC)639264068

## NOTES

LDR/18 [descriptive cataloging form] i = ISBD punctuation included

007/00 [category of material] t = text

040 $b [language of cataloging] eng = English

040 $e [descriptive conventions] rda = RDA]

245 $c statement of responsibility is CORE in RDA for serials (though not required by CONSER Standard Record)

300 $a [extent] "volumes" is spelled out

300 $b [illustrative content] "illustrations" is spelled out

300 $c [dimensions] "cm" is a symbol rather than an abbreviation; hence no full stop (However, if a series statement had been present in field 490, a full stop would have been required by the ISBD display syntax.)

336 [content type] (new for RDA)

337 [media type] (new for RDA)

338 [carrier type] (new for RDA)

362 [numbering area] Designations are transcribed as they appear in the source, abbreviated when abbreviated in the source but otherwise not

787 $i [relationship information] Although specific terms are not defined in RDA appendix J, online and print versions of the same serial may be related by explicitly recording "Online version:" or "Print version:" in [787] $i

## MICROFORM (MICROFILM REPRODUCTION)

[LDR]    01589cas#a2200409#i#4500

[001]    11152967

[005]    2007072050430.0

[007]    hd#afv—-baca

[008]    750929d18441845miuuu#p#a#####0###a0eng#c

[010]    ## $a mic60007197

[012] ## $a -3-7-0707190269-p-9111

[035] ## $a (OCoLC)1662183

[040] ## $a DC $b eng $c FGULS $d OCoLC $d PES $d OCoLC $d MnMULS $d DLC $d NST $d OCoLC $d SERSO $e rda

[042] ## $a msc

[050] 00 $a Microfilm 01104 no. 527 AP

[130] 0# $a Western literary journal and monthly review (Cincinnati, Ohio : 1844)

[245] 00 $a Western literary journal and monthly review.

[264] #1 $a Ann Arbor, Mich. : $b University Microfilms

[300] ## $a 1 microfilm reel ; $c 35 mm.

[336] ## $a text $2 rdacontent

[337] ## $a microform $2 rdamedia

[338] ## $a microfilm reel $2 rdacarrier

[362] 1# $a Issues published: Vol. 1, no. 1 (November, 1844)-vol. 1, no. 6 (April, 1845).

[490] 1# $a American periodical series, 1800-1850 $v ; 527

[500] ## $a Edited by: E.Z.C. Judson (real name of Ned Buntline) and L.A. Hine.

[588] ## $a Description based on: Vol. 1, no. 1 (November, 1844); title from caption.

[700] 1# $a Buntline, Ned, $d 1822 or 1823-1866, $e editor

[700] 1# $a Hine, L. A. $q (Lucius Alonzo), $d -1906, $e editor

[776] 0# $i Reproduction of (manifestation): $t Western literary journal and monthly review. $d Cincinnati :$b Published for the editors by Robinson & Jones, $c [1844]-1845. $h 1 volume. $n Monthly

[787] 0# $i Vol. 1, no. 3-6 also published in Nashville, Tenn., as: $t Southwestern literary journal and monthly review

[830] #0 $a American periodical series, 1800-1850 ; $v 527.

[850] ## $a DLC $a IaAS $a InLP

## NOTES

007 [coded data relating to microforms]

007/00-01 [category of material / specific material] c = electronic resource / r = remote

008/15-17 [place of publication of microform]

008/18-19 [frequency / regularity of microform]

008/22-23 [form of original item / form of item] # = none of the following / a = microfilm electronic / o = online

264 [Publication, etc., area pertains to microform]

300 [Physical description area pertains to microform. Ends with period / full stop because record contains series]

490 [Series pertains to microform]

776 [Structured description of the original publication (related manifestation)]

## CARTOGRAPHIC MATERIAL (ANNUAL ROAD ATLAS)

[LDR]   01194cas a22003854i 450

[001]   13556069

[005]   20040518140644.0

[006]   e

[007]   ad#canzn

[008]   040412c2003999scuar#m#######0eng#d

[010] ## $a 2004627374

[034] 0# $a a

[040] ## $a DLC $b eng $c DLC $d DLC

[042] ## $a pcc

[043] ## $a n-us—- $a n-cn—- $a n-mx—-

[050] 00 $a G1201.P2 $b M5

[052] ## $a 3701

[052] ## $a 3401

[052] ## $a 4411

[082] 00 $a 912.7 $2 22

[110] 2# $a Michelin North America, Inc.

[245] 10 $a Road atlas . . . USA, Canada, Mexico.

[246] 13 $a North America

[246] 3# $a Michelin road atlas . . . USA, Canada, Mexico

[255] ## $a Scales differ.

[260] #1 $a Greenville, SC : $b $b Michelin North America, Inc., $c [2002]-

[300] ## $a volumes : $b colored maps ; $c 28 cm

[310] ## $a Annual

[336] ## $a cartographic image $2 rdacontent

[337] ## $a unmediated $2 rdamedia

[338] ## $a volume $2 rdacarrier

[362] 0# $a 2003-

[500] ## $a Includes indexes.

[500] ## $a Includes maps of selected North American cities.

[588] ## $a Description based on: 2003; title from cover.

[650] #0 $a Roads $z United States $v Maps.

[650] #0 $a Roads $z Canada $v Maps.

[650] #0 $a Roads $z Mexico $v Maps.

[775] 0# $a Michelin North America, Inc. $t Large format atlas . . . USA, Canada, Mexico

## NOTES

006/00 [additional form of material] e = cartographic materials

007 [coded data relating to maps and atlases]

007/00-01 [category of material / specific material] a = map / d = atlas

034 [coded cartographic mathematical data] $a = category of scale (a = linear)

052 [Geographic classification] Library of Congress geographic area codes corresponding to areas in [650] $z

255 [Cartographic mathematical data] Main maps use more than one scale [RDA 7.25.1.4]

300 $b [illustrative content] May record "illustrations" or, alternatively, a more specific term [RDA 7.15.1.3]

## 6. ONLINE SERIALS AND CONSER PROVIDER-NEUTRAL RECORDS

An online serial is an interesting animal, so much so that it is worthwhile to examine them, along with some practices external to RDA, before looking at the way they are handled in RDA. This examination will involve the question of print and online versions and the related question of handling online versions from multiple sources.

### Title Changes: Online vs. Print (CONSER)

Nowadays serials tend to be "born digital" and are only subsequently issued in print, a reality that is extremely hard to digest for anyone who has spent most of his or her life in the pre-digital age. We would like to believe that the print version of a serial is the primary form, and in our cataloging we continue to treat it as such, though our rationale for doing so becomes thinner with each passing year.

Because this manual is designed for the cataloging world rather than the real world, it will maintain the fiction that print is the primary medium in all but exceptional cases. This means that events such as cessations and title changes will typically be recognized for online serials only when they occur in the print version. This will be true so long as evidence of this print version change is available in the online version. Any evidence will do, even if it involves scrounging around in an article PDF file looking for a running title. But if the online version shows absolutely no evidence of an earlier print title, it must be cataloged under the title it bears, even if this represents a later print title. To alert the user, a note and access point should be added for the earlier title proper (LC-PCC PS for RDA 2.20.2.4).

#### EXAMPLE

[245] 00 $a Legal medicine.

[247] 11 $a Legal medicine open file

[547] ## $a Issues published from 1992-1994 with the title Legal medicine open file have been reformatted with the new title: Legal medicine.

Note that this is not latest-entry cataloging, despite the provision of access to an earlier title proper. The description is still based on the earliest online issue. It's just that the title proper associated with that earliest issue has changed. Note also that this is not an integrating resource, in that the issues remain discrete and only the earlier title has disappeared, not any of the actual content.

The effort in these cases is always to try to align print and online versions (except when this simply can't be done, as in the example above). The FRBR conceptual model that underlies RDA will not function properly in the absence of such alignment because the print and online versions of a serial will fail to resolve to the same work.

## Provider-Neutral Records (CONSER)

We have used the term *version* advisedly here, in that online versions can represent, in FRBR terms, either manifestations or expressions, depending on the degree to which they differ from one another. While RDA is strict on the matter of manifestations and expressions, CONSER practice and the real world in which most online catalogs operate provide us some wiggle room and a way of accommodating the wide variety of forms in which a serial may appear online: the provider-neutral record.

A serial that appears one way in print may appear any number of ways online. One provider may provide text but no images, another may provide black and white images, and yet another color images. Each may provide its own supporting metadata. One may supply an audio file for the visually impaired (or for those who want to listen to it while they're out and about). The single print serial has morphed into a multitude of online versions. Text alone may be fine for a poetry journal, not so much for a newsmagazine. Black and white images may be fine for a journal devoted to macroeconomics, not so much for one devoted to heart surgery. What's a cataloger to do? And this doesn't even begin to address the problem that different vendors may provide access to different ranges of issues: perhaps all, but possibly just a few, possibly incorporating a moving window, moving wall, moving portcullis. One can quickly become overwhelmed.

The provider-neutral record solves this problem of an infinite variety of online versions by transferring responsibility for sorting it all out from the cataloger to someone else somewhere else, preferably the local manager of your electronic resource management system (ERMS) and a third-party vendor that supplies the knowledge base to that ERMS, hopefully keeping track both of the infinite variety of presentation and the infinite variety of access rights. In these cases, a single URL in the provider-neutral catalog record links to the corresponding data in the ERMS, enabling users to select the version most appropriate to their needs.

Although provider-neutral records represent all online versions of a given serial, the description represents a single version, selected according to a strict hierarchy aimed at identifying the version that would likely be preferred by users:

1. The version on the content originator's website (commercial publisher, learned society, etc.)
2. If hosted by a third party:
    a. The version on a website provided by that host to the content originator (commercial publisher, learned society, etc.)
    b. The version on the host's consolidated website
3. The print version
4. Any other version, including content aggregator websites
    a. Versions that keep issues intact
    b. Versions that do not keep issues intact

This hierarchy should be applied using cataloger judgment. For example, the version of the *Quarterly Journal of Economics* on the Oxford Journals website would be preferred over the archived version on JSTOR because Oxford Journals is the website of the publisher, Oxford University Press, and in this case contains all the issues back to 1886. If an institution does not subscribe to the issue archive on the Oxford Journals website but does subscribe to the archive on the JSTOR site, details from the earliest issue may be taken from that site. Likewise, while PMLA is available on a society-specific website hosted by Atypon, the site only includes issues from 2002 onward; the archive (and earliest issue) is on the JSTOR site, which would become the preferred site for cataloging.

In cases involving title changes, always prefer a site that gives issues under the title they bore when they were first published over one that gives all issues under the latest title. This facilitates gathering together the print and online manifestations of an expression (since issues of the print version will retain the title they had at the time of publication).

Links are provided to the website that serves as the basis of the description and, optionally, to other websites providing access to the content.

## REPRODUCTIONS VS. VERSIONS

One question that arises in the context of the provider-neutral record is whether one is cataloging a reproduction or a simultaneous publication. As with so much in serials cataloging, this is complicated. While retroactively, many serials will exist online as images of the print manifestation, they are seldom simple photographic reproductions in the way that a microform reproduction is. At the very least, mass digitization projects such as Google Books and the Internet Archive employ OCR software to create a searchable approximation of the text, enhancing the otherwise straightforward online reproduction. Beyond this, many online serials with a long history encompass a mix of more recent "born digital" issues and older digitized print issues. Given that provider-neutral records are meant to cover *all* manifestations of an online serial, and given that as the corpus of online serials grows, reproductions will represent a diminishing share of the total, the reasonable approach seems to be to catalog all online serials represented by provider-neutral records as though they were simultaneous publications.

## SPECIFIC INSTRUCTIONS

The preceding represents the context for cataloging online serials. In general, they are cataloged applying the same rules as are applied to print serials. The following addresses those instances where the instructions for cataloging online serials *differ* from those for cataloging print.

## SOURCES OF INFORMATION [RDA 2.2.2.2]

Most online serials that have corresponding print analogs consist of images of those print analogs or of their component parts (issues, articles). The preferred sources of information for these serials are the same as for the print analogs, and the related LC-PCC PS decisions apply. This means that the preferred source is the issue with the lowest/earliest numbering [RDA 2.1.2.3], regardless of which issue appeared first online (or, in the context of the provider-neutral record, whether the first issue is an original version or a reproduction).

Having said that, certain types of online serials—specifically those consisting of articles or similar separable content—tend to lack images of the preferred sources customarily used in cataloging their print analogs: title page, cover, etc. In these cases, RDA 2.2.2.2 prefers a source within the resource that bears a title, preferring a source where the information is *formally* presented (i.e., where it stands apart from the text). Sometimes, this may be the running title that appears along one of the edges of the page images of an article.

For older serials, with multiple online versions available to serve as the basis for the description, choosing a preferred source can present something of a challenge, as is illustrated by the following example.

### EXAMPLE

*The English Historical Review* is published by Oxford University Press and available online via the Oxford Journals website and the JSTOR website. On each website, the images begin with the first issue (January 1886), which is broken up into its component parts. Unfortunately, the cover and preliminary pages of individual issues were long ago discarded—a common practice prior to the middle of the twentieth century—leaving only a caption title. Ah, but the JSTOR copy also contains a volume title page, and the LC-PCC PS for RDA 2.2.2.2 says to prefer a volume title page when there is no source on an individual issue that is *sufficient for the description* of the serial. So this is good news, no? Alas, examination of the image reveals that it pertains not to the original publication but to a reprint volume published in 1962. But never fear! An image of the original volume title page is available, deposited in the Hathi Trust, digitized from a copy at the University of Michigan. So that volume title page becomes the basis for identification.

For details relating to more recent issues, the Oxford Journals website kindly preserves images of the "front matter" (cover and preliminary pages).

When an online serial does not consist of page images but rather of text embedded in the Web page itself, then the novel provisions of RDA 2.2.2.4 kick in. This instruction differs from its AACR2 predecessor (AACR2 rule 9.0B1) in preferring "embedded metadata in textual form that includes a title." This can prove problematical, in that such metadata is often imperfectly understood by those creating and maintaining the website. The most common place to find such metadata is in the <title> element at the head of the HTML source code for a web page. Because this element typically displays prominently in the bar at the top of a browser window, the owner of the website often uses it to do double duty: both identifying the serial and advertising its attractions to potential users.

**EXAMPLES**

> <title>The New York Times—Breaking News, World News & Multimedia</title>
> <title>News, Travel, Weather, Entertainment, Sports, Technology, U.S. & World—USATODAY.com</title>
> <title>Business News & Financial News—The Wall Street Journal—Wsj.com</title>

Usually we can get around this problem by treating the "advertising" text as introductory text [RDA 2.3.1.6] when it precedes what we think is the title and treating it as other title information when it follows it.

Unfortunately, this approach is worthless when it is evident from the content of the <title> element that the owner of the website has no clue as to the purpose of the element. For example, rather than containing the title of the resource, the element may simply give the name of the hosting entity and a generic characterization of the display, such as <title>OnlineJournalSite—Table of Contents</title>. In these cases, consider that no satisfactory metadata for the resource has been provided in terms of RDA 2.2.2.4 and so prefer, in the words of the instruction, "another source forming part of the resource itself, giving preference to sources in which the information is formally presented."

## VARIANT TITLES [RDA 2.3.6]

Two classes of title should be treated as variant titles for online serials:

- Variant titles that apply only to the online version of the serial
- Variant titles that apply only to the online versions provided by one or more (but not all) providers

Variant titles in the former class are handled in the same way as such titles appearing on the print serial. Variant titles in the latter class, however, must be characterized as not applying to all online versions.

**EXAMPLES**

> [246] 13 $a Silly journal online
>
> [246] 1# $i Issues from some providers have title: $t Silly journal of quantum mechanics

## NUMBERING AREA [RDA 2.6]

In some cases a print journal will not be available online in its entirety. In the context of the gradual migration of everything online, it is sensible to view this as a temporary situation, in anticipation that the entire run of the print journal will eventually become available. In the interim, the numbering statement can be fashioned with reference to the print version.

In MARC 21, the corresponding starting date in field 008, being based on the date in field 362, should likewise correspond to the starting date of the print version.

**EXAMPLE**

> [362] 1# $a Print version began with: Volume 1, number 1 (January 1984).

## PUBLICATION, DISTRIBUTION, ETC., AREA [RDA 2.8–2.10]

Recall that the online version is being described, not the print version. Whereas the title may be taken from the earliest image of a digitized print issue, the publication statement, etc., must be taken from a source on the journals Web site.

## PHYSICAL DESCRIPTION AREA

There is no physical description area required for an online serial that is not yet complete. If the online serial is complete, record its extent. (Recall that "volumes" refers to bibliographic volumes rather than physical volumes.)

**EXAMPLE**

> [300] ## $a 1 online resource (12 volumes)

## SERIES [RDA 2.12]

In the context of the provider-neutral record, do not record the name of a Web site (ScienceDirect, JSTOR, etc.) either as a series or as a related entity.

## RELATIONSHIPS BETWEEN ONLINE VERSION AND PRINT VERSION

Relationships between the online and print versions of a serial should be recorded as equivalent manifestations. While RDA J.4.2 gives the text "also issued as" for such relationships, prefer a more specific characterization.

**EXAMPLES**

> [776] 08 $i Online version: $t New scientist (1971) $w (DLC) 2010250720
> [On record for print version]
> [776] 08 $i Print version: $t New scientist (1971) $x 0262-4079 $w (DLC) 82644452
> [On record for online version]

## NOTES

While online versions exhibit noteworthy conditions and situations that print versions do not, the mechanisms for recording them are the same. In MARC 21, use the field that most closely approximates the condition or situation.

**EXAMPLES**

> [515] ## $a Successive articles are uniquely identified by a manuscript number and date.
> [When individual articles are numbered]
>
> [515] ## $a Articles are added to issues on a continuing basis; issues are complete after six months.
> [When individual issues accrete articles over time]
>
> [515] ## $a Numbering displayed in the language of the interface.
> [546] ## $a Interface available in English, Portuguese, and Spanish.
> [When issue captions vary with language interface: "number" on the English interface, "número" on the Spanish interface, etc.]

## Complete Record Examples

### ONLINE VERSION OF A PRINT SERIAL

[LDR]   01948cas 2200529 a 4500
[005]    20120107121537.0
[006]    m|||||o||m|#|
[007]    cr |||||||||||
[008]    010606c18699999enkwr#pso#####0###aeng#c
[010] ## $a 2005233250
[040] ## $a PIT $b eng $c PIT $d EYM $d OCLCQ $e rda
[022] 0# $a 1476-4687 $1 0028-0836 $y 1476-4679
[035]  ## $a (OCoLC)47076528 $z (OCoLC)41138435 $z (OCoLC)44300001 $z (OCoLC)47076626 $z (OCoLC)47079863 $z (OCoLC)52117460 $z (OCoLC)52308971 $z (OCoLC)60637826
[042] ## $a pcc

[050] 14 $a Q1

[210] 1# $a Nature $b (Basingstoke, Online)

[222] #0 $a Nature $b (Basingstoke. Online)

[245] 10 $a Nature : a weekly illustrated journal of science.

[264] #1 $a London : $b Nature Publishing Group

[310] ## $a Weekly

[336] ## $a text $2 rdacontent

[337] ## $a computer $2 rdamedia

[338] ## $a online resource $2 rdacarrier

[362] 1# $a Published issues: No. 1 (Thursday, November 4, 1869)-

[515] ## $a Some articles published online in advance of the issues containing them.

[525] ## $a Includes supplements.

[580] ## $a Vol. 229-246, Jan. 1971-Dec. 1973, issued in three parts. The two new parts, Nature: new biology, and Nature: physical sciences, continued the volume numbering of Nature in addition to carrying their own issue numbering. With vol. 246, Dec. 1973, Nature: new biology, and Nature: physical science, ceased publication and were absorbed by Nature.

[588] ## $a Description based on: No. 1 (Thursday, November 4, 1869); title from caption (Hathi Trust, viewed Jan. 7, 2011).

[588] ## $a Latest issue consulted: Volume 481, number 7379 (5 January 2012) (publisher's Web site, viewed Jan. 7, 2012).

[650] #0 $a Science $v Periodicals.

[650] #2 $a Science $v Periodicals.

[650] #6 $a Sciences $v Périodiques.

[776] 08 $i Print version: $t Nature $x 0028-0836 $w (DLC) 12037118 $w (OCoLC)1586310

[780] 15 $t Nature: new biology

[780] 15 $t Nature: physical science

[856] 40 $u http://www.nature.com/nature/index.html

[856] 40 $u http://catalog.hathitrust.org/Record/000637680


## NOTES

[no physical description: 300 field absent]

006 [coded data relating to electronic resources]

007/00-01 [category of material / specific material] c = electronic resource / r = remote

008/22-23 [form of original item/form of item] s = electronic / o = online

264 [publication statement] pertains to online version

336 [coded for the predominant content: text (stored in digital form)]

337, 338 [coded for an online resource]

515 [description of numbering peculiarities: articles published in advance of issues]

588 [basis for identification of the resource and title source in a combined note; specific Web site identified and date viewed]
856 [URI for resource] official site and catalog record on Hathi Trust site

## BORN ONLINE

[LDR]  02251cas#a2200493#i#4500
[005]  20100707063747.0
[006]  m|||||o||m|#|
[007]  cr |||||||||||
[008]  071003d20072010enk#x#pso#####0###aeng#c
[010] ## $a 2008204012
[022] ## $a 1754-0410 $1 1754-0410
[035] ## $a (OCoLC)ocn173650008
[040] ## $a CPT $b eng $c CPT $d OCoLC $d DLC $d CaQMU $d OCoLC $e rda
[042] ## $a pcc
[050] 00 $a QC770
[245] 00 $a PMC physics. $n A.
[246] 3# $a PhysMath Central physics. $n A
[246] 3# $a Phys Math Central physics. $n A
[246] 30 $a Physics. $n A
[264] #1 $a London : $b BioMed Central, $c 2007-2010.
[300] ## $a 1 online resource (4 volumes)
[310] ## $a Irregular (articles published individually)
[336] ## $a text $2 rdacontent
[337] ## $a computer $2 rdamedia
[338] ## $a online resource $2 rdacarrier
[362] 1# $a Issues published: 1:1 (2007)-4:1 (2010).
[515] ## $a Numbering identifies individual articles. Following the cessation of the journal, these individual articles remain accessible but links on the journal Web site no longer function; the journal as a whole remains accessible on various aggregator Web sites.
[520] ## $a "PMC Physics A is an international, peer-reviewed, open access journal that publishes articles on high-energy & nuclear physics, cosmology, gravity & astroparticle physics and also the instrumentation & data analysis of results in these areas"—Aims & scope (publisher's Web site, viewed Oct. 3, 2007).
[550] ## $a Sponsored by: CERN; and, DESY.
[588] ## $a Description based on: 1:1 (2007); title from journal home page (publisher's Web site, viewed Oct. 3, 2007).
[588] ## $a Latest issue consulted: 4:1 (2010) (publisher's Web site, viewed Jan. 29, 2008).
[650] #0 $a Nuclear physics $v Periodicals.
[650] #0 $a Particles (Nuclear physics) $v Periodicals.
[650] #6 $a Physique nucléaire $v Périodiques.

[650] #6 $a Particules (Physique nucléaire) $v Périodiques.

[710] 2# $a BioMed Central Ltd.

[710] 2# $a European Organization for Nuclear Research.

[710] 2# $a Deutsches Elektronen-Synchrotron (Center)

[787] 08 $i Complemented by: $t PMC physics. B $x 1754-0429

[850] ## $a DLC

[856] 40 $u www.biomedcentral.com/1754-0410/1/1

[856] 40 $u http://journals.academia.edu/PmcPhysicsA

## NOTES

006 [coded data relating to electronic resources]

007/00-01 [category of material / specific material] c = electronic resource / r = remote

008/22-23 [form of original item/form of item] s = electronic / o = online

310 [frequency describes article-by-article publication]

336 [coded for the predominant content: text (stored in digital form)]

337, 338 [coded for an online resource]

362 [numbering identifies articles]

515 [description of numbering peculiarities and post mortem access peculiarities]

520 [quoted note cites location, specific Web site, and date viewed]

588 [basis for identification of the resource and title source in a combined note; specific Web site identified and date viewed]

856 [URI for resource] official site (no longer giving journal-level access) and additional site giving journal-level access

# 7. ONGOING INTEGRATING RESOURCES

As a term, *integrating resources* made its official appearance in the 2002 revision of AACR2, when it was used to describe "a bibliographic resource that is added to or changed by means of updates that do not remain discrete and are integrated into the whole." Rules for describing integrating resources were added to chapter 12, which had formerly been restricted to serials. The introduction to the revised chapter noted that, though included in this chapter for "continuing" resources, integrating resources could be either finite or continuing in nature.

Integrating resources can be divided into two classes:

1. Print integrating resources (updating loose-leaf publications, though also applicable to any updating manual file such as a card file)
2. Online integrating resources (websites and components of websites that update in an integrating fashion, databases)

A third class existed briefly toward the end of the twentieth century: computer-output microfiche products comprising a base file of records and various indexes to those records. The indexes were updated on various schedules and always pointed to the latest image of a given record. This was an especially popular method for presenting library catalogs in the transitional period between card catalogs and online catalogs. Major examples were the National Union Catalog on microfiche, the CONSER microfiche, and the ISDS Register. Such products are now mainly of historical interest.

A fourth class is the manuscript. In fact, "integrating resource" is the natural state of a manuscript until its author shouts "Enough!" and stops revising it. Libraries and archives typically collect manuscripts that have ceased being updated, their original existence as integrating resources evident only from the crossed-out and inserted text.

In library cataloging, prior to online resources, the typical integrating resource was in print: the updating loose-leaf publication. Until the revision of AACR2 chapter 12 (serials), these publications were noteworthy for two exceptional cataloging practices:

1. In the physical description area, loose-leaf volumes were identified as such and recorded separately from bound volumes and transfer volumes.
2. If an updated title page was issued, then the bibliographic description was revised to reflect this. Important information from earlier title pages was retained in notes and added entries.

The arrival of online integrating resources disturbed this tranquil scene and led to the revision of chapter 12. As more and more print resources developed an online presence, many were transformed from a serial mode of issuance into an integrated mode. Although the process was accelerated by the expansion of the World Wide Web in the early 1990s, it actually predated it. Among the first library resources to develop an online presence were various abstracting and indexing services, many of them collected by early information retrieval services such as Lockheed's DIALOG and SDC's ORBIT. Services that published frequent paper issues, with larger cumulations coming out at various intervals, were accessible online as integrated databases. Users were able to search everything at once rather than carrying out the same search repeatedly in successive issues and cumulations.

As the World Wide Web has matured, online integrating resources have become more elaborate, many retaining serial components within a larger context that is increasingly one of databases and queries. Examples of these are the websites of government statistical agencies such as those of the US Census Bureau and the US Bureau of Labor Statistics, encompassing online versions of thousands of print publications even as their primary focus shifts from the publications themselves to the increasingly complex and interrelated databases that feed into those publications.

This chapter addresses the two classes of integrating resources—print and online—in turn, focusing upon the ways in which their cataloging differs from that of serials.

In terms of the FRBR conceptual model (and so RDA), the distinction between a serial and an integrating resource occurs at the work level, since a serial may include content that has been removed from the corresponding integrating resource and conversely may lack content later added to the integrating resource. Also, due to different means for handling title changes, successive serial descriptions (reflecting successive major title changes) may correspond to a single integrating resource description.

Note that integrating resources can be of limited duration; for example, a manual that will eventually be replaced by a new edition but is kept up to date by replacement pages in the interim. These are in the domain of the monograph cataloger. Here we are only interested in ongoing integrating resources, those serial-like resources intended to be kept up to date indefinitely.

This chapter will not address the diverting question of whether and when to catalog Web resources. That is best left to collection development staff at individual institutions.

## Cataloging Ongoing Integrating Resources vs. Cataloging Serials

There are only two major points one has to make about cataloging ongoing integrating resources:

- Unlike serials, the description is based on the *latest* iteration, not the *earliest* issue
- Unlike serials, when the title or responsible body changes, the existing description and authorized access point for the work are simply *revised* to reflect this [RDA 6.1.3.3.1–6.1.3.3.2]. Important information relating to earlier titles and responsible bodies is retained in notes and access points.

Note that changes in responsibility affecting the authorized access point for the work includes changes in the authorized access point for the creator (MARC 21 [1XX]) and changes in any name used as a parenthetical addition to the preferred title of the work (in MARC 21 [130] or [240]) [RDA 6.1.3.3.1]).

## Is This Resource a Serial or an Integrating Resource?

The key distinction between serials and integrating resources is whether or not new content remains discrete. If a database is issued on CD-ROMs or some other physical medium, and each issue represents a new version of the complete database, it is cataloged as a serial because the CD-ROMs are issued as discrete objects and remain discrete. Because their parts remain discrete, they are prone to be individually identified for inventory control and may be cited individually in the relevant literature. Consequently, they are best adapted to serial treatment.

In theory, one can keep the updates to an integrating loose-leaf discrete. In fact, updates to government manuals placed on deposit in a library are often treated in this manner because (a) that's the way they're received and (b) it's a pain to update the manuals, given the amount of effort involved and the low likelihood of use. However, just because one can treat an integrating resource as a serial doesn't mean it should be treated as a serial. Such resources should still be cataloged as integrating resources, though a local note should be added to warn the user that the updates are not integrated into the resource.

In rare instances, a journal published in discrete issues in print may become an integrating resource online if the articles are not collected into issues in the online version. If the journal website does not provide an easy means to present articles gathered into discrete issues, it should be cataloged as an integrating resource.

What constitutes an easy means? Typically, the default presentation for the journal will be in the form of issues, whether as a menu list of volumes and issues (common with scholarly journals) or a sequence of cover images (the default mode with Google magazines and newspapers).

Of course, for resources published online first, the situation is reversed, with articles published first on a website subsequently collected together to produce a serial print issue. Online, the articles may be revised, corrected, etc. (sort of an integrating resource within an integrating resource), in contrast to the static article that is published in print. For this reason, for example, online articles in the *New York Times* frequently end with the statement, "A version of this article appeared in print on [date], on page [page number] of the [edition name] edition with the headline: [headline]." In contrast to the discrete issues of the print edition, the online newspaper will contain a search box for finding articles not on the home page (including older articles). Additionally, online newspapers and newsmagazines will often bring together the content from multiple individual print editions, giving readers access to the editions in the form of particular arrangements of the consolidated content (such as favoring items with a particular regional emphasis).

## Is This Integrating Resource the Same as That Integrating Resource?

A major problem when cataloging a new integrating resource is that the cataloger may not recognize previous versions cataloged under earlier titles as the same resource. Fortunately, at least for online integrating resources, there is a tool to help supply this missing knowledge: the Internet Archive's Wayback Machine, www.archive.org/web/web.php. The Wayback Machine has been archiving hundreds of billions of Web pages since 1996, thus providing catalogers with snapshots of previous iterations of a given online resource. Simply enter a URL in the Wayback Machine's search box and click on the "take me back" button. You'll be presented with a hyperlinked calendar of all the available past snapshots of that website. (Of course, if the URL has changed, you're on your own.)

## At What Level of Analysis Should an Online Integrating Resource Be Cataloged?

Websites are infinitely extensible, so it is important to identify the object that is of most interest to one's users. For example, the website of the Bureau of Labor Statistics (BLS) is immensely complex, in some ways a world unto itself. Many publications that have a long history in print are brought together online with related materials. For example, should one catalog individual publications? This would probably be wise, if only to provide a connection between versions in print and online. BLS also supplies discrete websites for each of its publications—*Monthly Labor Review, Occupational Outlook Quarterly,* etc.—and these online versions are bona fide serials, organized by issue. On the other hand, some publications have been augmented online to such an extent that the publication may be less useful as a focus of the cataloging than the larger website that provides a context for it. For example, the Consumer Price Index page on the BLS website includes not just the online versions of the monthly print *CPI Detailed Report,* but a wealth of related resources: news releases, databases, an inflation calculator, tables, related publications, and FAQs. In such cases, it may be useful to ask the question: "Is the added cost associated with analyzing the resources accessible via the website—all of which in this case deal specifically with the Consumer Price Index—justified by the benefit that this level of access would provide? Or would it just create the equivalent of 'noise' in the catalog?" In many cases, individual resources (component parts) can be sufficiently identified by means of additional access points associated with the description of the larger resource, or a URL and note added to the description of the corresponding print resource.

In the end, these are all questions the individual cataloger must struggle with in the particular instance, an ongoing cost-benefit analysis.

## The Nitty-Gritty

The following instructions relate to those points on which cataloging an ongoing integrating resource differs from cataloging a serial.

## MARC 21 CODING (LEADER / 008)
- LDR/06 [bibliographic level] = i (integrating resource)
- 008/18-19 [frequency and regularity] = code for frequency and regularity of updating
- 008/21 [type of continuing resource]
  - Updating database = d
  - Updating loose-leaf = 1
  - Updating website = w
  - Updating other stuff = #
- 008/34 [entry convention] = 2 (integrated entry)

## BIBLIOGRAPHIC DESCRIPTION (TRANSCRIBED DATA)

Data transcribed in ISBD areas 1, 2, 4, and 6 (MARC 21 fields [245], [250], [264], [490]) should describe the latest available iteration of the resource. Although RDA provides instructions on this matter under each affected element, the instructions are essentially the same for each element and can be summarized as follows:

- If data to be recorded in a given element changes on a subsequent iteration of the resource, including the addition and deletion of data, change the data in the corresponding element to reflect this, ensuring that the data recorded represents the data as it appears on the latest available iteration.
- If considered to be important for identification or access, retain the earlier data, using the appropriate RDA element and MARC 21 field. When available, record any dates associated with this earlier data, enclosing a date in angle brackets when it is not known to be the earliest and/or latest such date. For online resources, these dates represent dates viewed. If data changes multiple times, record the changes in chronological order.
  - For earlier titles proper, use the *earlier title proper* element [247]
  - For earlier parallel titles proper, earlier other title information, and earlier other titles, use the *variant title* element [246]
  - For earlier persons or corporate bodies named in the statement of responsibility, formulate an appropriate note using [550] and, as necessary, an authorized access point for the person ([700]) or corporate body ([710]/[711])
  - For earlier edition statements, use a note [500]
  - For earlier publication, distribution, etc., data, use [264] with an appropriate first indicator value, and, as necessary, an authorized access point for the publisher, distributor, etc. ([710]/[711])
- If not considered to be important for identification or access, either ignore the earlier data or mention the change in a note [500], whichever seems most appropriate.

### EXAMPLES

[245] 00 $a Federal income taxation of intellectual properties and intangible assets.
[247] 10 $t Taxation of intangible assets $f 1997-1998

[245] 00 $a Washington state newsstand.
[247] 10 $t Washington newspapers database $f <Oct. 6, 1999>
Earlier title proper viewed October 6, 1999.

[245] 00 $a Managing environmental liability.
[247] 10 $t Environmental liability $f 1990-2001

[245] 00 $a Infobel world telephone directories.
[247] 10 $t Euroinfo international $f <May, 10, 1998>

[247] 10 $t Telephone directories international $f <Sept. 9, 1999>

Earlier titles proper viewed May 10, 1998 and September 9, 1999 respectively.

[500] ## $a Edition statement varies slightly.

Variations in the edition statement are numerous but not considered important for identification or access.

## PREDOMINANT FORM OF CONTENT (MARC 21)

Remember to code the type of record [LDR/06] for the predominant form of the content. In general, this will mean code *a,* since all loose-leaf publications and most websites are textual. However, use code *m* for online services, software (including programs, games, fonts), and materials that can be manipulated by computer program, such as spreadsheets and databases. (While texts can also often be manipulated by computer program—much to the annoyance of instructors asking students for original research—this is not their primary purpose.)

## BASIS FOR IDENTIFYING THE RESOURCE

For an integrating resource, the basis for identifying the resource is *a source of information identifying the current iteration of the resource as a whole* [RDA 2.1.2.4]. For a loose-leaf publication, this is the current version of the title page; for an online resource, this is the current version of the home page.

## OMISSIONS FROM THE TITLE PROPER

Remember not to transcribe words that serve as an introduction and are not intended to be part of the title [RDA 2.3.1.6].

### EXAMPLE

On resource: Welcome to Oklahoma's official Web site

[245] 00 $a Oklahoma's official Web site.

## FREQUENCY OF UPDATING

The frequency of updating is recorded in the same way as frequency of publication, but it should be made clear that the activity being described is updating [RDA 2.5.2.5, RDA 2.20.12.3–2.20.12.4].

### EXAMPLES

[310] ## $a Updated daily, except weekends

[310] ## $a Continually updated

Use "continually updated" only for resources that are known to update their content more frequently than daily, such as the websites of news organizations, stock market reporting services, etc.

[310] ## $a Frequently updated

[310] ## $a No longer updated

[310] ## $a Frequency of updates varies

## NOTES (GENERAL CAVEAT)

In general, do not make notes on minor attributes of the resource that may prove to be unstable, such as a particular file format.

## NOTE ON A SUSPENSION OF UPDATING

Make a note on a suspension of updating if considered to be important.

### EXAMPLE

[515] ## $a No updates issued from 1999 to 2001.

## NOTE ON THE ITERATION USED AS THE BASIS FOR THE IDENTIFICATION OF THE RESOURCE [RDA 2.20.13.4]

This note is used for updating loose-leafs. Although RDA 2.20.13.4 uses the formula "Identification of the resource based on: [designation of iteration]," continue to use the current formula, which uses a single note to identify both the iteration and the source of the title proper (when other than the title page; cf. RDA 2.20.2.3): "Description based on: [designation of iteration]; title from [source]." For online resources, include the date viewed [RDA 2.20.13.5].

Note that the "title from [source]" portion of the note is only needed for updating loose-leaf publications and online integrating resources consisting of images of multiple pages, leaves, sheets, etc., and then only if the title is taken from a source other than the title page [RDA 2.20.2.3].

If describing an online resource available from multiple sources, precede the date viewed by an indication of the source used.

### EXAMPLES

[588] ## $a Description based on 1994 ed. through update 10.

For an updating loose-leaf.

[588] ## $a Description based on version consulted Oct. 26, 2000.

For an online integrating resource.

[588] ## $a Description based on EBSCOhost version, viewed on Oct. 21, 1999.

For an online integrating resource available via multiple channels.

## RELATIONSHIPS

In the context of the relationships given in appendix J, only two sequential relationship pairs apply to ongoing integrating resources: supersedes (work) / superseded by (work) and supersedes in part (work) / superseded in part by (work) [RDA J.2.6]. These are coded in MARC 21 as 780 / 785 with a second indicator value of 2 (supersedes / superseded by) or 3 (supersedes in part / superseded in part by).

## Complete Record Examples

### PRINT (UPDATING LOOSE-LEAF)

[LDR]   00907cai#a2200277#i#4500
[001] 12368693
[005] 20011116134851.0
[008] 010403c19799999iluer#1 ##v####0###a2eng#
[010] ## $a 79122269
[040] ## $a DLC $b eng $c DLC $e rda
[043] ## $a n-us—-
[050] 00 $a KF1520 $b .C65 1979
[245] 00 $a Bankruptcy law reporter.
[264] 31 $a Chicago, IL : $b CCH Incorporated, $c c1979-
[300] ## $a volumes (loose-leaf), volumes (transfer) ; $c 25 cm
[310] ## $a Updated biweekly
[336] ## $a text $2 rdacontent
[337] ## $a unmediated $2 rdamedia
[338] ## $a volume $2 rdacarrier
[362] 1# $a Began in 1979.
[490] 1# $a Topical law reports
[588] ## $a Description based on: Number 830 (May 23, 2011).
[650] #0 $a Bankruptcy $z United States.
[650] #0 $a Bankruptcy $z United States $v Cases.
[710] 2# $a Commerce Clearing House.
[830] #0 $a Topical law reports (Commerce Clearing House)

### NOTES

LDR/06 [bibliographic level] i = integrating resource
008/18-19 and 310 [frequency (and regularity) of updating] e = biweekly / r = regular
008/21 [type of continuing resource] 1= updating loose-leaf
008/34 [entry convention] 2 = integrated entry
588 [basis for identification of the resource and title source in a combined note]

### MICROFORM (UPDATING MICROFICHE)

[LDR]   02431cai#a2200589#i#4500

[001]    11435533
[005]    20100311071115.0
[007]    he bmu—-buuu
[008]    790816d197819940ncar##bbb###f0###a2eng c
[010]    $a 94640682 $z ce 81079000
[016]    $a 810790009E
[016] 7# $a C45865500 $2 DNLM
[022] ## $a 0707-3747 $1 0707-3747 $2 4
[035] ## $a (OCoLC)ocm05279340
[040] ## $a NcD $b eng $c NcD $d DNLM $d OCoLC $d NSDP $d CaOONL $e rda
[041] 0# $a eng $a fre
[042] ## $a nlc $a isds/c $a pcc
[050] 00 $a Microfiche (o) 94/4561
[050] 14 $a Z6945 $b .C65
[060] 0# $a Z 6945 C753
[082] 00 $a 011/.34 $2 20
[210] 0# $a CONSER microfiche
[222] #0 $a CONSER microfiche
[245] 00 $a CONSER microfiche.
[246] 3# $a NLC/BNC CONSER/microfiche
[246] 30 $a NLC BNC CONSER microfiche
[246] 13 $a NLC/BNC CONSER microfiche
[264] 31 $a Ottawa : $b National Library of Canada, $c 1979-[1995].
[264] 32 $a [Washington, D.C.] : $b Distributed in the U.S. by the Library of Congress
[300] ## $a microfiches : |b negative.
[310] ## $a Updated annually
[336] ## $a text $2 rdacontent
[337] ## $a microform $2 rdamedia
[338] ## $a microfiche $2 rdacarrier
[362] 0# $a 1975/1978-
[362] 1# $a Ceased with 1994 issue.
[520] ## $a "A computer-output-microfiche listing of serial records created in the CONSER Project and authenticated by the National Library of Canada and the Library of Congress . . . [Base file] updated by supplements . . . consisting of added or changed register entries and cumulated indexes to [the most current version of] all authenticated records listed to date."
[588] ## $a Description based on: 1975/1978; title from eye-readable header.
[546] ## $a Text in English and French.
[650] #0 $a Periodicals $v Bibliography $v Periodicals.
[650] #0 $a Serial publications $v Bibliography $v Periodicals.
[610] 20 $a CONSER Program $v Bibliography $v Periodicals.
[650] #2 $a Union catalogs $z Canada.
[650] #2 $a Union catalogs $z United States.

[650] #2 $a Periodicals $v Bibliography $v Union Lists.
[710] 2# $a National Library of Canada.
[710] 2# $a Library of Congress.

## NOTES

LDR/06 [bibliographic level] i = integrating resource
008/18-19 and 310 [frequency (and regularity) of updating] a = annual / r = regular
008/21 [type of continuing resource] # = [none of the listed types]
008/34 [entry convention] 2 = integrated entry
588 [basis for identification of the resource and title source in a combined note]
Description was based on first iteration (base file) and was not revised since the descriptive data did not change.

## ONLINE (UPDATING DATABASE)

[LDR]   04362cai#a2200793#i#4500
[001]   13830248
[005]   20110910155706.0
[006]   m|||||o||e|f|
[007]   cr|||||||||||
[008]   050104c20009999mdu#x#doo#a##f0#a2eng c
[010] ## $a 2010228778 $z 2005567200 $z 2009219062
[016] 7# $a 101568487 $2 DNLM
[035] ## $a (OCoLC)ocm61201073
[037] ## $b Address: NCBI, NLM, 8600 Rockville Pike, Bldg. 38A, Bethesda, MD 20894
[040] ## $a N@F $b eng $c N@F $d DNLM $e rda
[042] ## $a pcc
[050] 00 $a R11
[060] 10 $a ZWB 100
[074] ## $a 0508-F-06 (online)
[082] 04 $a 025.174
[082] 04 $a 570
[082] 04 $a 610.7
[086] 0# $a HE 20.3627/2:
[245] 00 $a PMC / $c US National Library of Medicine, National Institutes of Health.
[247] 10 $a PubMed central : $b an archive of life science journals $f 2000-<Sept. 6, 2011>
[246] 30 $a Archive of life science journals
[246] 1# $i Title in HTML header: $a Home—PubMed—NCBI
[264] 31 $a Bethesda, MD, USA : $b National Center for Biotechnology Information, U.S. National Library of Medicine, $c [2000]-

[310] ## $a Updated frequently

[336] ## $a text $2 rdacontent

[337] ## $a computer $2 rdamedia

[338] ## $a online resource $2 rdacarrier

[516] 8# $a Digital archive, searchable database.

[520] ## $a "PubMed Central® (PMC) is a free archive of biomedical and life sciences journal literature at the U.S. National Institutes of Health's National Library of Medicine (NIH/NLM). In keeping with NLM's legislative mandate to collect and preserve the biomedical literature, PMC serves as a digital counterpart to NLM's extensive print journal collection. Launched in February 2000, PMC was developed and is managed by NLM's National Center for Biotechnology Information (NCBI)."

[588] ## $a Description based on last update: December 7, 2011; title from home page (viewed Dec. 31, 2011).

[610] 20 $a National Library of Medicine (U.S.) $x Periodicals $v Indexes.

[610] 22 $a National Library of Medicine (U.S.)

[650] #0 $a Medicine $v Abstracts.

[650] #0 $a Medicine $x Periodicals $v Indexes.

[650] #0 $a Life sciences $v Abstracts.

[650] #0 $a Life sciences $v Periodicals $v Indexes.

[650] #0 $a Life sciences literature.

[650] #0 $a Medical literature.

[651] #0 $a United States.

[650] 12 $a Clinical Medicine $v Abstracts $v Database.

[650] 12 $a Clinical Medicine $v Indexes $v Database.

[650] 12 $a Medicine $v Abstracts $v Database.

[650] 12 $a Medicine $v Indexes $v Database.

[650] 22 $a Bioethics $v Abstracts $v Database.

[650] 22 $a Bioethics $v Indexes $v Database.

[650] 22 $a Biological Science Disciplines $v Abstracts $v Database.

[650] 22 $a Biological Science Disciplines $v Indexes $v Database.

[650] 22 $a Dentistry $v Abstracts $v Database.

[650] 22 $a Dentistry $v Indexes $v Database.

[650] 22 $a Ethics, Medical $v Abstracts $v Database.

[650] 22 $a Ethics, Medical $v Indexes $v Database.

[650] 22 $a Nursing $v Abstracts $v Database.

[650] 22 $a Nursing $v Indexes $v Database.

[710] 2# $a National Library of Medicine (U.S.)

[710] 2# $a National Center for Biotechnology Information (U.S.)

[856] 40 $u http://www.ncbi.nlm.nih.gov/pubmed/

**NOTES**

LDR/06 [bibliographic level] i = integrating resource

008/18-19 and 310 [frequency (and regularity) of updating] # = no specified frequency / x = irregular

008/21 [type of continuing resource] d = updating database

008/34 [entry convention] 2 = integrated entry

247 [earlier title proper and associated dates, including most recent date viewed]

588 [basis for identification of the resource and title source in a combined note] Description based on iteration visible on latest date viewed.

**ONLINE (UPDATING WEBSITE)**

[LDR]    02395cai#a2200313#i#4500

[001]    14512638

[005]    20090616143308.0

[006]    m|||||o||m|f|

[007]    cr |||||||||||

[008]    060822c19949999dcu#x#w#o#####f0#a2eng##

[010] ## $a 2006586290 $z 2002564472 $z 00529706

[040] ## $a DLC $b eng $c DLC $d DLC $e rda

[042] ## $a pcc

[043] ## $a n-us—-

[050] 00 $a E173

[245] 00 $a American memory.

[246] 13 $a American memory home

[246] 1# $i Title in HTML header: $a American memory from the Library of Congress—home page

[264] 31 $a [Washington, DC] : |b Library of Congress, |c [1994]-

[310] ## $a Updated frequently

[336] ## $a text $2 rdacontent

[337] ## $a computer $2 rdamedia

[338] ## $a online resource $2 rdacarrier

[588] ## $a Title from home page (viewed on June 27, 2002).

[520] ## $a "American Memory is a multimedia web site of digitized historical documents, photographs, sound recordings, moving pictures, books, pamphlets, maps, and other resources from the Library of Congress's vast holdings. A historic initiative in its own right, American Memory currently makes available more than 100 collections and more than 9 million individual items to users in the U.S. and throughout the world."

[651] #0 $a United States $x History $v Sources.

[710] 2# $a Library of Congress.

[856] 40 $u http://memory.loc.gov

**NOTES**

LDR/06 [bibliographic level] i = integrating resource

008/18-19 and 310 [frequency (and regularity) of updating] # = no specified frequency / x = irregular

008/21 [type of continuing resource] w = updating website

008/34 [entry convention] 2 = integrated entry

336 [content type] text (content type applying to predominant part of resource [RDA 6.9.1.3 Alternative])

588 [basis for identification of the resource and title source in a combined note] Description based on iteration identified by "last updated" date.

---

**NOTES**

1. *IFLA Cataloguing Principles: Statement of International Cataloguing Principles (ICP) and Its Glossary*, ed. Barbara Tillett (München: K. G. Saur, 2009), principle 5.3 and footnote 11, www.ifla.org/files/cataloguing/icp/icp_2009-en.pdf.

2. Joint Steering Committee for the Revision of AACR, "RDA Implementation Scenarios," 5JSC/Editor/2, last modified January 14, 2007, www.rda-jsc.org /docs/5editor2.pdf.

3. "Transforming Our Bibliographic Framework: A Statement from the Library of Congress," last modified May 13, 2011, www.loc.gov/marc/transition/news /framework-051311.html.

4. Margaret F. Maxwell, *Handbook for AACR2* (Chicago and London: American Library Association, 1980); Margaret F. Maxwell, *Handbook for AACR2 1988 Revision* (Chicago and London: American Library Association, 1989 [reprinted with updates, 1993]); Robert L. Maxwell with Margaret F. Maxwell, *Maxwell's Handbook for AACR2R* (Chicago and London: American Library Association, 1997); Robert L. Maxwell, *Maxwell's Handbook for AACR2*. 4th ed. (Chicago and London: American Library Association, 2004).

5. Library of Congress, Network Development and MARC Standards Office, *MARC Code List for Countries,* 2003 ed., continually updated, www.loc.gov/marc/countries/.

6. Library of Congress, Network Development and MARC Standards Office, *MARC Code List for Languages,* 2007 ed., continually updated, www.loc.gov/marc/languages/.

7. Library of Congress, Network Development and MARC Standards Office, *MARC 21 Specifications for Record Structure, Character Sets, and Exchange Media. Character Sets and Encoding Options. Part 5, MARC-8 Code Tables,* last modified December 2007, www.loc.gov/marc/specifications/specchartables.html.

8. Most libraries in the United States have not followed AACR2 in this regard, continuing instead an older practice of describing the original and recording details relating to the reproduction in a note.

9. Joint Steering Committee for Revision of AACR, "RDA/ONIX Framework for Resource Categorization, Version 1.0," 5JSC/Chair/10 (last modified August 1, 2006, www.loc.gov/marc/marbi/2007/5chair10.pdf.

10. Library of Congress, Network Development and MARC Standards Office, *Term and Code List for RDA Content Types,* last modified April 5, 2011, www.loc.gov/standards /valuelist/rdacontent.html.

11. Library of Congress, Network Development and MARC Standards Office, *Term and Code List for RDA Media Types,* www.loc.gov/standards/valuelist/rdamedia.html.

12. "The ISSN Register," www.issn.org/2–22639-The-ISSN-Register.php (subscription required).

13. Ibid.

14. Library of Congress, Network Development and MARC Standards Office, *Term and Code List for RDA Carrier Types,* last modified March 5, 2012, www.loc.gov /standards/valuelist/rdacarrier.html.

15. Library of Congress, Network Development and MARC Standards Office, MARC 21 Format for Bibliographic Data, 1999 ed., regularly updated, www.loc.gov/marc/ bibliographic/.

16. Thanks to John Levy at the Library of Congress for supplying these numbers.

17. Library of Congress, Network Development and MARC Standards Office, *MARC Code List for Languages.*

18. Library of Congress catalogers will not be adding authority record control numbers to RDA records. It is anticipated that these will eventually be machine-generated; cf. *MARC 21 Encoding to Accommodate RDA Elements: LC Practice for the RDA Test: Original Cataloging* (Training Document #5), www.loc.gov/catdir/cpso/RDAtest /training2word8.doc.

# RDA AND
# LINKED DATA

**HIS MANUAL HAS BEEN WRITTEN FOR USE IN THE** environment of independent bibliographic and authority records known as RDA implementation scenario 3, using MARC 21 as its default record syntax. MARC 21 is also able to support RDA implementation scenario 2, which enables machine links between these records.

But MARC 21 will not be able to support RDA implementation scenario 1, an environment where rather than MARC records there will be aggregations of structured "linked data" representing, for example, instances of the several FRBR entities (work, expression, manifestation, person, family, etc.). That scenario still lies in the future.

Before venturing into that future, a caveat: Most people are terrible at predicting the future, and librarians are no exception. As evidence, we need only look back to a paper delivered by one of the titans of the profession, Charles Ammi Cutter, at the 1883 conference of the American Library Association in Buffalo, New York. There, Cutter bravely (or recklessly, depending on one's point of view) held forth on what it would be like to work in the Buffalo Public Library a hundred years hence.

According to Cutter, in 1983 the Buffalo Public Library building would be sensibly set back from the street to protect it from the "clatter" of traffic. (Clip-clop, clip-clop.) A researcher would no longer need wait for books to arrive from distant libraries, since the marvel of the telephone meant that a remote librarian would be able to *read* the relevant passages over the phone. (For longer passages, the librarian would mail the researcher a recorded reading on "foil," Edison's original recording medium.) Finally—and most important to Cutter—the physical environment of each reading room would be controlled by its own "thermometers and hygrometers and atmosferometers," their dials constantly monitored by the reading room librarians.[1]

Cutter's vision of 1983 appears strange to someone like me who actually *experienced* 1983. But I'm sure it would be familiar to my daughter, a devotee of steampunk (that genre of science fiction/fantasy where the future is dominated by steam power and elaborate mechanical devices). In fact Cutter's 1983 resembles nothing so much as 1883 on steroids.

So bearing in mind this all-too-common tendency to see in the future only a much-improved present, please take the following vision of our linked-data future with an appropriate measure of salt.

The purpose of this epilogue is to provide a very general overview of linked data, what it is, what it does, the role it may play in the future of bibliographic data, and the challenges it faces in getting from here to there.

## LINKED DATA AND THE SEMANTIC WEB

So what is linked data? In very simple terms, it's an attempt to do for data what the World Wide Web has done for documents. The idea was introduced to the broad public in an article in the May 2001 issue of *Scientific American*. There Tim Berners-Lee, the inventor of the World Wide Web, described a new extension of the web that he called the Semantic Web.[2] This new web would enable the linking of individual pieces of data into a "web of data" across which it would be possible to perform all sorts of complex calculations.

Berners-Lee made his case for this Semantic Web by describing what he hoped it would do. He took a case in which two people with very busy schedules were trying to make a medical appointment for their mother. In Berners-Lee's vision, they were able to use unobtrusive pieces of software called *intelligent agents* to navigate a rich "web of data" and seamlessly accomplish their joint task, bringing into perfect alignment: (1) their busy schedules, (2) the medical procedure needed by their mother, and (3) the equally busy schedules of the subset of medical providers who both (a) participated in their mother's health plan and (b) were able to perform the required procedure. (Actually, it was even more complex, but needless to say, the intelligent agents performed flawlessly, making anyone who has ever tried to schedule a medical appointment of any kind green with envy.)

More than a decade later, there has been a great deal of progress designing structures that can support this Semantic Web, structures that one hopes will ultimately enable the sort of complex interactions between diffuse data stores that Berners-Lee envisaged in 2001. But we're not there yet. Such a world still remains seemingly just out of reach, at least for those of us without smartphones.

But work is progressing, because various communities see advantages in the Semantic Web for their business models. These communities—including our own broad community of cultural heritage institutions (libraries, archives, and museums)—have been busy preparing the data under their control to function better in this world of linked data. And a lot of data—especially library-related data—has now been "exposed" as linked data on the Web. An increasing awareness of all this activity provided some of the impetus for the reorganization of the RDA draft in 2007, to make it more linked-data-friendly.[3]

In conjunction with this reorganization, in the spring of 2007 the British Library (BL) hosted a Data Model Meeting that examined RDA in the context of linked data and included representatives from the Dublin Core Metadata Initiative (DCMI).[4] DCMI was one of the early actors in the effort to develop the Semantic Web and in this context had already created core metadata vocabularies for resource management and discovery, including the eponymous Dublin Core. The participants at the BL meeting agreed that the RDA Committee of Principals and DCMI should work together to:

- Develop an RDA Element Vocabulary
- Develop an RDA Application Profile based on the Dublin Core Abstract Model (DCAM) and the FRBR and FRAD conceptual models
- Disclose RDA Value Vocabularies using RDF, RDF Schema, and SKOS

The BL meeting resulted in the creation of a DCMI/RDA Task Group "to define components of [RDA] as an RDF vocabulary for use in developing a Dublin Core application profile."[5] The task group has since been reconstituted as the Bibliographic Metadata Task Group and its charge broadened to defining "components of current and emerging library, publishing, and related bibliographic standards as RDF vocabularies for use in Dublin Core application profiles and semantic mappings."[6] Among these vocabularies are those RDA element vocabularies and value vocabularies mentioned above. RDA element vocabularies include FRBR entities for RDA, RDA Group 1, 2, and 3 elements, RDA relationships for Group 1 entities, and RDA roles. RDA value vocabularies identify the values—in general taken from RDA—that are valid for a given element. FRBR entities (classes) are defined in the FRBR Entities for RDA element set, while the attributes (properties) of these entities are defined in the three sets of Group 1, 2, and 3 elements, and the relationships among them (also properties) are defined in the RDA Relationships element sets.[7] (At the time the RDA element sets were created, there were no official FRBR element sets. These have since been created, and equivalences will now be established between elements in those sets and the corresponding elements in the RDA sets.[8])

All this constitutes the contribution of RDA to the web of linked data. One can get some sense of the extent of this web—at least in terms of discrete data collections—from the Linking Open Data cloud diagram at http://lod-cloud.net. At its core is DBpedia, a linked-data rendering of some structured information extracted from

Wikipedia articles. DBpedia calls itself "the nucleus of the web of data."[9] Other organizations are making commitments similar to those made for RDA.

But putting a lot of data out there is just one step. For linked data to flourish it must be linked, and this takes a bit more work.

## HOW DOES IT WORK?

Before proceeding further, let me assure you that what I am about to describe is what happens behind the scenes, under the hood/bonnet. It is *not* what you will encounter as a cataloger, any more than in today's environment you would encounter a raw MARC 21 record, which is a very ugly thing indeed. (What you see in OCLC, etc., is the cleaned-up user-friendly version.) As a cataloger, you will probably operate in a very *comfortable* environment, selecting elements (or groups of elements) from drop-down menus, typing a term and having it completed automatically—the sorts of things you've come to expect when working on the Web. The discussion that follows is to help you understand what's really going on underneath all that. You can read this, say to yourself "I see" (or not), and promptly file it away as interesting but not crucial to everyday existence. After all, you can drive a car without having been trained as an auto mechanic.

So how does linked data work? Basically, it works by publishing structured data so that machines can use it to do many of the things humans have done with unlinked data in the past. In theory, it's deceptively simple. For example, Berners-Lee reduces its best practices to four rules:[10]

1. Use URIs (uniform resource identifiers) as names for things.
2. Use HTTP URIs (essentially URLs) so that people can look up those names.
3. When someone looks up a URI, provide useful information, using standards.
4. Include links to other URIs, so that they can discover more things.

In practice, it has been easier to comply with the first three rules than the last. This is largely because complying with the first three rules can be accomplished by machine, at least so long as the data involved is well-formed and adheres to a defined structure (schema) and can be transformed into RDF—Resource Description Framework, the basic metadata structure of the Semantic Web—in one of its serialization syntaxes such as RDF/XML.[11] The last rule, however, requires the commitment of many more resources, so those links to other URIs will be built up slowly over time. Much depends on mapping from one schema to another, with its inherent fuzziness (see "Inference and Matching across Domains," below).

RDF is the basic language of linked data, and the fundamental expression in RDF is the *statement* or *triple,* consisting of a *subject, predicate,* and *object.* Ideally, all three are represented by HTTP URIs (adhering to Berners-Lee's rules 1–3), though objects must sometimes be represented by literals (plain text) when they represent elements without a controlled vocabulary (such as transcribed bibliographic data) or data outside the values in a so-called open vocabulary (a vocabulary identifying some, but not all, of its possible values).

RDF *subjects* are instances of a *class*. A FRBR entity such as *work* is an example of a class. Dante's *Divine Comedy* would be an instance of this class, as would the anonymous *Ethel the Aardvark Goes Quantity Surveying*. RDF subjects should always be identified by an HTTP URI, and for the time being URIs based on MARC record control numbers are a popular choice.

The *subject* of an RDF triple is followed by the *predicate* (*property*), which in our context may represent an RDA element (typically a FRBR attribute or relationship). Predicates are also represented by HTTP URIs, in this case drawn from the RDA element vocabulary (already referred to) or from a useful external vocabulary such as the Bibliographic Ontology (bibo) or Friend of a Friend (foaf).

The *predicate* is followed by the *object,* which contains either a literal (plain text) or an HTTP URI drawn from a vocabulary such as one of the RDA vocabularies (if the predicate represents a FRBR attribute) or from a dataset (if it represents a FRBR relationship with another entity). In the latter case, the URI would again likely be based (for now) on a MARC record control number.

Two simple (but hopefully illuminating) RDA examples are given below, each consisting of an RDF triple (subject, predicate, and object). The first identifies an attribute of an entity while the second identifies a relationship.

## Example 1 (Attribute of an Entity)

> http://d-nb.info/1018827005 http://rdvocab.info/Elements/languageOfExpression
> http://id.loc.gov/vocabulary/iso639-2/ger

## EXPLANATION

- The subject is the periodical "Macwelt XL : Sonderheft," represented by the Deutsche Nationalbibliothek record identified by the first URI.
- The predicate is the RDA Group 1 element "language of expression," identified by the second URI.
- The object is the value "ger," represented by the ISO 639-2 language code identified by the third URI.
- In this case, the object was represented in a vocabulary and so had a URI. However, had it been a transcribed element such as place of publication, the object would have had to have been represented by a literal.
- Also, the property "language of expression" can be defined with a domain of "expression" (meaning the subject must be an instance of a FRBR expression) and a range of "ISO 639-2 value" (meaning the object must be taken from

the ISO 639-2 vocabulary), enforcing rules on what can and cannot be the subject and object of the statement. In this case, the DNB bibliographic record is pre-FRBR, so one would not want to enforce such a constraint.

### Example 2 (Relationship between Entities)

http://bnb.data.bl.uk/id/resource/GBB1E3735 http://purl.org/dc/terms/subject
http://bnb.data.bl.uk/id/concept/ddc/e20/306.874305

### EXPLANATION

- The subject is the periodical "Gurgle," represented by the *British National Bibliography* (BNB) record identified by the first URI.
- The predicate is the DCMI metadata term "subject," identified by the second URI. (Note that this term was drawn from a non-RDA vocabulary.)
- The object is the DDC classification "306.874305," represented by the third URI.
- In this case, the relationship represented by the predicate in the RDF triple—a subject relationship—is not yet published in the RDA element vocabulary (or wasn't at the time). Since it is nonetheless a useful relationship in the context of the BNB, the predicate is taken from another vocabulary: DCMI metadata terms.
- In this case, the object was represented in a vocabulary and so had a URI. Note that DDC is not itself available as linked data (beyond the first three digits), so the URI refers to an internal dataset of DDCs used on records in the BNB). Should the DDC itself (the authoritative version) become available as linked data, values in this "internal" (and presumably incomplete) DDC might be linked to their corresponding values in the authoritative DDC, a process that might be accomplished by machine.

Berner-Lee's fourth rule—the "linking" in "linked data"—relates to what is known as *inference*. This is the subject of the next section.

## INFERENCE AND MATCHING ACROSS DOMAINS

Inference refers to the discovery of relationships. In the Semantic Web, relationships can be discovered via vocabularies, ontologies, etc. For example, RDA has an element called "identifier for the manifestation" [RDA 2.15] and this element is included in the RDA Group 1 element set as a property. The RDA Group 1 element set defines some other RDA elements—publisher's number for music, for example—as subproperties of "identifier for the manifestation" (that is, all publisher's numbers for music are also identifiers for the manifestation). Another vocabulary may define other specific classes of identifier such as ISBN, DOI, or EAN. (In fact, the Bibliographic Ontology [bibo] identifies bibo:isbn as a subproperty of bibo:identifier and bibo:isbn10 and bibo:isbn13 as subproperties of bibo:isbn.) If these are also defined as subproperties of rdaGp1:identifierForTheManifestation, then a machine can infer that any instance of bibo:isbn10 or bibo:isbn13 is also an instance of rdaGp1:identifierForTheManifestation.

Another vocabulary may assert that an ISBN is a transformation of an equivalent EAN (international article number), which is itself a transformation of an equivalent GTIN (global trade item number). (This is true, by the way.) However, while all ISBNs can be transformed into EANs and GTINs, the reverse is not true, and this constraint must be made explicit. This would enable EANs and GTINs in the appropriate ranges—for example, EANs beginning with 978 or 979—to be handled as the equivalent ISBNs. It also opens up the range of objects that may potentially be discovered when searching for an ISBN. Likewise, one can decide to search not just for ISBNs but all potential identifiers of manifestations by moving up the hierarchy of identifiers, from subproperty to parent.

Mapping of this sort can also be done probabilistically using the co-occurrence of terms in a given context. This is the machinery underlying matching in the Virtual International Authority File (VIAF), where equivalent name headings from different national authority files are tentatively identified based on their co-occurrence on bibliographic records representing a common set of resources. Problematic cases— where the expected co-occurrence falls below a certain critical threshold—can be referred to human editors for review.

One library-specific inferencing problem—at least in the context of RDA Scenario 1—involves structural differences between records created under RDA (based on the FRBR conceptual model) and those created under earlier cataloging rules. For bibliographic data, RDA elements are defined in terms of the associated FRBR entity (work, expression, manifestation, item) whereas data created under earlier rules is simply associated with a general "resource." This can cause problems for mapping between RDA elements and the analogous pre-RDA elements. The RDA vocabularies will attempt to address this by identifying the FRBR Group 1 entity-specific properties as subproperties of analogous resource-associated properties (for example, defining "place of publication [manifestation]" as a subproperty of "place of publication").

All this promises a high rate of successful mapping within the library community, not least because that community is largely committed to linked *open* data. If you look at the Linked Open Data cloud diagram referenced above, you will notice that there are already a number of library-related datasets present. These datasets are available for use by Semantic Web applications like Berners-Lee's intelligent agents. They're also available for mapping to other datasets.

But a major impediment to the achievement of a web of linked open data lies in the simple fact that data has value. This is a problem that is endemic on the Web, and organizations are still struggling over viable solutions. Data is expensive to create, requiring a considerable investment in time and resources, yet it is most efficiently used if it is made freely available. Thus while there is a considerable incentive to *use* other people's data, there is no similar incentive for those other people to *expose* their data. Consequently, most open linked data currently on the web is created by public authorities and communities (such as our own) with a vested interest in open data. The participation of commercial enterprises, on the other hand, tends to be more apparent on the consumption end than the production end. Hopefully, this will change over time.

Data can also be extremely complex, resulting in some compromises when it is exposed as linked data. Especially in the library community, "semantically rich" data sets such as the Dewey Decimal Classification (DDC) and LC Subject Headings (LCSH) are exposed as linked data in a much simplified state because the effort necessary to express the semantics is prohibitive in terms of cost. In the beginning, only the DDC summaries are being exposed as linked data, and LCSH is being exposed only to the extent that the semantics is already encoded in authority records. (Much LCSH semantics is *implicit* in the application of instructions in LC's *Subject Cataloging Manual* and is consequently absent from the finished MARC product.)

Nevertheless, this may change as there is more uptake of linked data. While the jury remains out on the broad application of linked data,[12] there is cause for optimism. As Tom Heath and Christian Bizer point out in their book *Linked Data:*

> Third parties . . . are consuming this data to build new businesses, streamline online commerce, accelerate scientific progress, and enhance the democratic process. For example:
>
> - The online retailer Amazon makes their product data available to third parties via a Web API. In doing so they have created a highly successful ecosystem of affiliates who build micro-businesses, based on driving transactions to Amazon sites.
> - Search engines such as Google and Yahoo! consume structured data from the Web sites of various online stores, and use this to enhance the search listings of items from these stores. Users and online retailers benefit through enhanced user experience and higher transaction rates, while the search engines need expend fewer resources on extracting structured data from plain HTML pages.
> - Innovation in disciplines such as Life Sciences requires the world-wide exchange of research data between scientists, as demonstrated by the progress resulting from cooperative initiatives such as the Human Genome Project.
> - The availability of data about the political process, such as members of parliament, voting records, and transcripts of debates, has enabled the organisation mySociety to create services such as TheyWorkForYou,

through which voters can readily assess the performance of elected representatives.[13]

But regardless of whether or not this broader uptake occurs, the migration to linked data can and will proceed within the library community. This is because even within a single community the advantages of linking data are substantial. Hence the Bibliographic Framework Transition Initiative.

## PLANNING FOR LIBRARY LINKED DATA: THE BIBLIOGRAPHIC FRAMEWORK TRANSITION INITIATIVE

MARC 21 is not designed to accommodate the structures envisaged in RDA implementation scenario 1, the Holy Grail of implementation scenarios. Aware of this, in May 2011 the Library of Congress announced its Bibliographic Framework Transition Initiative, to be undertaken in consultation with Library and Archives Canada, the British Library, and the Deutsche Nationalbibliothek, among others.[14]

The Bibliographic Framework Transition Initiative will address seven issues:

1. Determining which aspects of current metadata encoding standards, including MARC 21, "should be retained and evolved into a format for the future"
2. Experimenting with the Semantic Web and linked data technologies (see below) to see:

   - What benefits they offer in terms of the bibliographic framework
   - How current models need to be adjusted to take advantage of these benefits

3. Fostering maximum reuse of library metadata
4. Enabling users to navigate the relationships between entities (such as those set out in the FRBR model) to more precisely search in library catalogs and on the Internet
5. Exploring various approaches to displaying metadata
6. Making a cost-benefit analysis of the effect of various transitions, including the pace of transition, on the broader community
7. Accommodating the vast stores of legacy metadata "within the broader Library of Congress technical infrastructure"

The Bibliographic Framework Transition Initiative can be seen as an added caution against trying to predict the future, and it is that spirit that it is mentioned here. Bear in mind it's still early days, and much may change.

At the time of writing, the Library of Congress had issued a general plan for moving forward with the initiative, including requirements for a successor to MARC 21 as an exchange vehicle, but no further steps had yet been taken.[15] As set out in the general plan, the new "bibliographic framework environment" is expected to be:

1. Agnostic to cataloging rules (being intended for use by a variety of cultural heritage communities: libraries, archives, museums)
2. Able to support both bibliographic data and associated "supporting" data, such as authority, classification, preservation, and rights metadata
3. In conformity with RDF principles (see below), able to accommodate both textual strings and uniform resource identifiers (URIs) to represent attributes and relationships
4. Able to manage the relationships among:
   - Exchange format tagging
   - Record input conventions
   - System storage/manipulation requirements
5. Able to support the needs of all sizes and types of library
6. Able to continue maintaining MARC 21 until it is no longer needed
7. Compatible with MARC-based records
8. Able to provide a mechanism for converting MARC-based records into the new bibliographic framework environment

So in a way, we are embarked on a daring but necessary voyage from a known but increasingly fragile old world to a brave new world full of hope but whose contours currently must remain vague and uncertain.

## THE FUTURE CATALOGING AND CATALOG ENVIRONMENT

Now I will go out on a limb. I envisage a future cataloging environment where the creation of a catalog "record"—a collection of RDF triples relating to a given entity—will be an iterative process of selecting an appropriate predicate and then, operating within the constraints imposed by that predicate, either selecting an appropriate value from a vocabulary or dataset (presented once the predicate was selected) or supplying a text string (literal) when no such vocabulary or dataset exists or the vocabulary or dataset is not closed. Such an environment could be extremely efficient for producing and connecting entity records and then exposing them on the World Wide Web. Ideally, the elements in RDA element sets and values in RDA vocabularies would be mapped to and from similar element sets and vocabularies, both within the domain of bibliographic cataloging and without. Ideally, the selection of a given term would trigger links to other metadata collections, facilitating access to whole swathes of valuable metadata not traditionally part of a catalog record.

Much will depend on mappings between vocabularies. The Virtual International Authority File shows promise in this area, at least for those associated with mega-objects like books and serials. Links to data for persons in article-based files such as Elsevier's SCOPUS would vastly expand its coverage and so the interoperability of files of catalog metadata and files of article metadata, though this raises the thorny issue of proprietary metadata already alluded to and the negotiations that may have to take place to incorporate it into the matrix of linked open data. A similar challenge exists with the data store of the ISSN network.

Publisher data represents another potentially rich source of metadata. Linking to publisher metadata for serials would by definition ensure the most up-to-date metadata for subscription, package, and pay-per-view pricing. However, most of this metadata is not currently available in the form of linked open data, and publishers would have to be persuaded of the value of making it available in this form.

On the other hand, national bibliographic agencies such as the Library of Congress (LC), the British Library (BL), the Bibliothèque nationale de France (BnF), and the Deutsche Nationalbibliothek (DNB), are already making their metadata available as linked open data, and it is possible to envisage a world where much of the work of assembling a bibliographic record might be accomplished by intelligent agents of the sort envisaged by Berners-Lee.

To take one example, assume your library has purchased a subscription to a given serial. Armed with its ISSN, an intelligent agent could begin searching and assembling metadata from a variety of linked-data sources, using hierarchies of preferred sources for different classes of metadata. For example, the publisher and place of publication might be drawn from a DNB record, where these reside in RDF triples whose predicates are drawn from the ISBD vocabulary. The ISBD vocabulary would map to the RDA vocabulary at various levels of granularity, depending on the element. For example, unlike RDA, the ISBD vocabulary makes no distinction between publisher, producer, and distributor. So these elements would not be mapped directly to one element, but might be imported wholesale and flagged for visual inspection by a cataloger and assignment to one of the three corresponding RDA elements. (Fortunately, while the DNB record uses the ISBD vocabulary for place of publication, etc., and date of publication, etc., it uses the Dublin Core vocabulary term *publisher* to identify the publisher.)

Or useful non-RDA data may be harvested from such records. For example, DNB records include subject analysis based on the Dewey Decimal Classification (DDC). These are presented as RDF triples employing the Dublin Core term *subject* as predicate and a local URI for the DDC class:

http://d-nb.info/017604958 dcterms:subject http://d-nb.info/ddc-sg/070

Although this DDC element has a preferred label in German, it can be mapped by machine to a corresponding element from a DDC vocabulary such as the one at OCLC: http://dewey.info/class/07/, which has a preferred label in English.

On the other hand, an agency may employ elements from the RDA vocabulary without having used RDA to structure the corresponding data—a possibility with any vocabulary once it has been published. In this case, it will be necessary to understand the standards applied by the agency and the likely reliability of the data. For example, the BnF exposes a person's date of birth using the RDA element of the same name, though the BnF does not currently use RDA in its cataloging. In this case, the data is highly structured and will conform to RDA in most cases, while a machine analysis can flag exceptional cases. But all such exceptional practices will need to be investigated and evaluated. Adrian Stevenson discussed some of the challenges of linked data at the 2011 Semantic Web in Bibliotheken conference in Hamburg.[16]

So this is the world that is drawing near. As can be seen from the preceding, it holds both great promise and novel challenges, and libraries can expect to be in the thick of it. A brave new world indeed.

---

**NOTES**

1. Charles Ammi Cutter, "The Buffalo Public Library in 1983," in *Papers and Proceedings of the Sixth General Meeting of the American Library Association, Held at Buffalo, August 14 to 17, 1883* (Boston: Press of Rockwell and Churchill, 1883), 49–55. http://books.google.com/books?id=VdoDAAAAYAAJ.

2. Tim Berners-Lee, James Hendler, and Ora Lassila, "The Semantic Web," *Scientific American* 284 (May 17, 2001): 34–43, www.scientificamerican.com/article.cfm?id=the-semantic-web/.

3. Joint Steering Committee for Development of RDA, "A New Organization for RDA," last modified November 13, 2007, www.rda-jsc.org/rda-new-org.html.

4. "Data Model Meeting, British Library, London, 30 April–1 May 2007," www.bl.uk/bibliographic/meeting.html.

5. Dublin Core Metadata Initiative, "DCMI/RDA Task Group Wiki," accessed May 14, 2012, http://dublincore.org/dcmirdataskgroup/.

6. Dublin Core Metadata Initiative, "Bibliographic Metadata Task Group," last modified May 8, 2012, http://wiki.dublincore.org/index.php/Bibliographic_Metadata_Task_Group/.

7. A very good description of RDA linked data will be found in Diane Hillmann, Karen Coyle, Jon Phipps, and Gordon Dunsire, "RDA Vocabularies: Process, Outcome, and Use," *D-Lib Magazine* 16 (January/February 2010), doi:10.1045/january2010-hillmann; http://dlib.org/dlib/january10/hillmann/01hillmann.html.

8. A FRBRer element set has since been published at http://metadataregistry.org/schemaprop/list/schema_id/5.html.

9. DBpedia, blog, accessed April 4, 2012, http://dbpedia.org/About/.

10. Tim Berners-Lee, "Linked Data," last modified June 18, 2009, www.w3.org /DesignIssues/LinkedData.html.

11. "RDF/XML Syntax Specification (Revised)," W3C Recommendation, 10 February 2004, www.w3.org/TR/rdf-syntax-grammar/.

12. Janna Anderson and Lee Rainie, "The Fate of the Semantic Web," Pew Internet & American Life Project, 2010, http://pewinternet.org/Reports/2010/Semantic-Web. aspx; Sean Bechhofer et al., "Why Linked Data Is Not Enough for Scientists," Future Generation Computer Systems . Published electronically 19 August 2011. doi:10.1016 /j.future.2011.08.004 www.sciencedirect.com/science/article/pii/S0167739X11001439.

13. Those interested in developing a thorough understanding of linked data are referred to the excellent website of the same name at http://linkeddata.org. There they will find guides and tutorials, frequently asked questions, glossaries, presentations, tools, etc. An additional fine introduction is Tom Heath and Christine Bizer, *Linked Data: Evolving the Web into a Global Data Space* (San Rafael, CA: Morgan and Claypool, 2011).

14. "Transforming Our Bibliographic Framework: A Statement from the Library of Congress," May 13, 2011, www.loc.gov/marc/transition/news/framework -051311.html.

15. Library of Congress, "A Bibliographic Framework for the Digital Age," October 31, 2011, www.loc.gov/marc/transition/pdf/bibframework-10312011.pdf.

16. Adrian Stevenson, "The Highs and Lows of Library Linked Data" (paper presented at SWIB11, Semantic Web in Bibliotheken, Hamburg, Germany, November 29, 2011), www.scivee.tv/node/39218 (recorded presentation); http://swib.org/swib11/vortraege /swib11-adrian-stevenson.pptx (presentation slides).

# INDEX

## A

AACR1, 18, 19
AACR2
    changes from AACR2 to RDA
        access points, choice of, 40
        cartographic materials, 37
        continuing resources, 39
        description, general rules for, 35–37
        electronic resources, 38
        headings for corporate bodies, 41
        headings for persons, 40–41
        microforms, 39
        motion pictures and videorecordings, 38
        overview, 33–34
        references, 42
        sound recordings, 38
        uniform titles, 41–42
    corresponding RDA instructions, AACR2 rules linked to, 32
    overview, 21–23
    RDA compared, 27–29
AACR2-compatible headings, 21, 22
abbreviated titles, 14, 15–16, 20, 85–86
access points. *See* authorized access points
accompanying material, 116
accuracy, 33
alternative sequences, 103
Anglo-American cataloging code, 14–16
annual reports, 11

ANSI (American National Standards Institute), 18
appendixes in RDA, 31
approach of this manual, 32–33
associated institutions to corporate bodies, 162–163
attributes of resources
    content form
        changes from AACR2, 67–68
        examples, 70
        overview, 68–69
        spoken word, 69
        tactile text, 69
        text, 68
    editions
        changes from AACR2, 91
        changes in edition statement, 95
        designation of, 92–93
        multiple editions with minor differences, accommodating, 95
        as numbering, 94–95
        overview, 92
        parallel designation of, 94
    media type
        audio, 69
        changes from AACR2, 67–68
        computer, 69
        microform, 69
        overview, 69–70
        unmediated, 69

attributes of resources (cont.)
note area
frequency, 120–122
general notes, 120
language and script of
content, 123–124
overview, 120
summarizations of content,
122
titles that may lead to
confusion, 122
numbering serials
alternative sequences, 103
changes from AACR2, 96
chronological designation
of first issue or part of
sequence, 101–102
chronological designation
of last issue or part of
sequence, 103
CONSER examples, 97–100
multiple parts, issues in, 104
notes on, 103–105
numeric and/or alphabetic
designation of first issue
or part of a sequence,
100–101
numeric and/or alphabetic
designation of last issue
or part of a sequence,
102
overview, 96–97
pilot or sample issues, 104
physical description area
accompanying material, 116
carrier type, 114–115
changes from AACR2,
113–114
color content, 116
dimensions, 116
extent, 115
illustrative content, 115
publication, production,
distribution, etc., area
changes from AACR2, 105,
106
changes in statements
relating to production,
publication, distribution,
and/or manufacture, 112

copyright date, 112–113
date of publication, 110–111
distribution statements, 111
manufacture statements,
111–112
notes relating to publishers,
distributors, etc., 113
production statements,
106–107
publication statements,
107–109
publisher's name, 109–110
reproductions, 106
resource identifier and terms of
availability area, 124–126
series area, 117–120
statements of responsibility
changes from AACR2, 71
changes in, 90
identifying responsible
persons, families, and
corporate bodies, 91
overview, 86
parallel statement of
responsibility relating to
title proper, 90–91
serial as responsible entity,
89
title proper, relating to,
87–88
titles
abbreviated title, 85–86
changes from AACR2, 71
corrections and omissions,
71
earlier title proper of an
integrating resource, 84
earlier titles, titles that
mention or are
grammatically linked
to, 74
inaccuracies, 73
irreproducible results, 73
issuing body as substitute for
title, using name of, 74
key title, 85
later title proper, 85
omissions, 73
other title information,
80–82

overview, 72
of parts and sections, 74–75
of supplements, 75–76
title proper, 76–80
variant title, 82–84
audio (media type), 69
audio journal, 70
authorized access points
changes from AACR2 to RDA,
40
defined, 58
expression of a work with
creator, 137
expression of a work without
creator, 137
work with creator, 136–137
work without creator, 137

**B**
Berners-Lee, Tim, 194, 196, 198,
199
Bibliographic Framework
Transition Initiative, 201–202
Bizer, Christian, 200
BLvl field (workforms for serials
cataloging), 54
book catalog, 13
braille journal, 70
Buffalo Public Library, 193

**C**
Canby, Henry Seidel, 5
card catalog, 13–14, 16
carrier type, 114–115
cartographic materials
changes from AACR2 to RDA,
37
corporate bodies, 167–168
CAS Source Index (CASSI) Search
Tool, 125
*Cataloging Rules and Principles*
(Lubetzky), 16
changes from AACR2 to RDA
access points, choice of, 40
cartographic materials, 37
content form and media type,
67–68
continuing resources, 39
description, general rules for,
35–37

electronic resources, 38
headings for corporate bodies, 41
headings for persons, 40–41
microforms, 39
motion pictures and videorecordings, 38
overview, 33–34, 113–114
references, 42
sound recordings, 38
uniform titles, 41–42
Chemical Abstract Service, 125
chronological designation
  continuing resources, 39
  of first issue or part of sequence, 101–102
  of last issue or part of sequence, 103
CODEN, 125
color content, 116
common usage, 33, 34
compound surnames, 40
computer (media type), 69
Conf field (workforms for serials cataloging), 54
conferences, congresses, meetings, etc. (corporate bodies), 41
*CONSER Cataloging Manual*, ix
*CONSER Editing Guide*, ix
CONSER Project, 20
consistency and standardization, 33
Cont field (workforms for serials cataloging), 54
content form
  changes from AACR2, 67–68
  examples, 70
  overview, 68–69
  spoken word, 69
  tactile text, 69
  text, 68
continuing resources
  changes from AACR2, 39
  chronological designation, 39
  numeric and/or alphabetic designation, 39
  other title information, 39
  title proper, 39
convenience of user, 33
copyright date, 112–113

CORE elements for describing a resource, 58–59
corporate authorship, 14, 17, 18, 21
corporate bodies. *See also* headings for corporate bodies
  additions to, 162–168
  associated institution, 162–163
  cartographic material, 167–168
  change of name, 156
  date, adding, 162
  microform, 165–166
  names, additions to, 162–168
  notes
    cartographic material, 167–168
    microform, 166
    printed text, 165
  omissions, 156–157
  overview, 154–155
  place, adding, 162
  preferred name of, selecting, 155–156
  printed text, 164–165
  recording name of, 154–155
  related corporate bodies, identifying, 153–154
  searching by, 48
  subordinate and related bodies, 157–159
  terms to clarify, 162–163
  transliteration, 157
Cousins, Norman, 5
creator
  corporate bodies as, 140–143
  families as, 140
  overview, 58, 137–138
  persons or families as, 138–140
Ctry field (workforms for serials cataloging), 54–55
Currier, T. Franklin, 15
Cutter, Charles Ammi, 13, 193–194

**D**
date of publication, 110–111, 145
Dates field (workforms for serials cataloging), 55
DBpedia, 195–196

DCMI (Dublin Core Metadata Initiative), 195
DDC (Dewey Decimal Classification), 200, 203
Desc field (workforms for serials cataloging), 55
description
  changes from AACR2, 35–37
  creating
    for ongoing integrating resources, 61
    overview, 64–66
    for serials, 60
  dimensions, 37
  edition statement, 36
  extent of item (including specific material designation), 37
  general material, 35
  inaccuracies, 35
  language and script of, 35
  levels of detail in, 35
  name of publisher, distributor, etc., 36–37
  numbering within series, 37
  ongoing integrating resources, 182–183
  other physical details, 37
  other title information, 35
  parallel titles, 35
  place of publication, distribution, etc., 36
  statement of responsibility, 36
  subseries, 37
  title proper, 35
designations of function, 40
Dewey, Melvil, 14
Dewey Decimal Classification (DDC), 200, 203
dimensions
  changes from AACR2, 37
  microforms, 39
  motion pictures and videorecordings, 38
  overview, 116
  sound recordings, 38
distinguishing terms added to names, 41
distribution statements, 111
dollar sign ($), x

DtSt field (workforms for serials cataloging), 55
Dublin Core Metadata Initiative (DCMI), 195

**E**
EAN (international article number), 199
earlier titles, titles that mention or are grammatically linked to, 74
earliest-entry cataloging, 13, 14
economy, 33
edition statement, 36, 95
editions
    changes from AACR2, 91
    designation of, 92–93
    multiple editions with minor differences, accommodating, 95
    as numbering, 94–95
    overview, 92
    parallel designation of, 94
electronic resources, 38
ELvL field (workforms for serials cataloging), 55
EntW field (workforms for serials cataloging), 55
ERMS (electronic resource management system), 169
examples
    content form and media type, 70
    numbering serials, 97–100
    ongoing integrating resources
        microform (updating microfiche), 185–187
        online (updating database), 187–189
        online (updating website), 189–190
        print (updating loose-leaf), 185
    online serials
        online version of a print serial, 174–176
        originally online, 176–177
    RDF (Resource Description Framework)
        attribute of an entity, 197–198

relationship between entities, 198
exhibitions, fairs, festivals, etc., and headings for corporate bodies, 41
explanatory references, 42
expression. *See also* identifying works and expressions
    overview, 57
    of a work with creator, 137
    of a work without creator, 137
extent
    description, 37
    electronic resources, 38
    motion pictures and videorecordings, 38
    overview, 115
    sound recordings, 38

**F**
facsimiles and reproductions, treatment of, 66–67
families, identifying related, 153
Form field (workforms for serials cataloging), 55
FRAD (Functional Requirements for Authority Data), 28
FRBR (Functional Requirements for Bibliographic Records), 22–23, 28
*FRBR: A Guide for the Perplexed* (Maxwell), 33
Freq field (workforms for serials cataloging), 56
frequency
    ongoing integrating resources, 183–184
    overview, 120–122
Frost, Carolyn, 18
fuller forms added to names of persons, 41
future cataloging environment, 202–204

**G**
general instructions relating to serials cataloging using RDA and MARC 21
    bibliographic description, creating, 64–66

CORE elements for describing a resource, 58–59
    description, creating new
        for ongoing integrating resources, 61
        for serials, 60
    facsimiles and reproductions, treatment of, 66–67
    MARC 21 elements external to RDA, 53–57
    numbers expressed as numerals or words, 66
    responsibility for work, changes in, 64
    sources of information, 64–66
    terminology, 57–58
    title proper, changes in, 61–63
    transcribing data, 59–60
general material, 35
general notes, 120
GMD (general material designator), 34
governmental bodies, 160–161
GPub field (workforms for serials cataloging), 56
Green Book *(Rules for Descriptive Cataloging in the Library of Congress)*, 15–16
GTIN (global trade item number), 199

**H**
*Handbook for AACR2* (Maxwell), 21, 51
*Handbook for RDA* (Maxwell), 135
Hanson, J.C.M., 14
hash marks (#), x–xi
headings for corporate bodies
    changes from AACR2 to RDA, 41
    conferences, congresses, meetings, etc., 41
    different spellings of same name, 41
    exhibitions, fairs, festivals, etc., 41
headings for persons
    changes from AACR2 to RDA, 40–41

compound surnames, 40
different spellings of same name, 40
distinguishing terms added to names, 41
fuller forms added to names, 41
initials in personal name headings, 40
surnames, additions to names entered under, 40–41
Heath, Tom, 200
history of serials cataloging, 12–23

**I**

ICCP (International Conference on Cataloguing Principles), 17
ICP (Statement of International Cataloguing Principles), ix, 33, 51
identifier for manifestation, 124–125, 198–199
identifying related entities
corporate names, additions to, 163–168
joint committees, 159
persons, families, and corporate bodies, identifying related, 152–159
US political parties, local units of, 159–161
works and expressions, identifying related, 152
identifying works and expressions
authorized access points
constructing for expressions, 147–151
constructing for works, 147
expression of a work with creator, 137
expression of a work without creator, 137
work with creator, 136–137
work without creator, 137
overview, 135–136
preferred title for work, 143–147
illustrative content, 115

inaccuracies
description, 35
titles, 73
inference, 198–201
initials in personal name headings, 40
integrating resources
defined, 58
overview, 177–179
title proper, changes in, 40, 78
integration, 34
international article number (EAN), 199
International Conference on Cataloguing Principles (ICCP), 17
*Introducing RDA: A Guide to the Basics* (Oliver), 33
introduction of RDA, 29
ISBD (International Standard Bibliographic Description), ix, 51
ISBD(S) (International Standard Bibliographic Description for Serials), 19–20
ISBN (International Standard Book Number), 19
ISDS (International Serials Data System), 19, 127
ISSN (International Standard Serial Number)
locating, 47
overview, 19, 124–125
searching by, 46–47
of subseries, 119
ISSN History Visualization Tool, 6–7
ISSN Network practice, 134–135
ISSN Portal, searching by, 47
issuing body
searching by, 48
as substitute for title, 74
item, 57

**J**

joint committees, 159

**K**

key title, 85

**L**

Lang field (workforms for serials cataloging), 56
language and script
of content, 123–124
of description, 35
languages, adding, 42
later title proper, 85
latest-entry cataloging, 15, 17–18, 20
LC (Library of Congress), 13, 20, 201, 202, 203
LC-PCC PS (Library of Congress-Program for Cooperative Cataloging Policy Statement), 59–60
LCSH (Library of Congress Subject Headings), 200
legal works, 146–147
*Library School Rules* (Dewey), 14
linked data
Bibliographic Framework Transition Initiative, 201–202
DBpedia, 195–196
how it works, 196–197
inference, 198–201
metadata, 201–204
open data needed for, 199–200
overview, 193–194
and Semantic Web, 194–196
*Linked Data* (Heath and Bizer), 200
London Gazette, 9
Lubetzky, Seymour, 16–18

**M**

magazines, 9–10
major changes in title proper, 61–62
manifestations
identifier for, 124–125, 198–199
overview, 57
referencing related
guidelines for, 128–135
ISSN Network practice, 134–135
MARC 21 record syntax, 129–133

manifestations (cont.)
overview, 127–128
reproductions, 134
title changes out of sync, 133–134
manufacture statements, 111–112
MARC 21 format. *See also* general instructions relating to serials cataloging using RDA and MARC 21
elements external to RDA, 53–57
manifestations, referencing related, 129–133
ongoing integrating resources, 181
Maxwell, Margaret, 21
Maxwell, Robert, 33, 135
mechanization and international developments, effects of, 18–20
media types
audio, 69
changes from AACR2, 67–68
computer, 69
examples, 70
microform, 69
overview, 69–70
unmediated, 69
metadata, 202–204
microform
changes from AACR2 to RDA, 39
complete record example, 185–187
corporate bodies, 165–166
dimensions, 39
media type, 69
minor changes in title proper, 62–63
monographic series, 10–11
motion pictures and videorecordings
changes from AACR2 to RDA, 38
dimensions, 38
extent of item (including specific material designation), 38

multiple editions with minor differences, accommodating, 95
multiple parts, issues in, 104

**N**
newspapers, 9
NISO (National Information Standards Organization), 7
NISO/ANSI Z39.1, 7
NLC (National Library of Canada), 20
notes
corporate bodies
cartographic material, 167–168
microform, 166
printed text, 164–165
frequency, 120–122
general notes, 120
language and script of content, 123–124
numbering serials, 103–105
ongoing integrating resources, 184
online serials
online version of a print serial, 175–176
originally online, 177
overview, 174
overview, 120
publishers, distributors, etc., relating to, 113
summarizations of content, 122
titles that may lead to confusion, 122
NSDP (National Serials Data Program), 19
numbering
editions as, 94–95
within series, 37, 119
numbering serials
alternative sequences, 103
changes from AACR2, 96
chronological designation of first issue or part of sequence, 101–102
chronological designation of last issue or part of sequence, 103

CONSER examples, 97–100
individual elements, 100
multiple parts, issues in, 104
notes on, 103–105
numeric and/or alphabetic designation of first issue or part of a sequence, 100–101
numeric and/or alphabetic designation of last issue or part of sequence, 102
online serials, 173
overview, 96–97
pilot or sample issues, 104
numbers expressed as numerals or words, 66
numeric and/or alphabetic designation
of continuing resources, 39
of first issue or part of a sequence, 100–101
of last issue or part of sequence, 102

**O**
OCLC (Ohio College Library Center), 6–7, 20
Oliver, Chris, 33
omissions
corporate bodies, 156–157
titles, 73
ongoing integrating resources
bibliographic description, 182–183
cataloging ongoing integrating resources *vs.* cataloging serials, 179–180
complete record examples
microform (updating microfiche), 185–187
online (updating database), 187–189
online (updating website), 189–190
print (updating loose-leaf), 185
determining if resources are serials or, 179–180
frequency of updating, 183–184
identifying resource, basis for, 183

instructions for cataloging ongoing, 181–184
level of analysis for cataloging online, 181
MARC 21 coding, 181
notes, 184
predominant form of content, 183
previous versions, tool for recognizing, 180
relationships, 184
title proper, 183
ONIX exchange format, 68
online (updating database) example, 187–189
online (updating website) example, 189–190
online journal, 70
online serials
  complete record examples
    online version of a print serial, 174–176
    originally online, 176–177
  notes
    online version of a print serial, 175–176
    originally online, 177
  numbering, 173
  physical description area, 173
  print version and, relationship between, 173–174
  print versions, aligning, 168
  provider-neutral records, 168–174
  publication, distribution, etc., area, 173
  sources of information, 171–172
  title changes, 168
  variant titles, 172–173
open data needed for linked data, 199–200
organic nature of serials, 4–7
organization of RDA
  appendices, 31
  introduction, 29
  section 1, 29–30
  section 2, 29–30
  section 3, 30
  section 4, 30

section 6, 30–31
section 8, 31
Orig field (workforms for serials cataloging), 56

**P**

parallel designation of editions, 94
parallel statement of responsibility relating to title proper, 90–91
parallel title proper
  changes in, 79–80
  overview, 78–79
parallel titles, 35
Paris Principles, 17–18
parts and sections, titles of, 74–75
periodicals
  magazines, 9–10
  scholarly journals, 10
persons, families, and corporate bodies, identifying related, 152–159
physical description area
  accompanying material, 116
  carrier type, 114–115
  changes from AACR2, 113–114
  color content, 116
  dimensions, 116
  extent, 115
  illustrative content, 115
  online serials, 173
pilot or sample issues, 104
place of origin of work, 145–146
place of publication, distribution, etc., 36
preferred name of corporate bodies, selecting, 155–156
preferred source of information, xi
preferred title, 135, 136, 143–147
previous versions of ongoing integrating resources, tool for recognizing, 180
principal responsibility in works of shared responsibility, 40
print (updating loose-leaf) example, 185
print journal, 70

print journal with accompanying CD, 70
production statements, 106–107
provider-neutral records
  online serials, 168–174
  overview, 168–170
  reproduction *vs.* versions, 170–171
publication, production, distribution, etc., area
  changes from AACR2, 105, 106
  changes in statements relating to production, publication, distribution, and/or manufacture, 112
  copyright date, 112–113
  date of publication, 110–111
  distribution statements, 111
  manufacture statements, 111–112
  notes relating to publishers, distributors, etc., 113
  for online serials, 173
  production statements, 106–107
  publication statements, 107–109
  publisher's name, 109–110
  reproductions, 106
publication statements, 107–109
publisher's name, 109–110
punctuation, 35

**R**

RAK-WB (Regeln für die alphabetische Katalogisierung für wissenschaftlichen Bibliotheken), viii–ix
RDA
  AACR2 compared, 27–29
  corresponding RDA instructions, AACR2 rules linked to, 32
  implementation scenarios, viii
RDA Toolkit, 32
RDF (Resource Description Framework)
  examples
    attribute of an entity, 197–198
    relationship between entities, 198
  overview, 196–197

recording
    corporate bodies, name of,
        154–155
    title proper, 77–78
references, explanatory, 42
Regl field (workforms for serials
    cataloging), 56
related corporate bodies,
    identifying, 153–154
related entities, identifying. *See*
    identifying related entities
relationships between resources
    manifestations, referencing
        related
        guidelines for, 128–135
        ISSN Network practice,
            134–135
        MARC 21 record syntax,
            129–133
        overview, 127–128
        reproductions, 134
        title changes out of sync,
            133–134
    ongoing integrating resources,
        184
    overview, 126–127
representation, 33, 34
reproductions, 106, 134
resources. *See also* attributes of
    resources
    defined, 57
    resource identifier and terms of
        availability area, 124–126
responsibility for work, changes
    in, 64
*Rules for a Printed Dictionary
    Catalogue* (Cutter), 13
*Rules for the Compilation of the
    Catalogue* (Panizzi), 12

## S

S/L field (workforms for serials
    cataloging), 56
*Saturday Review*, 5–7
SBN (Standard Book Number), 19
scholarly journals, 10
searching
    by corporate body, 48
    hierarchy of searching
        techniques, 46
    by ISSN (International Standard
        Serial Number), 46–47

by ISSN Portal, 47
by issuing body, 48
before searching familiarizing
    yourself with minor title
    changes, 45–46
by title, 47–48
Semantic Web, 192–194
serials
    annual reports, 11
    boundaries of, 8
    defined, 3, 57–58
    magazines, 9–10
    monographic series, 10–11
    newspapers, 9
    ongoing integrating resources,
        determining if resources are
        serials or, 180
    organic nature of, 4–7
    overview, 3–4
    properties of, 4
    as responsible entity, 89
    scholarly journals, 10
    statistical, 11–12
    title changes, 7–8
    title proper, changes in, 40, 78
    types of, 9–12
serials cataloging
    AACR1, 18, 19
    AACR2, 21–23
    Anglo-American cataloging
        code, 14–16
    cataloging ongoing integrating
        resources *vs.* cataloging
        serials, 179–180
    CONSER Project, 20
    Cutter's rules, 13–14
    history of, 12–23
    Lubetzky's rules, 16–18
    MARC format, 19–20
    mechanization and
        international developments,
        effects of, 18–20
    overview, 53–57
    Paris Principles, 17–18
    workforms
        BLvL field, 54
        Conf field, 54
        Cont field, 54
        Ctry field, 54–55
        Dates field, 55
        Desc field, 55
        DtSt field, 55

        ELvL field, 55
        EntW field, 55
        Form field, 55
        Freq field, 56
        GPub field, 56
        Lang field, 56
        Orig field, 56
        overview, 53
        Regl field, 56
        S/L field, 56
        Srce field, 56
        SrTp field, 56–57
        Type field, 57
series
    changes in, 119–120
    ISSN of, 118
    numbering within, 119
    overview, 117
    statement of responsibility, 118
    subseries, 119
    title proper, 118
significance, 33
sound recordings
    changes from AACR2 to RDA,
        38
    dimensions, 38
    extent of item (including
        specific material
        designation), 38
sources of information, xi, 64–66,
    171–172
spellings of same name
    headings for corporate bodies,
        41
    headings for persons, 40
spoken word, 69
Srce field (workforms for serials
    cataloging), 56
SrTp field (workforms for serials
    cataloging), 56–57
SSN (standard serial number), 18
Standard Book Number (SBN),
    19
Statement of International
    Cataloguing Principles
    (ICP), ix, 33, 51
*Statement of Principles* (ICCP),
    17–18
statements of responsibility
    changes from AACR2, 71
    changes in, 90
    description, 36

identifying responsible persons, families, and corporate bodies, 91
overview, 86
parallel statement of responsibility relating to title proper, 90–91
serial as responsible entity, 89
series, 118
title proper, relating to, 87–88
statistical serials, 11–12
Stevenson, Adrian, 204
Stockholm Seminar (1990), 28
subordinate and related bodies to corporate bodies, 157–159
subseries, 37, 119
successive-entry cataloging, 16–17, 20
sufficiency and necessity, 33
summarizations of content, 122
superimposition, 18
supplements, titles of, 75–76
surnames
additions to names entered under, 40–41
compound, 40

**T**

tactile text, 69
terminology, 57–58
terms of availability, 126
title proper
changes from AACR2, 76
changes in, 61–63
continuing resources, 39
description, identifying basis of, 77
earlier title proper of an integrating resource, 84
later title proper, 85
major changes in, 61–62
minor changes in, 62–63
ongoing integrating resources, 183
overview, 35, 76
parallel
changes in, 79–80
overview, 78–79
recording, 77–78
selecting, 76–77

series, 118
statements of responsibility relating to, 87–88
of subseries, 119
titles
abbreviated titles, 14, 15–16, 20, 85–86
changes
manifestations, referencing related, 133–134
minor title changes, before searching familiarizing yourself with, 45–46
online serials and print versions, aligning, 170–171
overview, 7–8
changes from AACR2, 71
confusion, titles that may lead to, 122
corrections and omissions, 71
earlier titles, titles that mention or are grammatically linked to, 74
inaccuracies, 73
irreproducible results, 73
issuing body as substitute for title, using name of, 74
key title, 85
omissions, 73
other title information, 80–82
overview, 72
of parts and sections, 74–75
preferred title, 136
searching by, 47–48
of supplements, 75–76
variant title, 82–84
transcribing data, 59–60
transliteration, 157
Type field (workforms for serials cataloging), 57

**U**

*Understanding MARC Authority Records: Machine-Readable Cataloging* (Library of Congress), 33
*Understanding MARC Bibliographic: Machine-Readable Cataloging* (Library of Congress), 33

uniform titles
changes from AACR2 to RDA, 41–42
languages, adding, 42
overview, 21
works created after 1500, 41–42
unmediated (media type), 69
US political parties, local units of, 159

**V**

variant titles, 82–84, 172–173
VIAF (Virtual International Authority File), 199, 203

**W**

Wayback Machine, 180
workforms for serials cataloging
BLvL field, 54
Conf field, 54
Cont field, 54
Ctry field, 54–55
Dates field, 55
Desc field, 55
DtSt field, 55
ELvL field, 55
EntW field, 55
Form field, 55
Freq field, 56
GPub field, 56
Lang field, 56
Orig field, 56
overview, 53
Regl field, 56
S/L field, 56
Srce field, 56
SrTp field, 56–57
Type field, 57
works. *See also* identifying works and expressions
created after 1500, 41–42
with creator, 136–137
defined, 57
of shared responsibility, 40
without creator, 137

# You may also be interested in

## RDA
### Strategies for Implementation

MAGDA EL-SHERBINI

Every cataloger will want this volume close at hand as a comprehensive roadmap to the changes already underway.

**ISBN: 978-0-8389-1168-6**
**240 PAGES / 8.5" x 11"**

**MAXWELL'S HANDBOOK FOR RDA**
Explaining and Illustrating RDA: Resource Description and Access Using MARC21

ROBERT L. MAXWELL

**ISBN: 978-0-8389-1172-3**

**RDA AND CARTOGRAPHIC RESOURCES**

PAIGE G. ANDREW AND MARY LARSGAARD

**ISBN: 978-0-8389-1131-0**

**CATALOGUE 2.0**
The Future of the Library Catalogue

EDITED BY SALLY CHAMBERS

**ISBN: 978-1-55570-943-3**

**PRINT RDA**
Resource Description and Access Bundle

**ITEM NUMBER: 7000-0931**

**RDA TOOLKIT**
rdatoolkit.org

**RDA**
Resource Description and Access Print

**ISBN: 978-0-8389-1093-1**

## Order today at **alastore.ala.org** or **866-746-7252!**

ALA Store purchases fund advocacy, awareness, and accreditation programs for library professionals worldwide.

Lightning Source UK Ltd.
Milton Keynes UK
UKOW06f0154310115

245450UK00007B/87/P